STORYING RELATIONSHIPS

STORYING RELATIONSHIPS

Young British Muslims Speak and Write about Sex and Love

Richard Phillips, Claire Chambers, Nafhesa Ali,
Kristina Diprose and Indrani Karmakar

I.B. TAURIS
LONDON • NEW YORK • OXFORD • NEW DELHI • SYDNEY

I.B. TAURIS
Bloomsbury Publishing Plc
50 Bedford Square, London, WC1B 3DP, UK
1385 Broadway, New York, NY 10018, USA
29 Earlsfort Terrace, Dublin 2, Ireland

BLOOMSBURY, I.B. TAURIS and the I.B. Tauris logo
are trademarks of Bloomsbury Publishing Plc

First published in Great Britain 2021
This paperback edition published 2022

Copyright © Richard Phillips, Claire Chambers, Nafhesa Ali, Kristina Diprose
and Indrani Karmakar, 2021

Richard Phillips, Claire Chambers, Nafhesa Ali, Kristina Diprose and Indrani
Karmakar have asserted their right under the Copyright, Designs and Patents Act,
1988, to be identified as Authors of this work.

For legal purposes the Acknowledgements on p.xi constitute
an extension of this copyright page.

All rights reserved. No part of this publication may be reproduced or
transmitted in any form or by any means, electronic or mechanical, including
photocopying, recording, or any information storage or retrieval system,
without prior permission in writing from the publishers.

Bloomsbury Publishing Plc does not have any control over, or responsibility for,
any third-party websites referred to or in this book. All internet addresses given
in this book were correct at the time of going to press. The author and publisher
regret any inconvenience caused if addresses have changed or sites have ceased
to exist, but can accept no responsibility for any such changes.

A catalogue record for this book is available from the British Library.

A catalog record for this book is available from the Library of Congress.

ISBN HB: 978-1-7869-9846-0
      PB: 978-1-7869-9847-7
      ePDF: 978-1-7869-9845-3
      ebook: 978-1-7869-9843-9

Typeset by Integra Software Services Pvt. Ltd.

To find out more about our authors and books visit www.bloomsbury.com
and sign up for our newsletters.

This book is dedicated to the young people from Muslim backgrounds who participated in the Storying Sexual Relationships project as interviewees, writers, performers, facilitators, tutors and critical friends.

CONTENTS

List of Figures — ix
List of Tables — x
Acknowledgements — xi

INTRODUCTION — 1

Chapter 1
SINGLE — 17

Chapter 2
MEETING — 31

Interlude 1
COMING TO TERMS — 45

Chapter 3
DATING — 59

Chapter 4
LOVE — 73

Interlude 2
SPEAKING TO STEREOTYPES — 85

Chapter 5
PRESSURE — 101

Chapter 6
MARRIED — 115

Interlude 3
(NOT SO) DIFFERENT — 128

Chapter 7
SEX — 143

Chapter 8
DREAMING 157

CONCLUSION 171

Guide to Literary Sources 186
References 191
Index 201

FIGURES

0.1 Creative writing journal written by Bilal, who took part in a series of workshops in Bradford in 2018. This extract from Bilal's diary, with its beautiful writing and crossings-out, is at once elegant and uncertain, still searching 5

2.1 A scene from the animated film *Halal Dating*, which was made by the participants in Workshop Series 1. This shows an imaginary Muslim dating gameshow. The presence of all family members acts as a humorous illustration of the collective rather than individualistic approach to relationships. The participants in this workshop described this as a common experience for British Muslims, particularly for those with South Asian heritage 32

3.1 'To date or not to date: Halal is the question'. This still from the animated film *Halal Dating*, which was made by the participants in Workshop Series 1, visualizes the conundrum faced by many young Muslims: the question of whether or not dating can ever be religiously permissible 63

3.2 Traditional first meetings between potential brides and grooms are symbolized by the tea and biscuits which are typically served by the young woman, with all eyes on her. Tea and biscuits are, of course, also symbols of Britishness, Pakistaniness, and wholesome hospitality. This still image is from the animated film *Halal Dating*, which was made by the participants in Workshop Series 1 64

3.3 Those who entertain the possibility that dating can be religiously permissible tend to agree that it should not involve physical contact and that it should be chaperoned. Given the challenges of the former for two young people who are drawn to each other but find themselves anxious about the awkwardness of being chaperoned, some young Muslims speak of dating over the phone and online. This image, illustrating such virtual dating, is from the animated film *Halal Dating*, which was made by the participants in Workshop Series 1 64

6.1 In this light-hearted depiction of marital conflict, a woman throws a shoe at her husband for his smoking habit. This scene is taken from the animated film *Halal Dating*, which was made by the participants in Workshop Series 1. This image, and the storyline accompanying it, express realistic rather than idealistic ideas about marriage. The young animators acknowledge the existence of conflict and exasperation, even in marriages that generally work 126

TABLES

0.1	Storying Workshops: these series of workshops, each involving around six meetings, were conducted between July 2017 and April 2019	15
1.1	Interviews quoted in Chapter 1, 'Single'	28
1.2	Workshop participants and convenors quoted in Chapter 1, 'Single'	29
2.1	Interviews quoted in Chapter 2, 'Meeting'	44
2.2	Workshop participants and convenors quoted in Chapter 2, 'Meeting'	44
I1.1	Interviews quoted in Interlude 1, 'Coming to Terms'	58
I1.2	Workshop participants and convenors in Interlude 1, 'Coming to Terms'	58
3.1	Interviews quoted in Chapter 3, 'Dating'	71
3.2	Workshop participants and convenors quoted in Chapter 3, 'Dating'	72
4.1	Interviews quoted in Chapter 4, 'Love'	84
4.2	Workshop participants and convenors quoted in Chapter 4, 'Love'	84
I2.1	Interviews quoted in Interlude 2, 'Speaking to Stereotypes'	98
I2.2	Workshop participants and convenors quoted in Interlude 2, 'Speaking to Stereotypes'	99
5.1	Interviews quoted in Chapter 5, 'Pressure'	113
5.2	Workshop participants and convenors quoted in Chapter 5, 'Pressure'	113
6.1	Interviews quoted in Chapter 6, 'Married'	127
6.2	Workshop participants and convenors quoted in Chapter 6, 'Married'	127
I3.1	Interviews quoted in Interlude 3, '(Not So) Different'	141
I3.2	Workshop participants and convenors quoted in Interlude 3, '(Not So) Different'	141
7.1	Interviews quoted in Chapter 7, 'Sex'	155
7.2	Workshop participants and convenors quoted in Chapter 7, 'Sex'	155
8.1	Interviews quoted in Chapter 8, 'Dreaming'	169
8.2	Workshop participants and convenors quoted in Chapter 8, 'Dreaming'	170
C.1	Interviews quoted in Conclusion	185
C.2	Workshop participants and convenors quoted in Conclusion	185

ACKNOWLEDGEMENTS

This book is informed by a research project entitled 'Storying Sexual Relationships: The Stories and Practices of Young British Pakistani Muslims' (https://www.sheffield.ac.uk/storyingrelationships). We gratefully acknowledge the support of the Arts and Humanities Research Council (AHRC), which funded this research (Grant Number AH/N003926/1).

We would like to thank the young people who participated in this project, and to thank them for their time and the trust they invested in us, particularly in interviews and creative workshops. For their trust and support, then, we are grateful to all those who agreed to be interviewed (mostly by Nafhesa) or to interview others, including friends and members of their communities. These 'community interviewers' included Maryah Khan, Anas Makda and Raeesa Hussain.

We also want to acknowledge those – too numerous to list here – who attended creative workshops, encouraging each other with feedback, camaraderie and constructive criticism. Special thanks to those who led these workshops: the playwright Sara Shaarawi, novelist Safina Mazhar, bloggers Talat Yaqoob and Faiza Yousaf, and the artist Stacy Bias and writers Afshan D'souza-Lodhi, Mohammed Barber, Atta Yaqub and John Siddique. Also to those who convened and hosted the workshops. We extend particular gratitude to Syma Ahmed, the Women's Project Development Worker at the Glasgow Women's Library (GWL). This is a library we have come to love and admire, and which has itself been a key partner in this project. Others who nurtured these workshops and young writers, and who we regard as friends of the project, include Kamal Kaan, Syima Aslam (Bradford Literature Festival) and Sheraz Mohammed (Hamer Youth Group, Rochdale).

Some of the stories printed in this book and others told within the broader project have also been brought to life on the stage and through the medium of film. For this work we wish to acknowledge Edinburgh's Stellar Quines Theatre Company, and filmmakers Cathy Giles and Ben Giles (https://www.matobo.co.uk/). Short films about the project and readings of a selection of stories by authors in this book, and others too, can be viewed online (follow links through www.sheffield.ac.uk/storyingrelationships). Thanks also to BBC Radio and TV for their coverage of this research, including through the BBC Asian Network, BBC Radio Sheffield and BBC Look North.

We owe a debt of gratitude to others who contributed to this project. Kasia Narkowicz coded interviews and brought valuable insights to the interpretation of findings. Jo Britton commented insightfully and generously on the text. Freya Liddle, Michal Kupis and Gill Eyre provided valuable administrative support. Team members presented work in progress in numerous settings and meetings, and we are grateful to audiences and organizers for their feedback, encouragement and invitations to speak. These include BBC Radio 4's Woman's Hour (4 September 2020), the Media in Muslim Contexts Conference (Aga Khan University, 2016), Postcolonial Studies Association Convention (2017), Nordic Geographers Meeting (Stockholm 2017 and Trondheim 2019), Kings College London, the University of Glasgow, the Department of Communities and Local Government (Home Office, London), and other events. Warm thanks are due too to the Alwaleed Centre, University of Edinburgh, and to Stellar Quines Theatre Company, who helped fund the performance at the Glasgow 'Women Making Choices' event. Actors and performers included the wonderful Atta Yaqub, Taqi Nazeer, Maryam Haidi, Mandy and Lubna Kerr. Thank you to all those who engaged with these events. Special thanks are due to Kirsten Simonsen and Lasse Martin Koefoed for their inspirational keynote paper in a session at the Nordic Geographers Meeting, Trondheim in 2019.

We are grateful to Kim Walker, Melanie Scagliarini, Olivia Dellow and colleagues at Zed/Bloomsbury for their support and vision, and to the anonymous reviewers whose constructive criticisms of the proposal and manuscript have greatly improved this book.

INTRODUCTION

'I would have liked more time to get to know my husband, but we could only talk over the phone.'

'I think I'm gay, but I can't tell my mum.'

'I fancy her but how can I meet her?'

'My husband doesn't seem sexually attracted to me. What should I do?'

'My mum goes to *rishta* parties. I think it's funny.'

'Is it okay to date?'

'I don't want to marry … yet.'

'My parents knew I was being abused by my uncle, but they kept it hidden.'

'Two girls at school were caught holding hands. One of their parents found out about it and sent her to Pakistan.'

For many young people, it is difficult to speak about sexual relationships, to know what they want and to put experiences and desires into words. Particularly when it comes to young Muslims born and living in Western countries, there are added complications. On the one hand, these women and men write or speak in the shadow of stereotypes about them. Islamophobic and racist tropes are found in political arguments, in newspapers and on TV, and in what passes for common knowledge: things people think they know about Muslims' attitudes towards issues such as homosexuality and marriage. On the other hand, the things that young Muslims can say about sexual relationships and the things they can do are shaped, and in some cases constrained, from within their communities by religious understandings and social and cultural norms, and more directly by older family members and community members. And so, while trying to get on with the wonderful and difficult business of living sexual lives – making sense of and learning to express desires; losing their virginity; finding a partner to love; negotiating the expectations and prejudices of friends, family and strangers; attempting to make relationships and marriages work; struggling through break-ups – young Muslims face added pressures.

The fragments quoted above – memories, statements, dilemmas and questions – point to some stories that young British Muslims are beginning to tell about sex and relationships. These stories have a threefold significance: for those who are telling them, for their communities and for the wider societies in which they live. In his study of sexual stories, sociologist Ken Plummer reflected that the telling of stories can be personally therapeutic and socially transformative. He explained that although some stories narrate events, they can do more than advancing coherent accounts of what has already happened. At very least, they encourage interpretation of those events because of their selection and ordering, all the while making meaning. Plummer argues that '*[w]hatever else a story is, it is not simply the lived life.* It speaks all around the life: it provides routes into a life, lays down maps for lives to follow, suggests links between a life and a culture' (1995: 168; emphasis in original; see also Adams 2016). Since a story does not simply or necessarily represent, its potential is to 'play with possibilities' (Cameron 2012: 585). When young Muslims write and tell stories of sex and love, they identify and make choices about the kinds of relationships they may or may not want for themselves, and sometimes confront anxieties about the relationships others may want for them. In so doing, they distil and explore experiences, reflect upon desires and open up possibilities.

While it may be empowering for individuals to tell their own stories, and perhaps also explore the forward momentum of their lives, their storytelling often has a wider significance within their communities. When young people tell their stories, they may challenge intergenerational dynamics in which younger people tend to be spoken for and talked over. Older relatives and sometimes so-called community leaders typically have a powerful hand in shaping the lives of young Muslims, particularly in deciding when, whether and to whom they will marry. When young people speak for themselves, this intergenerational order may be disrupted.

Their stories of sex and love have a wider significance still, for they speak to representations of Muslim minorities in Western societies. They speak to stereotypes that permeate through mainstream journalistic, media and political discourse: stereotypes of the loveless Muslim marriage, the sexually tyrannical Muslim man and the passive Muslim woman, to name but a few. We do not want to say too much about these stereotypes now, since the stories we share in this book represent so much more than knee-jerk reactions to Islamophobic and racist stereotypes. We discuss this later in an interlude on the ways in which young Muslims are 'speaking to stereotypes'.

So, there is a lot going on when young Muslims speak about sex and relationships. To paraphrase Plummer, they are speaking about their lives, envisaging routes into their lives, laying down maps to follow and suggesting 'links between a life and a culture' (Plummer 1995: 168). At the same time, their stories have a value of their own, an imaginative and in some cases literary value, which goes beyond any social or political purpose they might have. This value rests within their words, and within writing and reading, telling and hearing as ends in themselves.

Stories

In the stories we have quoted, young people speak of being single, dating, feeling lonely, loving and being loved, and making relationships work (and, in each case, struggling with these things). They allude to the experiences of individuals who are sexually active and those who are celibate, of those in relationships and those who are single, of straight and LGBTQ+, unmarried, married and divorced, and of those who know what they want and those who do not. These are tantalizingly brief points of departure, some of which leave the listener or the reader wanting more, curious about the fictional or nonfictional characters in the story and possibly identifying with them. To expand upon these fragments and introduce the three kinds of sources that we will focus upon – published fiction, amateur creative writing and conversations – we now turn to three more sustained stories.

Love in a Headscarf: Muslim Woman Seeks the One

Love in a Headscarf, a work of creative life writing by Shelina Zahra Janmohamed, recounts the female protagonist's wearisome relationship journey. She deals with aunties and matchmakers, hopelessly unsuitable boys and internet dating – all the while striving not to compromise her faith. Reflecting the author's own experiences – Janmohamed is a practising Muslim with East African Asian heritage who covers her hair and sometimes leads discussion at her local mosque – this book communicates deep religiosity and the prejudice with which it is sometimes received.

Claire Chambers (2013), Rehana Ahmed (2015) and Lucinda Newns (2017) have already discussed the way in which Janmohamed's memoir circulates in the global literary marketplace as a positive twist on what Gillian Whitlock has termed the 'veiled bestseller': books which typically feature a veiled woman on the cover and revolve around misery and oppression (2007). The design of the paperback edition identifies this book as mainstream 'chick lit'. The cover art, with its glamorous heroine wearing fashionably huge shades and a flowing pink hijab while driving an open-top sports car through London's mosque- and Ferris wheel-lined streets, sends out the important message that practising Muslim women can be as happy and fun-loving as any heroine of mainstream chick lit. The *Daily Mail*, a conservative mainstream tabloid newspaper, praised Janmohamed's volume as 'a wonderfully funny romantic adventure' (qtd in Janmohamed 2009, back blurb). The *Daily Mail* article implicitly endorsed the book's portrayal of a Muslim woman who, if not necessarily belying the stereotype of the passive and unhappy spouse, demonstrates that Muslim women need not submit to that way of being.

Love in a Headscarf's narrative arc departs from the individualistic underpinnings of other works in life writing, chick lit and related genres: 'My marriage', declares

Janmohamed, 'was a collective endeavour' (2009: 64). This theme recurs throughout the novel, for example in a chapter on Muslim speed dating, in which the whirling pairs at the dating tables dissolve into the throngs encircling the sacred Kaaba at Mecca on Janmohamed's subsequent Hajj pilgrimage, prompting reflection on individual and communitarian love:

> I knew that I was different because I was me, but I was also the same as everyone, because I was a human being. Each of us occupied so many spaces and identities, and that made us multiversal, not identical.
>
> I had been searching to find a partner to love and had been trying to learn about Divine love. In front of me now I realised that there was one more kind of love that was essential: the love for other human beings.
>
> (246)

Two ideas that are repeated in *Love in a Headscarf* are, firstly, that marriage is 'half your faith' (56). As one chapter heading puts it, men and women are 'From a Single Soul, Created in Pairs' (178), so to get married completes the circle. Moreover, in Islam, Allah is supposed to be gender-neutral, unlike in Judaism and Christianity which have their father God. Secondly, Janmohamed makes it clear that love can come after marriage, contrary to Hollywood portrayals of what she terms 'Finding the One, Falling in Love, Getting Married, and Living Happily Ever After' (53). She privileges a hard-headed, exhaustive selection process in the choosing of a life partner, rather than believing in love at first sight.

For all it does say, there are silences in this book. One specific issue, which is emblematic of the limitations some Muslims experience in their sexual lives and which speaks to the existence of desires that cannot be contained within conventional marriage, is same-sex sexuality, the existence of which is ignored in this book, but taken up in others, as we shall see.

'A Day of Love'

A second story is handwritten by a young Muslim man, a twenty-two-year-old student. This was written in the second in a block of six creative writing workshops held in Bradford in March 2018, organized by the authors of this book and led by the British Muslim-heritage author John Siddique. This handwriting is elegant and articulate – beautiful to look at – and tellingly messy. Its crossings-out speak of a search for the right words, and a struggle to find them. Like some other pieces by this young man, written within these workshops, the story is ambiguous, addressed to a gender-neutral 'you', and it is both tentative and suggestive. Here, in a preliminary piece of creative writing, the writer is exploring possibilities of sexual love.

As the subtitles to 'A Day of Love' suggest, this piece was written in response to clear instructions issued by John as the workshop leader. This was the most demanding task participants were invited to complete in the session. It involved them doing 'free writing' for two to three minutes on a topic before switching to spend the same length of time on a different but related topic. Students started with 'A memory of love', moved to 'A memory of a colour connected to that love', 'A sound or song relating to the love', 'A picture of the person', 'A meal with that person' and so forth. In multisensory detail, students built up a rounded depiction of their protagonist's love interest. In this particular student's case, extra dimensions are revealed by the adjectives he chose to gesture towards or rebel against the clandestine nature of the relationship described: 'The stifled giggle [...] unburdened curiosity. A guarded kindness. But an open friendship. An even more open mind!' Here, in the first draft of a piece of creative writing, we get a stylistically raw but tender and confessional sense of a young man exploring sexual love and desire.

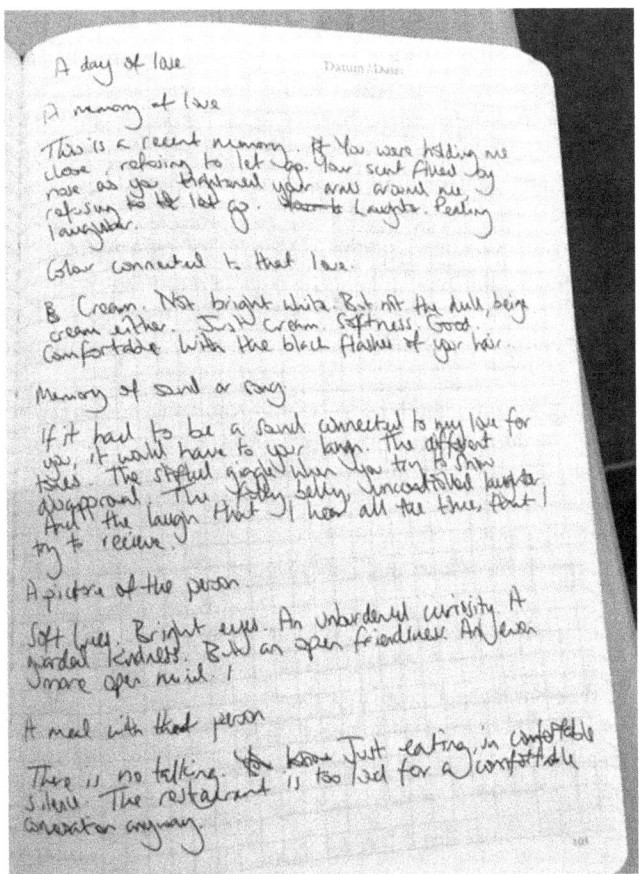

Figure 0.1 Creative writing journal written by Bilal, who took part in a series of workshops in Bradford in 2018. This extract from Bilal's diary, with its beautiful writing and crossings-out, is at once elegant and uncertain, still searching. Reproduced by permission of the author (Bilal).

Cautionary tales

Alongside the stories that are printed and read, and those jotted down in notebooks and diaries, other stories circulate in everyday life, in conversations with friends, family members and others. For the purposes of this project, we invited young Muslims to retell some of the stories they had previously heard and shared, and to tell others for the first time, drawing upon their own lives. Since they are conversational, these spoken words are inevitably less coherent and confident than published fiction and writing notebooks. However, spoken words can also be more vivid and revealing, in keeping with oral traditions of storytelling. Two of the stories that we collected in this way include vignettes about unplanned trips to Pakistan. They signal ideas about the transnational lives of many British Muslims, and of Pakistan in particular as a place of importance and symbolism, if not always affection or aspiration, among these young people.

One young woman – twenty-three-year-old Dua – spoke of a friend who had been dating another British Pakistani, a young man of around her age. One day, the boyfriend disappeared from her life. He had been sent to Pakistan for an arranged marriage, and later returned with a wife. The young woman took revenge by sending black roses to the home where he lived with his extended family. She left messages for him and expressed her anger that he should be so compliant with his family's wishes, at her expense.

Where would one even buy black roses? Such a flower may not exist in nature but is undeniably vivid in the imagination. What is important to note here are not points of factual detail but some fundamental (and universal?) truths about love, betrayal, jealousy and revenge, all of which are real and eloquently expressed in this story.

Another young woman, eighteen-year-old Saamiya (whom we will hear more from in the course of this book), identifies as a lesbian and lives in Glasgow. Saamiya recounted a story that made an impression on her when still in school, and has haunted her ever since. Like the tale of the black roses, this story 'about a friend' may or may not be accurate, but that does not undermine its power and significance to the young woman telling the story:

> A couple of months back when I was in my last year of school, two girls who are both Muslim got like caught holding hands, or just like kissing each other's cheek, and their parents got called up because it is a Catholic school, so they are quite strict about these kinds of things. And like once their parents found out they were completely separated: one was sent off to Pakistan with her family for a good couple of months.

The story seems to have functioned as a warning, threatening any girl who might hear it with a one-way ticket to Pakistan, should she step out of line and resist the heteronormativity not only of her family and community but also the religious – Catholic – school in which she was being educated. This was not an empty threat. Parents, older relatives and community members do sometimes send young people to Pakistan, hoping this will bring them into line (Samad and Eades 2002). Elders arrange and sponsor 'punitive, correctional or rehabilitative visits' to Pakistan for sons and daughters whom they see as wayward (Bolognani 2014: 110; Shaw 2000).

Stories of, by and for young Muslims

These overviews and fragments of stories – a novel, a page or two from a creative writing journal and some snippets from interviews – open windows onto the lives of Muslims in Britain. Of course, these small stories should not be seen as representative of towards three million Muslims living in Britain, nor of the stories they might tell. British Muslims are diverse in terms of their ethnic affiliations and family backgrounds, as well as their ages, sexualities, gender and class. Still, these small stories do resonate, telescoping into a constellation of broader stories and issues. In this way, they introduce themes that will become important in this book.

First, each of these stories speak of the centrality of religion in young Muslims' relationships. *Love in a Headscarf* describes a search for love, conducted within a religious framework which the author–narrator has not simply inherited through her birth and upbringing; she has also chosen this for herself, deciding what it should mean. Those who are brought up in Muslim families and communities tend to experience certain sexual attitudes and expectations, which take variable forms but share in common certain features. These include assumptions that men and women will marry a person of the opposite sex while they are young, and that these marriages are not just a matter for them but also their families, who play a part in arranging and sanctioning them (Pande 2014). Conversely, these expectations leave little room for same-sex relationships (Yip 2004b), premarital relationships, dating that includes sexual intimacy, and individualistic relationships. These are broad generalizations, of course, but they capture some of the experiences of sex and love that many different Muslims recognize. That said, individuals make choices about the ways in which they position themselves as Muslims, and the ways in which they follow this through in relation to sex and love, and in other areas of their lives (Hall 1990; Alexander 2000). In *Love in a Headscarf* Janmohamed actively portrays herself as Muslim, which percolates into the religiously principled (but never dour) way in which she searches for a man. Though some readers might find her romantic adventures tame and inhibited, this reading does not stand up to scrutiny. Pnina Werbner explains one of the attractions of Islam for the many young women in Britain who (like many of their male counterparts) are increasingly positioning themselves as Muslims (see also Mondal 2008; Lewis 2007): 'The girls argue that Islam accords equality to men and women, that it requires young people's consent to a marriage and allows them to choose their own partner, and even to associate with their fiancés before marriage. Islam also opens up a much wider marriage market for young people' (Werbner 2007: 161). Thus, many Muslims find that their religion can be an enabling resource rather than exerting limitations on their search for a life partner.

Second, as the stories of unplanned visits to Pakistan illustrate, transnational family and community ties and histories also have a strong bearing on the lives of young British Muslims. Pakistan is particularly important in this context, given that more British Muslims trace their heritage to that country than to any other (43 per cent of English Muslims have Pakistani heritage; the figures for Wales and Scotland are 33 per cent and 67 per cent, respectively (Office for National Statistics 2015)). Conversely, most (over 90 per cent) of British Pakistanis are Muslims (Change Institute 2009: 7–8; Muslim Council of Britain 2015). Pakistani marriage customs have an impact in Britain, as we shall see as this book unfolds. For some, this means following marriage traditions; for others, it extends to marrying men and women from Pakistan (Casey 2016; Qureshi, Charsley and Shaw 2014; Mohammad 2015; Shaw 2006). Meanwhile, many other British Muslims identify with other homelands and diasporic communities, including Bangladesh, India, Somalia, Nigeria and other parts of South Asia and Africa, which bring marriage customs and traditions of their own.

Although the stories we have begun to analyse shadow forth the power of religion and cultural heritage in the lives of young people, their authors and protagonists are not simply constrained. The fictional or real girl in Saamiya's story, sent off to Pakistan against her will, does not have any real choice. But many young people do make decisions about whether and how to be Muslim and/or relate to Pakistani heritage, and about which of these identity components to prioritize in particular contexts. Particular young men and women may come to very different conclusions about the implications of being a Muslim or a member of a Pakistani or other primarily Muslim community, in terms of the ways in which they marry and react to any sexual desire they may feel.

It is therefore necessary to situate the specific stories, with which we have begun this book, within a bigger picture, a wider set of stories about the sexual lives of Muslims in Britain and other Western countries. A series of recently published, groundbreaking books, TV documentaries and dramas, newspaper articles and online commentaries have started to explore and confront stereotypes of variously oversexed or undersexed Muslims. In doing so, they are putting something happier and more ordinary in their place. Examples include a collection of essays that promise to 'dispel the narrow image of what a Muslim woman [...] looks and lives like' – *The Things I Would Tell You: British Muslim Women Write*, edited by Sabrina Mahfouz (2017: 8). Another book along these lines is Mariam Khan's *It's Not about the Burqa: Muslim Women on Faith, Feminism, Sexuality and Race* (2019). Ayesha Nattu and Nura Maznavi, working with stories from the United States, have also edited two books about the sexual lives of Muslims in the West: *Love, InshAllah: The Secret Love Lives of American Muslim Women* (2012) and *Salaam, Love: American Muslim Men on Love, Sex, and Intimacy* (2014) shift attention from the sensational and the stereotypical to the experiences of ordinary Muslims who 'present complex lives and identities', telling tales of 'romance, sex, and their sense of self' (Mattu and Maznavi 2012: x). Other books attend more directly to the lives of gay and lesbian Muslims, including Shanon Shah's *The Making of a Gay Muslim* (2017).

The challenge in representing the sexual lives of Muslims is to steer a course between the extremes of stereotypes and counter-stereotype, Islamophobia and Islamophilia. This means moving beyond negative stereotypes of sexually constricted and miserable lives, without resorting to equally simplistic representations of happy Muslims. It means reaching beyond the clichés that dominate the mainstream media on the one hand, and reactive, Islamophilic interventions on the other (Shryock 2010).

An accordingly low-key approach to this highly charged issue has been pioneered in a number of measured and scholarly studies of the sexual attitudes and practices of Muslims. Some instances are Fida Sanjakdar's *Living West, Facing East: The (De)construction of Muslim Youth Sexual Identities* (2011), which is primarily concerned with sexual and religious education and curricula, and Umm Zakiyyah's *Let's Talk about Sex and Muslim Love: Essays on Intimacy and Romantic Relationships in Islam* (2016). The premise of the latter is that 'sex, intimacy, and love remain taboo topics in many Muslim circles today' and that it would be better if these issues could be discussed more openly (Zakiyyah 2016: n.p.). These books sit alongside others that explore the experiences of Muslims in non-Western and Muslim-majority societies, for example *Sexuality in Muslim Contexts: Restrictions and Resistance*, edited by Anissa Hélie and Homa Hoodfar (2012).

But more remains to be done if the sexual lives of young Muslims are to be demystified and seen more clearly by themselves and others. Accordingly, this book presents an unsensational picture of the sexual lives of Muslims through stories told by young Muslim men and women themselves. Their stories are at once specific and ordinary. In their specificity, they speak of the circumstances of Muslims and particular Muslim communities. For young Muslims trying to tell stories about sex and love, this means being careful with language, weighing up what can and cannot be said and done within their families and communities. But their stories are not unique; they have much in common with those of other young people. As such, these stories neither reproduce nor crudely contradict stereotypes. So, when young Muslims story their sexual relationships, they necessarily face in two directions and with two audiences in mind. In this book, we explore some of the words that they are choosing as they perform this challenging balancing act. Crucially, stories are instrumental in all this.

Storying: Researching stories

The stories with which we opened this book are diverse: they include an extract of life writing, a reflection on love and some conversational hearsay. As a body, they indicate the eclecticism of stories and the variety of forms that 'storying' can take. This includes so much more than storytelling and narrative (Gubrium and Holstein 2008). Storying incorporates but reaches beyond the various types of storytelling identified by Robert Atkinson: 1) ordering experiences and events; 2) affirming and validating experiences, relationships, morality, order; 3) evoking mystery and awe, as in religious storytelling; 4) interpreting and ordering the world or other wider structures (1998: 9–10). Storying also goes beyond conventional storytelling media – the spoken and written word – to include other media. It offers many ways to describe, explore and reimagine experiences and relationships. Stories, in their manifold forms, are central to how people make sense of experiences and construct narratives of the self (Fraser 2012).

For researchers and storytellers alike, storying is a powerful way of getting at things that many people consider sensitive or private. Whether as a literary device, social practice or research method, it speaks to areas in which direct questions and answers are awkward or uncomfortable. Sensitive subjects, where storying and other forms of arts-based research have been effective, include eating disorders (Leavy 2010), grief (Vickers 2002), sexual abuse (Harvey et al. 2000) and sex itself. Storying can be blunt – recounting experiences and describing memories. It may equally approach subjects with delicate indirectness, such as through fictional characters and scenarios, and via allusive rather than explicit content (Plummer 1995). Hence, the power of storying as a means of exploring sex and love (Bochner, Ellis and Tillmann-Healy 1997). Sexual stories encompass such forms as autobiography and fiction, as well as distilled or embellished accounts of desire, first meetings, relationship tensions, sexual encounters, unrequited and problematic love.

In this book we follow Australian researchers Louise Phillips and Tracey Bunda's lead in framing 'research through, with and as storying' (Phillips and Bunda 2018, title quoted). Relationships are 'storied' across contrasting spheres of life, from sustained works of fiction to scribbling in diaries, and from narrative storytelling to unstructured conversations with family and banter with friends. As such, it is appropriate to draw upon a range of sources, bringing appropriate methods to each, with expertise from across the social sciences and humanities. Accordingly, for the purposes of this book, we elicited, collected and interpreted three kinds of spoken and written material. Together, these methods and sources reach stories that people are not yet telling as well as those that they are (Sandelowski 1991). Our first method involves reading published 'relationship stories' including fiction and blogs which are about, by and for young British Muslims, particularly those with Pakistani heritage. Second are stories crafted by young British Muslims of Pakistani heritage through writing workshops convened as part of the Storying Sexual Relationships research project. Third and finally are conversations with young British Muslims of Pakistani heritage in the form of individual and group interviews, and exchanges in reading groups and performance events, all of which were conducted through this project.

The contrasting methods and sources that we introduce in more detail below are complementary in the sense that they speak to but do not simply echo each other. Fiction can sometimes be more outspoken and dramatic than stories told in person, the former confronting issues such as forced marriage and premarital or extra-marital sex. Creative writing, too, can move more decisively from the prosaic facts of life, as young people live or might expect to live these out, and can freely explore realms of possibility. This imaginative literature has greater tolerance for ambiguity and uncertainty, raising issues without necessarily taking a stand on them. Meanwhile, the spoken word has a form and a power of its own, allowing for spontaneity and dialogue, and sometimes breaking free of the genres and conventions of the written word. Together, these different stories paint an illuminating, composite picture of some young people's lives and futures: a picture of sexual relationships as they are and as they might be.

Published stories

Sexual relationships are prominent in fiction, nonfiction, poetry, blogs, screenplays, essays and other published literature of and by British Muslims. In our readings of published literature, we are primarily interested in fiction: specifically, novels that explore sex and love from the perspectives of young Muslims. Specialist genres with which we engage include Muslim 'chick lit', young adult (YA) fiction and what might be termed queer Muslim fiction.

Muslim chick lit, which includes creative memoirs such as *Love in a Headscarf*, shares many of the traits of its wider genre, including an interest in sex, love and relationships, as well as a lightness of touch and playful style. YA fiction is 'age appropriate' to some of the younger Muslims with whom we are concerned in this book, and in some cases was formative reading for others when they were younger. Many YA novels are also concerned with sex and love. Moreover, YA writing remains a relatively unexplored field, especially when it comes to ethnic minority authors and Muslims in Britain. Examples of relevant YA books published by Muslim-heritage authors in Britain include Sufiya Ahmed's *Secrets of the Henna Girl* (2012), which explores forced marriage and a young woman's abduction to Pakistan, and other novels with British Pakistani and Muslim themes including Muhammad Khan's *I Am Thunder*.

A third body of imaginative literature, which we shall tentatively call queer Muslim fiction, explores a wider range of sexual possibilities, tackling the heteronormative blind spots of works of life writing such as *Love in a Headscarf*, and disrupting sexual expectations and conventions (hence the term queer, which is more than a synonym for gay). This literature is exemplified in novels such as Amjeed Kabil's *Straightening Ali* (2007), which tells the story of twenty-four-year-old Ali Mirza, a gay Pakistani-heritage man from Birmingham, and Fatima Bhutto's *The Runaways* (2019a), one of whose three protagonists, Sunny Jamal, is attracted to other men. Other books from this broadly defined literary landscape explore extra-marital affairs, as for example in Hanif Kureishi's *The Black Album* (1996/1995) and Nadeem Aslam's *Maps for Lost Lovers* (2004), as well as sexual questioning and coming of age, as in Kureishi's *The Buddha of Suburbia* (1990) and Zahid Hussain's *The Curry Mile* (2006).

In evaluating these works, we employ the standard English Literature methodology of close reading, which examines works for their minute connotations, larger significance and writerly techniques, as well as placing them in a broader field of (con)texts (Federico 2016). We have selected two or three texts to focus upon in each of the substantive chapters of this book. Being selective in this way allows us to critically analyse these books, setting them alongside the other stories which we collected in creative writing workshops and interviews, as explained below.

Creative workshops

The page from a creative writing notebook reproduced above (Figure 0.1) introduces a second set of sources and methods which we discuss in this book. These include stories crafted by young British Muslims through a series of creative workshops which we convened from 2017 to 2019. In these workshops, we collaborated with established writers and bloggers, and with an animator and a playwright, all of whom facilitated writing workshops (Table 0.1). We also worked with schools and community groups, who drew on their networks to invite young Muslims to these workshops. The views of particular groups – which varied in terms of gender, age, educational background and occupation – were canvassed to determine the kinds of creative activities they would like to engage in, and to tailor the activities to suit them. These workshops were conceived as a form of participatory research (Kindon, Pain and Kesby 2007). We worked with participants not to extract stories from them but to enable them to find and recount their own stories. Our aim, to quote Canadian researcher Patrick Lewis, was to 'create a space for the storyteller and her story' (Lewis 2011: 506).

Each set of workshops began with an open taster session at which the research team introduced themselves and the project, and ran an exploratory activity at which potential participants could get a feel for the style of the forthcoming workshops. For example, the taster session for the animation workshops included a screening of previous work by the facilitator, and discussion of a text that served to introduce the possible topics for the activities that would follow: an essay entitled 'Islamic Tinder' by Triska Hamid (2017). A taster session at a high school (known locally as a college) in Sheffield was arranged by a teacher who wanted to encourage these young people to read and write more confidently. This session included presentations by two young Muslim authors, both in their twenties, one reading from his blog posts, the other from a short story. These writers additionally spoke to the participants about their earlier experiences of writing and publishing. Some of the other workshops involved less formal introductory sessions, and relied more on one-to-one meetings and conversations to gradually establish trust and build up viable groups, each of around six to twelve participants.

The full list of workshops is shown in Table 0.1. All drew in young Muslims in their late teens and/or twenties, though several older participants joined the women's playwriting and men's fiction workshops in Glasgow. These participants came to the sessions with younger friends, and we did not want to exclude them from the sessions.

The sets of workshops included between four and six sessions, at which participants learned and practised creative writing and explored the content they wanted to express through their newfound creative skills. Each group was given the opportunity to round off the workshops with an event enabling participants to present their creative work to audiences that included friends, family, community and members of the public. These included a film screening and public forum at a theatre in Huddersfield in 2017 and a celebration of Muslim women's writing at the Glasgow Women's Library in 2018.

Alongside the facilitator, a member of the research team attended each workshop, supporting, participating and observing in the activities. Researchers kept diaries of proceedings, taking participants and facilitators aside for short, optional interviews designed to explore their experiences and perspectives, and bringing the group together periodically for informal focus groups on the same subject. Similarly, we also recorded and in some cases – with participants' consent – filmed the discussions that took place at the taster sessions and end-of-workshop performances. We attend to these records over the course of this book. Films – including an animation entitled 'Halal Dating', several short documentaries about the writing workshops in Glasgow, and 'talking heads' style monologues in which participants read out their work – have all been posted on YouTube and are available to view (through the Storying Sexual Relationships channel on YouTube, https://www.youtube.com/channel/UCFwFkLcS80D7cxXZk4-3dTg).

Conversations

Informal interviews with participants in creative workshops, mentioned above, introduce the third set of sources and methods which we draw upon in this book. Alongside ad hoc informal interviews with individuals and in groups, which took place during and alongside creative workshops, we also arranged a more systematic programme of in-depth interviews. Interviews can be seen and directed as conversations in which stories are told and retold, and in which narratives are explored and co-constructed (Leavy 2015: 46).

We interviewed individuals whom we had accessed through our personal and project networks, and through leafleting and outreach. In total we interviewed around sixty young Muslims, aged between sixteen and thirty. We spoke to roughly equal numbers of men and women, across three British regions with particular concentrations of Muslims: Yorkshire, Glasgow and the Newcastle area (Tyne and Wear). In the interest of focus, we worked primarily with one strand of Britain's diverse Muslim communities: British Muslims of Pakistani heritage. These interviews preceded the creative workshops explained above, and took place over a twelve-month period beginning in June 2016. Not all the interviews we conducted will be quoted in this book; some were more fruitful than others. Each chapter ends with a table of interviewees who are quoted in that chapter, with some relevant information about them.

Interviews were consistent with standard social science ethical codes, which the project team readily embraced. We explained the project to participants verbally and in writing through an information sheet, allowing them every opportunity to withdraw at any stage. Participants who agreed to interviews read and signed a consent form. We refer to them through pseudonyms and preserve anonymity where possible. The only exceptions are where authors of creative work wished to take credit for their work and to have their names mentioned in this book and/or other publications coming out of the project.

The interviews began with discussions of the participants' backgrounds and identities, before moving on to focus primarily upon relationship attitudes and experiences. We were interested to see how and why these young people speak about relationships. And, when they do so, we wanted to know: how do they choose their words? What conversations are they enacting, practising, repeating and reworking? What choices are they making?

We did not explicitly ask interviewees to tell stories, and nor did we push them to reveal anything too private or personal. These young people alluded both to the facts about their lives, as they saw them, and also the choices they could make. But much of the time they also talked *around* the issues of sex, love and relationships, rather than confronting these head on. This often meant stepping out of the first person and the confessional, speaking instead of 'you' or 'they', 'he' or 'she'. Sometimes, it meant telling stories, some of which were mere fragments of happenings, rumours or ideas, rather than sustained or well-developed oral histories. As we have explained, stories involve more than chronicles of happenings, and this is true of the stories told within the interviews and other conversations, which we conducted and will discuss.

What follows

This book is comprised of two different kinds of chapter: substantive chapters and interludes, which are positioned at key junctures. The ideas, arguments and significance of the book are set out most explicitly in the interludes. The first of these – 'Coming to Terms' – takes its title from the Scottish poet Edwin Morgan (2000), who came to see his own struggle to write about and around his homosexuality as at once difficult and creative. Many of the young Muslims whose stories are explored in this book have had a parallel struggle. Their words – often preliminary and exploratory – reflect a search for language capable of breaking silences, bringing experiences and possibilities into view, while negotiating expectations, conventions and sometimes constraints. This interlude traces some different ways in which they break these silences in their spoken and written words. Second, when young Muslims speak about sex and love, they do so amid a penumbra of stereotypes, which we draw out in the second interlude: 'Speaking to Stereotypes'. We have deliberately chosen to defer this interlude until later in the book rather than starting out with it because we wanted the Muslim storytellers themselves to frame this book. Though we do not underestimate the power of stereotypes, and the racism and Islamophobia behind them, we do not want to privilege these baneful forces as our points of departure. Third, though we combat stereotypes about how and how much Muslims are different, we are not trying to claim that Muslims are not distinctive when it comes to sex and relationships. Accordingly, the third interlude – '(Not So) Different' – examines some religious and cultural norms that young Muslims negotiate in their love lives. These include particular norms surrounding marriage – when, whether, who – and the implications they contain for other sexual possibilities, whether with a person of the same or the opposite sex.

The remainder of the book – and the majority of chapters – are more directly composed around stages and themes in relationships. The themes are: Single,

Meeting, Dating, Pressure, Love, Sex, Married and Dreaming. As a reader, you may choose to go straight to chapters that interest you most rather than following a linear path through the book. That said, we have arranged the chapters intentionally, to follow the chronological order that many but not all British Muslims experience in their lives, with carefully timed pauses for reflection, in the form of the interludes. Each chapter revolves around the three types of sources – published works, new writing and interviews – which we have sketched in this introduction.

In writing this book, we wanted to acknowledge specific experiences – including those of gay and lesbian Muslims and members of particular Muslim-identified communities such as British Pakistanis – but we did not want to segregate them into chapters of their own; rather, we integrate them in the broader discussions. The chapters are not in any firm order. Mainstream relationship stories do take a linear course: beginning with desires, hopes and dreams, followed by first contact, leading sooner or later to sex, possibly love, then marriage, which is by no means the end of the story. For those whose stories are told here – and who tell their stories here – things tend to happen in a different order, and in some distinctive ways: being introduced to eligible men or women; making contacts of one's own; getting married, in most cases young; dating and getting to know a husband or wife; all this followed, sometimes, by love; consummating the marriage, when the time is right and the opportunity arises; coping with the expectations of family members; and, in some cases, life after (a first) marriage. Other young Muslims miss out some of these stages or put them in a different order. Some date before marriage, and some marry the person they already love.

Our aim, particularly in these substantive chapters, has been to allow the stories to 'breathe' and to allow the young people who have written and told them to speak for themselves in all their complexity. To this end, we have attempted to write with a light touch, avoiding jargon and minimizing distracting academic references. We hope, in this way, to have written a book that is not just about, but with and for young Muslims, and a book in which they may recognize themselves.

Table 0.1 Storying Workshops: these series of workshops, each involving around six meetings, were conducted between July 2017 and April 2019.

Series	Location	Medium	Facilitator	Gender	Ages
1	Sheffield	Animation	Stacy Bias	Mixed	18–30
2	Bradford	Creative writing	John Siddique	Mixed	18–30
3	Sheffield	Creative writing	Afshan D'souza-Lodhi	Mixed	16–18
4	Glasgow	Playwriting	Sara Shaarawi	Women	18–40
5	Glasgow	Fiction	Safina Mazhar	Women	18–30
6	Glasgow	Blogging	Talat Yaqub and Faiza Yousaf	Women	18–30
7	Rochdale	Fiction	Mohammed Barber	Men	18–30
8	Glasgow	Fiction	Atta Yaqub	Men	17–46

Chapter 1

SINGLE

Across the green stands his crush, alone. This is it. This is his opportunity to say what he has felt for months and let it out into the open, to be free of the burden of 'What if?'

(Yusuf, twenty-two, synopsis for story, 'What If?')

As a young woman, I have concerns about entering into a relationship. Most of us do, it's a given. Will it work? Will it be magical? Will we argue? The biggest fear before entering a relationship is the worry that it won't be equal. The biggest fear, for me, is losing myself. But most young Muslim women face that challenge nearly every day […] The fear of losing our voice in a relationship, the ability to make our own decisions, but most importantly, our freedom. That's what is at stake.

(Noura, twenty-eight, blog post, 'Finding Your Power')

Being single can be a time of freedom and exploration, but it can also be a time of fear – of loneliness, of pressure, of worry about whether the right (or wrong) person will come along. This chapter explores young Muslims' diverse experiences of singlehood, how they talk about being single and how they write about their own experiences and the single lives of fictional characters. The first extract above is from the synopsis for a short story, which the author went on to complete with support from the research team. Written by Yusuf, 'What If?' follows a gay Muslim man trying to work up the confidence to approach his first serious love interest. The story's protagonist Mateen navigates his love life amid the stress of university deadlines, job applications and sometimes low self-esteem. The second extract is from a blog piece written in a creative writing workshop at Glasgow Women's Library, in which Noura speaks more positively of singlehood as an opportunity for self-discovery. The testimony and stories in this chapter offer multiple perspectives on being young, single and Muslim, from enjoyment, self-fulfilment and planned singlehood, to ambivalence, uncertainty and anxiety about being single, to fears of single life coming to an abrupt end.

'My focus is to sort myself out right now'

For some young Muslim men like Tahir, quoted in the heading above, being single is a good thing – a chance to decide what he wants from life and prepare for what might follow. In no hurry to enter a serious relationship, he said: 'My focus is to sort myself out right now. Stop smoking and stuff like that. But if I do meet someone at college, I will be all right with it.' Others similarly spoke of enjoying single life as an opportunity to focus on themselves. Faisal, who was approaching an age to start thinking about relationships, said he didn't want to 'mess about'. Encouraged by family members, he has been prioritizing his studies; marriage may come later:

> As I have gotten older like now I am sixteen he [Dad] knows I am like, I am pretty much like, I don't like go out, mess about [...] [Auntie] treats me like her own kid and like every time I see her when I come down to see her, she will be like, 'Attend to your studies, then after you do your studies then you can do what you want. Don't mess it up right now'.

Here, singlehood is envisaged as a temporary state, with these young men articulating their openness to the possibility of future relationships when the time is right. Meanwhile, education offers a good excuse not to enter into anything serious. On the subject of marriage, Waheed observed, 'I've not thought about it yet to be honest because I've got my uni stuff and all that'.

A few years older, Salim looked back on his single days as an important time to mature and fulfil ambitions. Nearing the end of his university degree and having been single by choice for a few years, he explained that he was coming around to the idea of marriage:

> I used to be scared [laughs], like because in my head I was like I'll graduate when I'm like twenty-two, twenty-three and then I'll work for a couple of years and then I'll be twenty-five and then I'll consider marriage. But now that I'm still at uni, it was like oh no, like it's too soon like, I want to like maybe enjoy myself single a little bit first. But not in a bad way, like just like explore with your friends and do that sort of thing. But now like as I'm like getting through uni, I kind of think like I actually wouldn't mind marriage so soon, like I don't see it as such a scary thing any more [laughs].

Salim's repetitive use of the filler word 'like' and seemingly nervous laughter contrast with the seriousness of what he is talking about. Though it is not straightforward to interpret, this laughter seems to speak of embarrassment in relation to the topic of relationships, and fears about fast-approaching marriage, which he does not feel ready for.

In the light of strict rules regarding sex before marriage – rules imposed by others and adopted voluntarily by many young Muslims – the 'free and single' period is not generally a time for sexual experimentation; though some do use it this way. For many, it is a time for putting off daunting decisions and making an unrushed transition to adulthood. As Salim suggests, being single affords time to spend time with friends and focus on other goals until such a time as marriage seems less 'scary'.

'Because she didn't want to get married she just kept studying'

The above stories from Tahir, Faisal, Waheed and Salim speak to a common theme among our interviewees, and among young British Muslims in general. Time spent studying and settling into a career can be a way of putting off early marriage. Speaking about her older siblings, Rabia said there is no parental pressure to get married while they are still studying. Of her brother, she observed that 'Mum just wants him to study just now', and similarly her sister 'has only just gone to uni, so nothing like that'. Waheed said his parents won't look into arranging his older brother's marriage until the latter settles into a more permanent job: 'My parents I think just want a bit of stability in his life and then from there on in they can get to sort a relationship out for him'. This contributed to Waheed's own view that he doesn't need to turn his thoughts to marriage just yet, and can instead focus on university. In these accounts, families expect that education and work will be triaged before relationships.

Other interviewees reflected candidly on friends who are pursuing higher education as a deliberate strategy for delaying marriage for as long as possible. Safa, recently married and in her early twenties, said: 'My friends that are not married, it is only because they are in education', speaking in particular of one friend who had gone on to do a PhD. Noor, in her late twenties, said she has a lot of single female friends of a similar age. She revealed how one of these friends had confided in her about not wanting to marry the man her family has arranged for her to marry. This friend found in postgraduate study an acceptable reason to delay the marriage, rather than tell her family the truth:

> I actually know one girl, because she didn't want to get married ... um ... she just kept studying, so she just did a degree and did a master's, but the reason she is really doing it is because she didn't want to get married to the person that her family had found for her. And she knew that they won't get her to get married until she is out of studies. So I know people on both sides use study as like a – a blame kind of a reason that you can't get married.

These accounts suggest that some young British Muslims are engaged in a kind of strategic singlehood, which enables them to extend their transition to adulthood. Through indefinitely deferred educational goals, they are able to justify being single well into their twenties.

It is necessary to acknowledge, however, that while for some this continuation of singlehood is an active choice, others may feel under pressure in work or study that leaves little time or money for relationship commitments. Noor's account of her single brother, for example, emphasized his hectic work schedule as a junior doctor as an obstacle to marriage: 'the first two years of Medicine is so full on, it is like you just about eat at the end of the day. So I think it is a lot of those things, rather than him actively not wanting to get married.' In other words, pursuing education and career goals while single can be a frustrating experience, when there are self-imposed or external expectations about what needs to be done before settling down.

'I chose a string of boyfriends over one solid partner'

Young Muslim women, as well as men, spoke about being single by choice. Amilah, now married and in her late twenties, described singlehood as a time of 'freedom' and 'independency' that is increasingly common among 'strong-minded' young women, adding affirmatively: 'you know, I think that's how women should be, they shouldn't be shut down'. Likewise, Noura's blog title emphasizes the importance of 'finding your power' through singlehood, reflecting its author's resistance to early marriage:

> I'm the non-traditional Western Muslim girl. You know, that chick at family gatherings that everyone looks at and wonders why is she still single? What's wrong with her? Why hasn't her mother married her off? [...] I chose a string of boyfriends over one solid partner. But only because I believe I can find my partner after I have found my power.

Noura is somewhat atypical in being open about having had a 'string of boyfriends', owning her sexual agency and 'non-traditional' or 'Western' view of casual relationships that can be explored while single. But she is not alone in this. Fatima also expressed a notably laidback attitude to non-marital relationships:

> I'm not so much into putting conditions down on people, like you have to marry me or this is what goes on in society, blah blah blah [...] I think yeah, that comes from my family in the way I was brought up with two parents that were split up and whatever but I don't necessarily see it as a bad thing because I don't feel like I'm bound to what society thinks I should be doing.

In these accounts, Noura and Fatima speak of refusing to follow a particular script and of being in no hurry to find a husband. Together with Amilah's view of the importance of independence for her and her peers, these accounts challenge the stereotype of the submissive Muslim woman who has no say in her life, with these young women confidently staking a claim to an extended period of singlehood.

Other young women's accounts of single life are more ambivalent, often looking forward to a new life with anticipation and simultaneously worrying about what happens next. This includes accounts in published fiction and nonfiction, where singlehood is storied as a time of uncertainty, anxiety and possibility. Sometimes, following familiar tropes of the romance genre, this takes the form of a quest to find 'the One', as in Shelina Janmohamed's memoir *Love in a Headscarf*. Other narratives, such as Tabish Khair's *Just Another Jihadi Jane*, chronicle their fictional characters' strategies for avoiding marriage and protecting their freedom.

'From being one, to being part of a pair': Surviving singlehood in Love in a Headscarf

Shelina Janmohamed's memoir *Love in a Headscarf: Muslim Woman Seeks the One* (2009) follows a classic (auto)biographical Bildungsroman narrative arc to relate the author's experiences growing up as a young British Muslim in the 'bubbling ethnic mix of North London' in the 1980s (34). As the title suggests, the memoir concerns the author's quest for love: her search for a husband who will match up to her high ethical, spiritual and intellectual standards. As such, it records Janmohamed's journey through singlehood in which faith and love – both romantic and spiritual – take centre stage. All the while, she 'negotiates the perils of match-makers' and aunties' etiquette, hopelessly unsuitable boys and internet dating' (Chambers 2013: 84). Here, single life is storied around uncertainty, sometimes anxiety, but also eventfulness and always possibility.

The memoir opens with Janmohamed's family formally meeting a suitor for her. Recalling this first unsuccessful meeting with a potential groom and his relatives, she writes:

> In the process of making a decision to turn down one suitor, I had set in motion a greater journey: to look for the love of my life. The precedent was set: Finding the One was my mission, and in looking for love, I would find myself, my faith and Divine Love along the way. I had declared the search officially open.
>
> (2009: 30)

These lines set the tone for the memoir's content, pithily encapsulating the connection of faith and love that she seeks in her journey through single life. Her parents are supportive of her decision to say no to this first *rishta* (relationship or suitor) upholding the fundamental Islamic values of choice and consent. Yet, singlehood, for Janmohamed, is not devoid of its trials and tribulations, conveyed mainly in the form of her inner struggle. There are also external pressures, such as when Janmohamed becomes the subject of gossip among relatives and neighbours as she grows older and less eligible. She finds herself being showered with unsolicited advice from 'buxom aunties' (48), who apprehend that her increasing age and academic degrees may impede the effort to find a good match. Nonetheless, with time she develops a sympathetic view of these women, managing to divine genuine concerns underneath their apparently presumptuous remarks and 'mannerisms' (92).

Reluctantly single, Janmohamed details a series of meetings arranged by aunties, religious elders and others that – despite their promising origins – prove unsuccessful. Throughout this time, Janmohamed's unwavering faith sustains her. In the following passage, she explains why she persists in her quest:

> I had learnt to be philosophical about these meetings. I had to be. It was important for my sanity to keep alive a small glimmer of hope that one of these Y-chromosome unmarried individuals might have something to tease me into marrying them. For weren't human beings full of surprises? This continuing optimism, coupled with a good old-fashioned British stiff upper lip, meant that I ploughed on with the search with stoic determination.
>
> (86)

This passage effectively captures her single life, one that is rife with anxiety but not devoid of possibility. Despite such enforced optimism, readers also witness vulnerable moments, often during prayer, in which she cannot help expressing her desperation. For example, she addresses Allah in an accusatory tone:

> I really want to get married. Have a husband, settle down. Haven't you told us that getting married means to complete half of our faith? I want to follow your guidelines and I'm trying hard, so hard, to find someone. Why don't you send me someone?
>
> (91)

Her yearning is palpable and, more importantly, it is her faith that she turns to for emotional refuge.

In another passage, Janmohamed reflects on how single life can result in profound loneliness. Here, the author expresses how she felt, having been disappointed by many suitors' attempts to label her for choosing to wear a hijab:

> My heart was disintegrating in the solitude, in my increasingly lonely, empty inner world. Would I be able to find a man to share these questions with? Where was the one who could empathise with me on this journey, who was also determined to throw over the stereotypes and live his own path?
>
> (152)

Relating specifically to the Muslim context, these passionate lines betoken the isolation that an extended singlehood sometimes entails. However, we witness that the author, steadfast in her faith, develops the strength to look at 'singledom' with greater humour and understanding: 'I decided that if I couldn't find a man, then I would have a wedding anyway. I hadn't lost hope – just started to prepare myself for the idea that it might not happen' (237). This shows the degree of quiet acceptance that many single people acquire over time.

'I had not thought of marriage': Staying single in *Just Another Jihadi Jane*

Unlike the quest for love that characterizes the singlehood depicted in Janmohamed's memoir, the difficulties that accompany the single life in Tabish Khair's novel *Just Another Jihadi Jane* (2017/2016) are more material in nature.

This luminous novel follows the lives of Jamilla and Ameena, two teenagers in northern England, who become radicalized because of a range of personal and social circumstances. They end up joining ISIS in Syria, only to experience intense regret and remorse. At the beginning of the novel, Jamilla narrates their early teenage years in a way that sheds light on the complexities of her single life, marked as it is by a curious blend of faith, fear and freedom.

Ameena is a plain but daring teenager who loses her virginity at the age of fifteen or sixteen and gets into a relationship with their David Beckham-lookalike classmate Alex. Beautiful Jamilla, on the other hand, maintains a safe distance from relationships. She is intelligent enough to perceive Alex's interest in her but remains unresponsive to his implicit invitations. She is, to use Ameena's words, tinged with a strong Yorkshire accent, 't'most solemn girl in t'class' who does not even 'joke […] with t'boys' (2). Their friends do not believe that she has ever slept with a man. Jamilla's dislike of such apparently frivolous relationships owes much to her conservative, orthodox upbringing and strong sense of religious morality. While recalling her reactions to Ameena's relationships, she declares: 'In those days I was obsessed with rights and wrongs – my Islam was still a minefield of rights and wrongs' (99). Although she says this in response to Ameena's so-called 'promiscuity', these religiously inflected morals account for her own decision to remain single and a virgin. She wants to remain faithful to the particular kind of Islam that she has been taught at home, especially by her father.

However, when it comes to marriage we see Jamilla desperately trying to remain single. Like some of the young people who spoke to us for this project, she turns to higher education to delay her inevitable nuptials. This is somewhat out of kilter with her usual obedience to family values and instructions:

> I had not thought of marriage. Not one of the girls from my class had married yet. Some of them were living with partners, but these were not Muslim girls. Marriage had been something like the rumour of a distant war; now, suddenly, the cannons were at my doorstep. I did not know what to do, and simply hoped that one of my applications would get me a scholarship […] I could postpone the marriage by two or three years, until I got my degree […]. It is just that the idea of getting married right now sent me into a kind of panic.
> Oh, how I prayed for one of my applications to be successful!
> (65)

What is especially interesting about this passage is its figuration of marriage using martial imagery. This portends the day when 'the rumour of a distant war' becomes adjacent fact after Jamilla goes to Syria, where the cannons really are at her doorstep. That war and marriage are linked in this way signals the violence Jamilla believes attaches to the widespread expectations about her romantic future. The girl's life, from this point on, carries with it the constant fear of an imminent end to her singlehood. Her insistence on education has more to do with avoiding marriage than fostering her career ambitions. Despite this, she has to meet a potential groom and his family, and that makes her even more anxious. She foresees that her life will swiftly follow a dreary path of compliance and conformity, like that of her mother. She asks herself: 'Was that all I could do with my life in this world where there was so much that called out to be done? Was all my reading and piety to end in a kitchen, denying the role that a woman of true faith had to play in this life […]?' (73). This reflection suggests that singledom accords Jamilla some sense of freedom – however circumscribed it might be – which is likely to end after marriage. Her urge for self-exploration shows singlehood in a positive light.

'Forever alone'

Not all of the young people who spoke to us for this project viewed being single through such a rosy glow. Some admitted to feeling frustrated. This is evident in some responses to a screening questionnaire, which they completed before taking part in an interview. One of the questions asks about the respondent's relationship status. As an alternative to 'single', some women wrote that they were 'not-married', while others were more elliptical or mischievous, playful or evasive, identifying as 'forever alone', 'single pringle' and 'only relationship is with my books'. This suggests self-consciousness about the stigma of singlehood, which the women acknowledge but also deflect with self-deprecating humour.

Such responses were more prevalent among women than men, reflecting gendered anxieties about the urgency of finding a suitable match. Unmarried men seemed relaxed about describing themselves as single. When pressed on the subject of finding a partner, they claimed to be unflappable. One said he was 'not fussed' and 'not really thinking about it too much just now'. Talking about the possibility of future relationships, men tended to express casual optimism. Pervaiz said 'like I might – maybe find one through uni […] that's probably what I'll do. I don't have a plan', and Faisal similarly said that he will 'probably find someone myself, then get to know them better'. Compared to their female counterparts, these young men are laidback about their single status.

The prospect of remaining alone seemed increasingly real to Nabila, a divorcee who had recently turned thirty. She said that she has become 'fussier' as a result of being single for so long, making it more difficult to find someone she can settle down with:

> I don't think my expectations have lowered ever; in fact, I think they have increased. And I think that has probably been because as I have grown up you develop an understanding of life better. So – and obviously when you make your own personal achievements you don't want somebody who is going to be bringing you down. So I think for me I would want somebody on par with myself you know. I think – I would need somebody who could understand me and vice versa. You know life is a challenge on its own, and you need somebody there – to be fighting that battle with you, really. So I wouldn't say that I have lowered my expectations, in fact I think I have got more fussier as I have got older. I think I probably would have settled for somebody that you know friends have

recommended or my parent selected when I was younger, you know around the age of 16 to 24, do you know I would probably have thought that is fine.

With echoes of Janmohamed's *Love in a Headscarf*, Nabila offers an insight into extended single life and the mixed feelings it brings. On the one hand, she would prefer to have 'somebody there' to support her; on the other, she expresses a strong sense of self-worth and unwillingness to compromise in her search for a life partner. She believes that she might have 'settled for somebody' if pushed toward marriage at a younger age, but her choice of vocabulary suggests relief rather than regret in not having done so.

Other women around the same age voiced similar anxieties. Janan, also thirty, reflected on her recent experience of trying to find a husband. She felt that her confidence is off-putting to some men:

> Yeah, I think Pakistani men are actually intimidated by confident women. You know, they'll try to break you and they'll try to – I find that a lot of – you know, there's been a couple of situations now, obviously like I'm trying to get married and trying to find somebody, so I've spoke to a few people here and there. And you know, I get things like you know, 'You tick all the boxes, so I assume you're divorced.'

Here, although Janan's verbal tic (like Nabila's) of 'you know' underscores some hesitation, her expectations of Pakistani, implicitly Muslim, men are clearly quite low. However, at the end we catch a glimpse through the sometimes broken syntax of the pessimism these men may also feel. She reports that men often assume that a woman who looks so good on paper may be hiding something, such as a divorce. Taken together, these accounts present mixed pictures of singlehood, of coming to understand what you want from life and then fearing the (imagined) choice of being forever single or submitting to an unequal or unhappy match.

'He might even like you'

Some lesbian and gay Muslims enjoy being young and single, taking the opportunity to explore their sexuality, as we shall see in a later chapter on sex. Others, however, have less positive experiences. For some, singlehood may be experienced as self-censorship rather than self-discovery, as they attempt to conceal their sexuality from friends and family members. Written from the perspective of a gay Muslim man, Yusuf's short story 'What If?' documents the frustration of unspoken desire. It follows Mateen in his final days of university as he comes to terms with his feelings about a classmate and tries to work up the confidence to tell his crush how he feels. Following on from the extract that opened this chapter, Mateen decides to reveal all on graduation day, but his declaration of love does not go as planned:

> *Be cool. Be cool. He might even like you. He won't – but he might.*
>
> I start walking over, hearing my feet hitting the ground, crushing the grass beneath with every step. My heart starts to race, pounding ever faster and harder in my chest. I wring my hands continuously to wipe away the sweat.
>
> With his back still to me I say 'Hey,' to catch his attention, but my voice gets stuck in my throat so nothing comes out. I try again, but this time it sounds more like a shriek than a greeting. He certainly hears that.
>
> Tony turns around to face me. An uncertain look brought on by the shrill shriek morphs into a smile.
>
> 'Hi,' he says to me.
>
> The two of us look at each other, smiling.
>
> I don't reply immediately, stretching the pause for a moment too long. This is partly deliberate and partly because I'm awestruck that Tony is smiling; smiling at seeing me.
>
> And then I reply, finally, 'Great weather.'
>
> *The weather? Very smooth.*

Mateen's real purpose is betrayed by his all-too-obvious nerves. It is of course difficult for any young person to reveal their feelings and risk rejection, but this is made harder for Mateen by the tense backdrop to his story. Yusuf elaborates on some of this in the subplot, in which a close Muslim friend, DC, expresses his religiously justified refusal of homosexuality:

> The disgust in his voice is unmistakable.
>
> 'You're either gay or Muslim. You can't be both. It's so clear in the Qur'an as well. Completely unambiguous! Clear as day. How can they not understand this? People are free to choose what they want, so choose one. Don't force the two together. Can't square a circle.'

Knowing how this Muslim friend would react to him liking another man, Mateen feels that he cannot confide in anyone. In this story there are tantalizing moments of possibility, but singlehood is ultimately storied as an unhappy time of self-doubt, hesitation and missed opportunity. After his abortive attempt to speak his mind on graduation day, Mateen never sees Tony again. Despite these tensions and failures, Yusuf's story breaks silences, both for him and within his community. Even the protagonist's fraught conversation with his disgusted friend DC is a faltering first step.

'She pictured herself sinking into the ground, disappearing'

This chapter has told stories of young Muslims who relish their singlehood alongside those who long for an end to unpartnered loneliness. There are others for whom single life comes to an abrupt and early conclusion with their marriage. Fears of curtailed singlehood appear in creative fiction, as in Tabish Khair's *Just Another Jihadi Jane*, as well as in the stories people tell about their own experiences and those of friends and acquaintances. Responding to a prompt during a creative writing workshop at Glasgow Women's Library, Heena captured the moment a young woman arrives at the realization that her family is beginning to consider arranging her marriage:

> Alisha walks into the room and notices her gran and mother looking at her strangely. She realizes why this is when they start speaking to her about getting married. She does not feel ready for this conversation. They tell her that there were three aunties who noticed her at her cousin's wedding and asked her gran to speak with Alisha to discuss marrying their sons. Alisha felt sick. Her gran and mother were relentless. They bombarded her with questions, pressuring her to respond. Asking which one? Why not? They were emphasizing the importance of these decisions yet demanding a quick response. Alisha couldn't respond. She pictured herself sinking into the ground, disappearing and therefore not having to deal with this conversation.

In this story, Heena portrays the ephemerality of singlehood for a young woman suddenly confronted with the question of marriage and family matchmaking. From this moment, her protagonist is unable to relax and enjoy being single, even if she is able to decline or defer marriage offers. Alisha's previous obliviousness and current panic reflect the rapidity with which thoughts of marriage have been thrust upon her at a time when she does not feel ready.

Teenage Farooq recalled, with some concern, a former classmate who disappeared after her family arranged a marriage for her in Pakistan. These more serious stories, voicing young Muslims' fears about arranged or forced marriage, are crucial to recognize while resisting the temptation to generalize. For others, like Waheed, the threat of singlehood coming to an abrupt end in this way is little more than a family in-joke. Acknowledging the stereotype, he told us: 'My dad does kind of poke fun at me saying that we're going to find you a girl from Pakistan or whatever'. It was clear that in no way did he feel this was a true reflection of parental intent. Speaking casually about how he might meet someone in the future, he said: 'My parents have always told me that if you like someone, if you do it the right way then that's not a problem'.

This illustrates how some young Muslims are afforded more freedom to enjoy singlehood, and more time to be single, than others. There are also, of course, those who can't wait for singlehood to end. 'I do want to get married young [...] I need to get married soon', enthused Hanifa, opening up about her longing for a partner and a sex life. Together, these accounts speak of diverse experiences and views of singlehood and what may come after.

Conclusion

The stories recounted in this chapter have explored mixed experiences of singlehood. For some young Muslims, some of the time, these stories tell of freedom and possibility. For others, and at other times, stories of singlehood are marked by anxiety, loneliness and uncertainty. Strains of a single life are evident in Yusuf's story, 'What If?' and in Tabish Khair's novel. While being single can be lonely, it can also be a time of yearning for connection, a time of intense non-sexual friendships, and also of reflecting on relationships, laying out 'maps for lives to follow' – one of the functions of a good story, according to sociologist Ken Plummer (1995: 168).

This chapter has shown that, whether singlehood is storied positively, negatively or somewhere in between, it does exist. Muslims are often portrayed as passing from childhood to married life in the blink of an eye. Certainly, for some young Muslims, single life is shorter than for many other young people in Britain. But, contradicting the stereotype of the Muslim who is either a child or a married adult, the stories told here have illuminated a liminal stage. This does not apply to all: some Muslims may never find the right person to marry, or the right circumstances or opportunities; gay and lesbian Muslims may not feel marriage is for them, even though British law now says it is. For these and other reasons, for some Muslims single life is more than a window between childhood and marriage; it is more enduring, and extends into later life, where it takes on new meanings and brings new experiences. For young Muslims, then, single life takes different forms, lasts different lengths of time and comes with different feelings. Across this range of experiences, though, the presence and significance of singlehood, as a time of relative freedom and exploration, should be acknowledged, and in some cases celebrated.

Table 1.1 Interviews quoted in Chapter 1, 'Single'

Name	Gender	Age	Relationship Status	Location
Tahir	Male	20	Single	Glasgow
Faisal	Male	16	Single	Glasgow
Waheed	Male	21	Single	Glasgow
Salim	Male	24	Single	Newcastle
Amilah	Female	29	Married	Glasgow
Fatima	Female	21	In a relationship	Glasgow
Pervaiz	Male	18	Single	Glasgow
Nabila	Female	30	Divorced	Newcastle
Janan	Female	30	Single	Glasgow
Rabia	Female	17	Single	Glasgow
Safa	Female	22	Married	Yorkshire
Noor	Female	27	Married	Yorkshire
Hanifa	Female	22	Single	Glasgow
Farooq	Male	17	Single	Yorkshire

Table 1.2 Workshop participants and convenors quoted in Chapter 1, 'Single'

Name	Gender	Age	Workshop Series	Role in Workshop	Title
Yusuf	Male	22	7. Fiction, Rochdale	Participant	'What If?'
Noura	Female	28	6. Blogging, Glasgow	Participant	'Finding your Power'
Heena	Female	25	4. Playwriting, Glasgow	Participant	'Untitled'

Chapter 2

MEETING

> The air was smoky with sandalwood and musk, every room lit up welcomingly and to its best advantage. Aisha's mum paced the corridor, vacillating between reception and kitchen, making sure everything was prepared to perfection. Aisha stood before the mirror, having arranged and rearranged her scarf to frame her face flatteringly, and having winged her eyeliner with far more care than usual.
>
> (Liba, twenty-five, creative writing exercise)

> There's so many different ways nowadays, especially with social media and uni, you could be out shopping and you might meet someone, you never know, the families or something.
>
> (Masood, twenty-one, interview)

This chapter explores various ways in which young Muslims are embracing, questioning and reinventing the protocols around finding a partner. It includes stories of traditional introductions, like the one vividly described by Liba, above, in a creative writing exercise, in which family members play a prominent role. Some young Muslims look forward to these meetings; others scorn them; some – like the gay protagonist of Amjad Kabil's novel *Straightening Ali* (2007) – reluctantly go along with them. Other encounters, as Masood suggests above, are led by young people themselves, from online matchmaking to casual meetings at school, college, university, at work or out socializing. For some, such meetings can complement, help to reform or even supplant formal introductions by family members. In sum, these stories illuminate diverse perspectives on ideal ways of meeting: as two people interested in one another and as whole families; formally and informally; by chance or by design; with an express view to marriage and in passing moments of attraction.

'The meeting of two families'

In an animation made by a group of young Muslims on halal dating – a subject and a film we explore further in the 'Dating' chapter – one scene imagines a

Figure 2.1 A scene from the animated film *Halal Dating*, which was made by the participants in Workshop Series 1. This shows an imaginary Muslim dating gameshow. The presence of all family members acts as a humorous illustration of the collective rather than individualistic approach to relationships. The participants in this workshop described this as a common experience for British Muslims, particularly for those with South Asian heritage.

Muslim dating gameshow in which each contestant is backed by their family team (Figure 2.1). Zarah explains the animators' thinking behind this scene in an accompanying voiceover: 'in a Muslim community it's usually meeting *families* rather than just spouses'. This speaks to the ways in which the search for a partner is traditionally a family affair, with young people, their parents and siblings all engaged in the matchmaking process through supervised meetings.

In a creative writing exercise at Glasgow Women's Library, Liba described the careful preparation that goes into these meetings by all family members. Her protagonist, Aisha, makes the final adjustments to her appearance as her mum paces their immaculate, optimally lit and perfumed house. In this short, vivid scene, we sense a whole household in a state of anticipation: 'The house was waiting, the flurry of activity over. The food was ready – all ten dishes – as well as the sparkling flavoured water, not to mention the completely new set of crockery.' Liba gently jests at the extravagance, whilst acknowledging the significance of this moment for a young woman and her family eager to make a good impression. One draft of this scene ends with Aisha taking a last look in the mirror: 'scimitar eyebrows and a stubborn mouth looked back at her with some nervousness. The courtship had begun.' An alternative ending, from a second-person draft, takes the reader back into the extended household: 'Sudden surprise as the doorbell rings, almost as if you hadn't all been preparing for this moment all week. The entire house holds its breath as your dad walks towards the door.' In this exercise, Liba deftly oscillates between the personal and household presentational rituals that a sanctioned meeting entails.

The inclusion of all family members in meetings, with knock-on effects for those indirectly involved, is explored in a short story entitled 'A Simple Nature'. Written by Sareena, another participant in the Glasgow Women's Library creative writing workshops, the story opens with her protagonist, Mariam, feeling overlooked as she helps to tidy the house in preparation for a *rishta* visit for her half-sister, Hanna. Mariam complains to her mother:

'Mum, I feel like you guys don't want me to get married.'
'What makes you think that, beta?' asked Mum.
'Well, you guys are so focused on getting Hanna a rishta that I feel you've forgotten about me,' Mariam's voice cracked almost imperceptibly.
'Beta, I have told you many times that after we get Hanna married, we will do the same for you. Anyway, there's no rush. You've got plenty of time,' Mum reassured her.
'Come on, I'm twenty-five years old, coming up twenty-six! How am I going to find someone if you and Dad are only focused on getting Hanna a rishta?'

Mariam is impatient to get married herself. Though she shares in the household preparations and anticipation of her sister's marriage, she does so with a heavy heart and a longing to meet her own future husband.

Men, too, can look forward to meetings arranged by their families. Hassan, an interviewee in his late twenties, shared the fictional Mariam's frustration. Hassan said he worries he will be 'too old' for marriage in another few years, and that he has given his parents an 'ultimatum' to set him up, laughingly complaining: 'I have been left to fend for myself!'. In a creative writing exercise at a men's workshop in Rochdale, Shezad imagined a young man's excitement when his mum suggests making some introductions:

One day my mum called me into the room for a chat. She told me she spoke to some girls about me and then showed me some potential rishta pictures. I felt amazed! I was buzzing. I liked this girl because of her looks and she is Muslim. The girl had dark hair, brown eyes. She is also tall and she is wearing a burka and flip flops.

The narrator's enthusiastic language makes it clear that he welcomes his mum's matchmaking efforts. Set before a meeting has taken place, this story also highlights how first impressions can be based on scant and superficial details. There are, of course, contradictions in this account. If the woman were wearing a burka, as he claims, her hair would not be visible. Clearly, the subject of the photograph is a projection of the young man's contradictory desires: she is at once religiously modest, and physically attractive, visually available to him.

Of course, not all young Muslims meet through arranged introductions. Later in this chapter, we explore the stories of those who are finding love and flirtation through other avenues. A common thread, though, is that – in the words of Masood, who also contributed one of the epigraphs to this chapter – families 'inevitably' become involved at some point if meeting leads to something more serious. Whereas Masood and others were relaxed about the circumstances of initial meetings, some take a more conservative approach. Amir considered a hypothetical example of meeting someone you like at work. He felt that it wouldn't be 'proper or respectable' to meet informally. Rather, he said, 'the first meeting should be done in an Islamic way' by speaking to both families. Here, as is often the case, the possibilities for meeting the opposite sex are circumscribed by religious boundaries.

'Forced small talk': Formal meeting in The Tea Trolley

Rehana Alam's novel *The Tea Trolley* (2017) is about a young woman, Amna, who has a series of meetings with potential suitors. Although the novel is set in Pakistan, it is relevant for a discussion of meetings in the British Pakistani Muslim context because many of the meeting conventions travel from Pakistan to the diaspora and back again. There are also diasporic characters in the novel, including two of Amna's suitors who are based in the UK and US respectively. As the title of this book suggests, the tea trolley becomes a character in itself because of its association with these meetings. A formal introduction is often performed over tea and snacks, and it is generally the potential bride who brings in the tea trolley to serve guests.

The novel begins with Amna reaching the marriageable age of eighteen, and her mother suggesting she begin the search for a husband. Amna's first suitor is a doctor who has just completed his medical qualifications to work in the UK. Amna takes great care over her appearance for this first meeting, wearing 'a cream colored *shalwar qameez* and a chiffon *dupatta* of my mother's in swirls of three shades of pink' (24; emphasis in original). Unfortunately, this meeting quickly sours when Amna's mother takes an immediate dislike to her potential son-in-law who, according to her, is poorly dressed. Amna recalls, 'my mother disliked the doctor on sight. He was wearing socks and sandals. "At age twenty-seven if he doesn't even know how to dress," my mother opined, "there is no hope for him"' (24). Although trivial and funny, this incident shows the snap judgements of family members and the significance of the smallest details.

Later in the novel Amna's aunt, Tahira Khala, comes over with her daughter, Sofia, for whom a meeting has been arranged. Interestingly, Saif, Sofia's potential groom, has a relaxed chat with Amna while Sofia is busy preparing herself. Consequently, the boy's family informs Sofia's family that Saif has taken an interest in Amna instead. Tahira Khala's friend, Guddi, who set up the meeting, intervenes to lighten the situation; she says, 'It is not a rejection [...] It is a proposal for the other girl in the family' (75). The young protagonist feels delighted to have been noticed over her beautiful cousin. Narrated in a light-hearted manner, this incident shows that despite their scripted nature, meetings can bring surprises and take unexpected turns.

While Amna's family is considering Saif's proposal, meetings with other prospective matches continue. The following passage vividly captures the formula of the meeting process:

> At home the job of getting me settled went on apace. Ammi screened out the unacceptable suggestions and about once a fortnight I had to present myself, pushing the tea trolley, to interested parties. But no one came up to my parents' standards. In some cases, which I made a point of forgetting quickly, I didn't please the visitors. For the health of my ego, thankfully that didn't happen too often.
>
> (84)

On first glance, this passage describes these meetings in a nonchalant way, highlighting their routine occurrence. Nonetheless, it also shows the rigorous selection process that precedes and follows each meeting. Besides, however mundane this process might be, rejections inevitably hurt one's feelings.

After many such meetings, Amna grows philosophical about them, comparing yet another stilted conversation with her chance encounter with Saif: 'As we made forced small talk, I realized how different my response to Saif had been. Since I was not the protagonist of that show, I had been easy and relaxed with him. That was probably why he had preferred me over Sofia, not my looks' (94). There are theatrical overtones in her description of the meeting, especially evident in her use of the words 'protagonist' and 'show'. Another insight that can be gleaned from this extract is how such a meeting, by its very air of seriousness, can put a stifling pressure on the prospective couple.

By the end of the novel, Amna's mother defers all meetings for a while, as Amna is about to pursue higher education in the UK. Amna is no longer annoyed with the meetings; rather, she has developed a mature way of thinking about them: 'Ammi's desire to settle me had allowed me to meet such diverse people and hear such astonishing stories that it had awakened in me an interest in my fellow creatures' (196). This remark shows the process of formal meetings – their attendant complexities and even absurdities – in a philosophical and intermittently sympathetic light.

'She shall walk in and place herself in the centre of the room'

The themes explored in *The Tea Trolley* are also prominent in stories, real and imagined, told to us by young Muslim women in the UK. More so than men, some women described ambivalent or negative feelings about arranged meetings. In a short story called 'First Part', Sofina describes a young woman's second meeting with her potential in-laws. Her protagonist, Amal, assesses the situation as she makes her way over 'to *their* house': 'If it wasn't obvious before, it was now frighteningly clear that this is becoming serious. They liked Amal – a lot. Of course they would: a decent-looking twenty-two-year-old, ripe age for marriage and potential baby machine, why wouldn't they?' Amal's suitor is scarcely mentioned, other than when Amal concedes, 'Okay. She knew she was being unfair. The rishta that had come knocking on her doorstep three weeks ago was a good one.' Her reservations are not about the match per se, but the feeling of being superficially judged, rather than of being an equal partner in the matchmaking process. Sofina explains that Amal can't help but feel 'on edge' because 'this was her *life* that everyone was discussing'.

Aqeelah, who met her husband online, had serious reservations about arranged meetings because of the experiences of her friends and relatives. She warned that they can expose young women to uncomfortable situations if parents aren't 'savvy' enough to protect them:

> [O]ne auntie asked my friend all of her measurements when she came over, like, she was like 'What's your chest size? What's your waist size?' and things like that, which is really creepy. I think someone asked my middle sister to walk up and down the room [...]. She had a lot more meetings and a lot more of this sort of superficiality and judging and literally like aunties coming to our house and really blatantly looking her up and down. And I don't know, making comments about her looks or 'Oh, she's very skinny, I don't know about that'.

Like Sofina's fictional account, Aqeelah's real-life examples highlight how relatives can complicate meetings. She describes how an older woman may, under the auspices of measuring up wedding clothes, let her potential daughter-in-law know whether or not she looks the part. Others are more direct in body-shaming younger women in 'creepy' interactions, asserting matriarchal dominance.

Aqeelah also observed that there is scant opportunity to get to know someone through a formal introduction: 'I found that there was very little involvement of the guy and the girl, like they would maybe go into the other room and chat by themselves for ten to fifteen minutes but really it was the families doing most of the talking.' Aisha, another interviewee, similarly felt that the prospective couple not having time alone to get to know one another is a problem. She said it is hard 'meeting the whole family before you actually get to know the guy'. They both observed that these meetings focus almost exclusively on making a good impression on your potential in-laws. Echoing the formality of meetings described in *The Tea Trolley*, Aisha said 'the most difficult bit' of a *rishta* visit is serving tea:

> So you have got to put like all this stuff in a tray, and if you drop it, they are all looking at you, or if you spill the tea the mother's looking at you and giving you [an] evil look, like 'Why have you spilled the tea? Don't you know how to pour tea from a teapot?' And that just makes you more nervous because they are watching you pour the tea and then you will spill it because their eyes are burning, watching you.

As in Aqeelah's account, it is the judgement of other women – the burning and watchful eye of a future mother-in-law – that Aisha most fears; the *rishta* himself is of peripheral concern.

Asmah's short story, 'The Entry', likewise centres on the pivotal moment a young woman, Sara, must enter a room and serve tea. It begins with Sara eavesdropping outside the door and waiting for a cue from her parents:

> 'Yes, yes Raj has several companies located around the country …' Along came a rehearsed giggle from Raj's mother.
> 'Sara is a wonderful cook and has excellent preparation and time management skills …' replied her father. And all that was required was for Sara to walk into the room and place, gently, the silver tray onto the coffee table. Her grip around the handles of the tray tightened as reality dawned on her. She shall walk in and place herself in the centre of the room …

Asmah observes with subtle humour how orchestrated this meeting is, from Raj's mother's staged laughter to Sara's appearance on cue with the silver tray. She highlights the gendered focus of the parents' conversation, and Sara's self-consciousness as she enters the room wishing she could speak more freely and sit close to Raj. Embarrassed at being the centre of attention, she places the tea tray down 'gently, but with elegance' and misses the table!

'No spark': Unsuccessfully Straightening Ali

An unsympathetic account of formal meetings from a male perspective appears in Amjeed Kabil's *Straightening Ali* (2007), which has been described as 'somewhere between a thriller and modern tragedy, ending with survival tainted by despair' (Meghani 2015: 177). The novel follows the life of twenty-four-year-old Ali Mirza, a gay British man of Pakistani descent living in a Muslim family in Birmingham. Readers quickly learn that Ali has come out before the beginning of the novel. Despite knowing this, Ali is pressured by his family to agree to an arranged marriage that, to all intents and purposes, is forced. As the novel progresses, we see him being routinely harassed and abused by his family members. Ali's mother fakes a heart attack to trick him into formally meeting twenty-year-old Sajda, whom she has chosen as her daughter-in-law. A guilt-ridden Ali gives in to his mother's demands only to abandon his wife soon after the marriage. Although it relies heavily on stereotypes, the novel nonetheless makes some effort to 'alter' the 'typical British-Asian marriage plot' by using 'the backdrop of non-heteronormative sexuality' (Chambers et al. 2018: 20). As an early instance of 'queer Muslim' fiction (Carbajal 2019), *Straightening Ali* merits a closer look.

Soon after the novel begins, Ali is given the news of a meeting that has already been arranged without his knowledge or consent. This news is delivered abruptly by his younger sister, Aneesa: 'Wake up, Ali, Ammi's arranged for you to see your in-laws' (Kabil 2007: 23). Ali is completely unprepared. When he refuses to get up, Aneesa says:

> Listen, Ammi says that she's arranged for you to meet Sajda, so you've got to get up […] It's a chance for you to meet your fiancée and not everyone

gets the opportunity to do that. Ammi's trying to be modern about your wedding because you've got a degree. You're so lucky.

(23)

Aneesa's emphatic instruction that Ali rouses himself makes it clear that the meeting is mandatory. However, the second part of the excerpt gives the impression that, with a university education, one can perhaps acquire a little liberty to reshape the rules of formal introduction. Ali is reminded of this concession again when his sisters tell him that he can see his potential in-laws at any time. Usually the groom would not be able to meet his fiancée once the marriage date has been fixed, but his mother has generously 'sorted' this; because Ali is a 'modern man who was born in England; they have to do things differently'. In this way, the family is 'bend[ing]' some of the meeting rules (25). What all of this demonstrates is the seriousness around the rituals of meetings – their importance for the individual and the families involved. This also assumes an ironic valence: as the narrative unfolds, very little 'bending' of the rules actually takes place.

Aneesa also tries to convince her brother by alluding to the practical necessity of meeting as she asserts: 'You can't trust photographs these days, not with all that digital imaging and camera lighting' (24). The particularities of the ritual are described in the following passage, in which Ali's mother gives him a number of instructions while 'ignoring his protest':

> You must go. I have arranged it. It is part of our custom for you to take clothes for your fiancée and to meet your in-laws. They need to speak to you and make sure that you are happy with the match. You must behave when you go to see them, be respectful and don't talk back at them. They are a very good family, very big in our community. Please don't do anything to bring shame on us when you visit them.
>
> (26)

The authoritative tone of this passage demonstrates the general compulsion exerted on Ali, and the particular codes of conduct he is expected to follow during the meeting. It also suggests that the decision to hold a meeting entails many considerations relating to family and community. Since matrimonial matters involve the wider community, such a meeting brings with it concerns of social shame and the stigma of deviation from the prescribed rules.

At the meeting, after a conversation with his future father-in-law, Ali is given five minutes to talk to Sajda under the supervision of a chaperone who watches them from a distance. For Ali, the moment of meeting crackles with tension and fear:

> In those few minutes, Ali had realized that he had nothing in common with Sajda. Their short conversation had been very stilted. She had appeared young and naïve. He'd expected some connection with her at any level, but there had been nothing. No spark, no meeting of minds. Nothing! As he

stepped back into the house, he became acutely aware of just how much of his happiness he was sacrificing to keep his mother happy.

(52)

What is evident in this passage is that Ali interprets the meeting as a tangible reminder of his misery. His encounter with Sajda only serves to augment his unfortunate situation, as the entire arrangement has been made against his wishes. Finding himself face to face with his much-dreaded future, Ali realizes in a profound way how terribly unhappy he is going to be. Ali has particular reasons for this – being gay – but his sense of powerlessness and impending unhappiness is not unique to gay men.

From these stories of traditional meetings, we now turn to more modern ways that young Muslims are seeking one another out in ways that can function as a supplementary channel to formal introductions by family members.

'Meeting in coffee shops'

Some young Muslims eschew the traditional route of family introductions to make their own decisions about who they want to meet and how. Nabila believed that ideal matchmaking comes 'through friends of friends […] because I think there is always an effective safety element there'. She highlighted how meeting through social networks in this way can be more 'personal', offering a space to get to know one another on an equal footing:

> I know that [meeting] is probably something that has always been quite traditional over the last few decades, but I think now it has moved on vastly, where people are meeting in coffee shops. Arranging meetings through friends […] and seeking potential, marriage potential in other contexts. Well in a modern concept they are now meeting in coffee shops. The female is no longer making a cup of coffee [laughs] so it is actually promoting equal opportunities shall we say […] where she is not having to feel pressured to bring out a tray of delights to potential strangers.

This account subverts traditional 'tea trolley meetings', with their formality and overbearing parents, instead picturing a scene where two young people simply chat on their own over coffee.

Others also emphasized the importance of social networks. Azeem, who is gay and openly dating, said he meets new partners 'through kind of peers and friends really. People who – who come from a similar background'. Arshad, in his second marriage after an arranged marriage ended in divorce, reflected on the different ways that people can meet outside of family introductions:

> [T]here's a big wide world out there […] You know, you can meet anybody in the street, you meet people who go out, you socialize, you go to events you know,

you go to Islamic talks you know, there's plenty – there's a lot of things happen in this day and age that you can meet people.

These two men have different reasons for eschewing the formal matchmaking process, but they have come to the same conclusion: that there are plenty of other opportunities to meet someone. Ifrah, studying away from home at university, said she previously would have been 'quite happy just to be introduced to people by my parents', but now thinks 'maybe it is not so bad to have known the person longer'. As she has matured, she said, her attitudes have changed about 'whether I would talk to guys'. She fancied that it could be 'nice' to meet someone 'whether from university or from work […] and you might be friends and if you think like there may be potential and then tell your parents about it, and go from there'. Careful to speak in hypotheticals, Ifrah described becoming more open to things she would have previously considered off-limits, such as meeting the opposite sex through conversations and friendships.

Aqeelah felt that she had struck a good compromise by being open with her parents about arranging meetings herself, initially through an online matchmaking service: 'I've always told them "Oh, I'm speaking to this person now" or "I'm speaking to that person now"'. When going to meet the man who would later become her husband, she told her dad: 'Oh, I'm going to go meet this guy and we've been talking this way'. Aqeelah suggested that she take a chaperone to this meeting, but – according to her – her dad advised: 'Don't worry about it, you know, you're in a public place and I trust you enough to know what you're doing and to know your boundaries.' Aqeelah herself felt that meeting requires some self-discipline 'when it's not in such a sort of sterile environment as a rishta visit' and said it can be challenging 'keeping things halal'. She dealt with this by seeking her parents' advice. Aqeelah's story of meeting a husband on her own terms oscillates between both traditional and modern ideals.

'Like going shopping'

Other stories of meeting are more casual, emphasizing everyday encounters and moments of attraction. Short stories from teenagers of both sexes who took part in a creative writing workshop at their sixth-form college highlight the simplicity and ordinariness of first meetings. They focus on characters who are in the same class but never speak to one another, characters who meet in the summer holidays and bond over 'walking and enjoying nature', characters who are reunited by chance in a cafe, and attraction that grows over time, until the protagonist realizes there's someone they look forward to seeing every day. These stories demonstrate that meetings can be both unremarkable and exciting, innocent and unburdened with expectations. Such meetings might develop into something more, or could lead nowhere in the long run. Nonetheless, they are thrilling at the time.

Rabia fantasized about meeting a romantic partner in a serendipitous way: 'I kind of want to find somebody myself […] maybe in like uni, so I can know them for a couple of years.' Faisal similarly felt optimistic that he will make a special friend while studying: 'Just at college and at school like you are going to meet someone, get to know them better. And then you go from there.' In these accounts, meetings happen in the routine course of life. In a creative writing exercise at a workshop in Rochdale, Mobeen wrote about a young couple in love who first meet in school:

> Adam met Shanice when he was at high school. They were in the same year. Adam liked the look of her, he thought she was pretty. She was really popular. She had black hair, hazel eyes, was slim, small diamond earrings. They were in the same class. One day he just asked her out.

This story illustrates how relationships that later become emotionally intense can begin casually, out of passing physical attraction. Young Muslims spoke of school, college, university and work as places where they can get to know new people, without the initial complications and formalities of dating and family introductions.

This more spontaneous way of meeting has its attractions, but can be daunting for some. 'I'm not very good at talking to girls', admitted teenage Daud. 'I never understand what's going through their head and so I never am able to'. Janan said that she finds meeting people difficult due to her shyness. She liked the idea of meeting 'naturally'; for example, if two people were to meet 'just in work or whatever … because the conversation flow is different and it's not forced'. Yet, single at thirty, she worried that this might not happen for her. Similarly, Dua shared her feelings of frustration and uncertainty about how to meet someone:

> Like how do you go about finding someone? People are like just put yourself out there [laughs], it's like not that easy just putting yourself out there. I think you find it a bit harder when you're working with the *goray* because they go out partying and stuff like that and it's normal for them, but it's like I'm Muslim I don't go out and party [laughs]. I don't do that kinda of thing.

Here, Dua reflects on her limited opportunities to get to know people in a way that she feels comfortable with. In her workplace's social networks, which are dominated by *goray* or white people, she is in the minority as a young Muslim who refrains from alcohol-fuelled nights out.

Others are more confident. Tahir recounted a time he approached a group of girls while out with friends: 'I was with my friend and they called some girls to come and hang out. And then I met one of the girls through that. It wasn't really like a date, it was just: go out and have fun.' Aisha, single at the time of our interview though later married, said she seizes opportunities for meeting the opposite sex which arise in such everyday situations as shopping trips. She hinted at how she enjoys flirting for men's attention:

> I approach it probably the same way like going shopping, something like that. Accidentally bumping into them because it is easier in shops when you are

trying to get past and it is busy, there are opportunities just waiting for you to go on and just bump into him. And they will notice you, and if he is with somebody else, then it is his loss. They will come after you when they go out of the shop, when they have seen and then they will kind of follow you and go 'Oh, are you all right there? You know I have not seen you about. Are you not from here?' So even if they don't speak to you in the shop, you wait five seconds outside the shop and they will, they normally do.

For Tahir and Aisha, meetings can be enjoyable encounters, presenting opportunities to have fun and test their powers of attraction. Aisha's account of 'going shopping' for dates is in stark contrast to her story of serving tea at a formal introduction, describing a completely different setting in which she had more agency as a single woman enjoying casual meetings.

'You can develop a relationship with somebody you've never met'

Like others of their generation, young Muslims are also turning to dedicated marital and matchmaking sites, apps and social media to meet. Hassan reflected on the 'huge demand' for these services:

> I think that these days there is more awareness and attitudes have changed. And that is why I think you get lots of like you know Singlemuslim.com and Shaadi. com and stuff like that. And that is a growing market, because there is a demand for it. There is a huge demand for it. And I think there is a huge demand for people to meet in an Islamically appropriate way, and develop a relationship in an Islamically appropriate way. And then get married.

His comment highlights a particular attraction of meeting online for young Muslims, as a way to circumvent the taboo of premarital dating by getting to know someone at a distance. Shafiq similarly discussed how online spaces offer new opportunities for people to meet: 'You can now develop a relationship with somebody you've never met, you can develop a relationship with somebody who's not in the same country: online, apps, websites, social media. That seems to now be at the forefront of developing relationships'. Shafiq emphasized the importance of these kinds of meeting spaces in developing a connection 'purely based on communication' rather than just physical attraction.

While some sign up to matchmaking websites, other online meetings are more casual. Mainstream social media and dating apps are used with a view to friendship and flirtation. Bashir said:

> I was considering actually getting Tinder because my friends have it and at the end of the day it's a fun thing to do really […]. Especially because Tinder is very popular among uni students, so it's a way to just meet other friends as well.

The sometimes frivolous nature of online meeting apps was highlighted by Pervaiz, who observed: 'not many people I know take it seriously. Like all my friends took Tinder as a joke, they were like joking about, seeing if they maybe see anyone they recognize, which is funny.' These comments reveal the influence of peers, and illustrate that not all online meetings are conducted with an earnest view to finding a relationship.

Young Muslims, like others, have mixed feelings about internet dating. Some are sceptical of the sincerity of connections made online. Zohaib said that some of his friends 'find it easier to meet girls' through social media apps, but he feels 'I can't trust something I see like over the phone, like the little pictures, they could be just like all them filters and stuff [...] I have to meet them in person.' Speaking from a more mature perspective about online dating with marriage in mind Shahid, later engaged, said:

> The only problem with finding spouses on social media is you don't get to know them the way you should actually get to know them [...] they could just be saying what you want to hear, they could be catering it to obviously meet what they think you're after.

Nabila and Janan similarly spoke about the risk of meeting people online who turn out to be very different on the phone or in person. Janan recalled one recent disappointing encounter: 'it was really off-putting because clearly he was lying just to get girls' numbers and I cut the call short and told him I wasn't interested'.

Conclusion

The contrasting stories in this chapter open windows on young Muslims' experiences of introductions and meetings. From formal *rishta* arrangements involving families and communities, to coffee shop dates and online trysts, meeting means putting yourself out there and taking a risk. As such, accounts of meeting are replete with anxiety and excitement. Asmah's short story 'The Entry', for example, alternates between these two impulses in the moment her protagonist tightens her grip on the tea tray and enters the room. The tighter the grip, the more likely she is to drop it – and she does. This story of mixed and heightened emotions is simultaneously specific and generic. As a story of elaborate arrangements for meeting, it will resonate with others who have experienced a first date, feeling many things at once: hope, desire, embarrassment, nerves, self-consciousness, anticipation ... and possibly a little amusement.

Several of the stories in this chapter highlight the intergenerational dynamics of meeting, encapsulated by the imaginary of the Muslim dating gameshow in which each contestant is backed by their family team. What the audiecne doesn't see, or have time to explore in this brief scene (Figure 2.1), is the dynamic between these family members. Asmah's story – with her mother's rehearsed giggle and her father's conversational gambits – speaks of the different roles that family members can play in meetings, and the sense that family members bring several things to the mix. In other chapters, including 'Pressure' and 'Married', we see some difference and disagreement between family members, developing this picture of the generational and gendered powerplay of relationships and relationship stories.

Table 2.1 Interviews quoted in Chapter 2, 'Meeting'

Name	Gender	Age	Relationship Status	Location
Masood	Male	21	Single	Yorkshire
Hassan	Male	29	Single	Yorkshire
Janan	Female	30	Single	Glasgow
Aisha	Female	27	Single	Yorkshire
Nabila	Female	30	Divorced	Newcastle
Azeem	Male	26	Single	Newcastle
Ifrah	Female	21	Single	Yorkshire
Rabia	Female	17	Single	Glasgow
Faisal	Male	16	Single	Glasgow
Aqeelah	Female	29	Married	Glasgow
Dua	Female	23	Single	Yorkshire
Shafiq	Male	29	Married	Newcastle
Bashir	Male	19	Single	Glasgow
Pervaiz	Male	18	Single	Glasgow
Zohaib	Male	19	Single	Newcastle
Shahid	Male	24	Engaged	Yorkshire
Amir	Male	22	Single	Yorkshire
Tahir	Male	20	Single	Glasgow

Table 2.2 Workshop participants and convenors quoted in Chapter 2, 'Meeting'

Name	Gender	Age	Workshop Series	Role in Workshop	Title
Liba	Female	25	5. Fiction, Glasgow	Participant	'Untitled'
Sareena	Female	20	5. Fiction, Glasgow	Participant	'A Simple Nature'
Shezad	Male	28	7. Fiction, Rochdale	Participant	'Untitled'
Sofina	Female	21	6. Blogging, Glasgow	Participant	'First Part'
Asmah	Female	24	5. Fiction, Glasgow	Participant	'The Entry'
Mobeen	Male	26	7. Fiction, Rochdale	Participant	'Untitled'
Zarah	Female	23	1. Animation, Sheffield	Participant	Animation voiceover
Daud	Male	17	3. Creative writing, Sheffield	Participant	Focus group discussion

Interlude 1

COMING TO TERMS

The stories in this book range from fragments of spontaneous conversations to more sustained interviews, and from the scribblings of free-writing exercises to refined stories, plays and poems. In each, there is something preliminary and exploratory, the search for a language capable of bringing experiences and possibilities into view, and in some cases breaking silences. The struggle to articulate sex and love is played out in different ways, from the proficient and fluent to the broken and stumbling.

To begin to explore these different ways of 'coming to terms', we shall turn to a series of fragments of speech. The first is from a play called *The Funeral Director* (by Imam Qureshi, 2018) and is spoken by the grieving boyfriend of a Muslim man named Ahad, who has killed himself.

> He fucking loved Bollywood, that man. The dances, the drama, the moustaches, and saris, but the songs especially. He'd sing them sometimes. I'd wake up to it some days. Smell of coffee from the kitchen, and the sound of him singing away. Wish I'd recorded it now.
>
> (65)

An interview with Janan, a thirty-year-old woman who lives in Glasgow, also touches upon the subject of Bollywood:

> It's kind of cliché but you know, at high school we did watch Bollywood and we did watch all the Disneys and you know, you watch fairy tales and it's all perfect and you think 'oh yeah, I want that'. But yeah, no I don't at all. I just want somebody to, well, be decent, to be honest with you, and I think that comes from also experiences of just different guys I've been introduced to and talked to and met as well and I've just thought oh God, you know, like you have no respect for women, you don't know how to talk.

Another interview, this time with Hassan, a man in his late twenties, revealed a different way of speaking about relationships. Hassan spoke more seriously and less smoothly than Janan:

In an ideal world ... um I would say in an ideal kind of perfect world, I don't know ... it is like ... I think, I think there is like, there is two ways of ideal way. Which is probably an Islamic-legitimate Islamic way ... and then there is the more perhaps realistic way, which is: it might not be like that. Does that make sense? So in an ideal way, because like ... um so in an ideal it could be perhaps through a family, an introduction through a family member, a friend and ... and yeah, so ...

These three fragments describe a continuum from the seemingly uncomplicated romantic ideals of a Bollywood fan; through the more sceptical words of a woman who has learned to manage her own expectations, enjoying popular love stories for what they are but not taking them too literally; to the halting speech of a man who is self-consciously inarticulate when he tries to talk about marriage.

For each of these three people, in their very different ways, speaking about sexual desire and love is difficult and complicated. It can be a vehicle for exploring rather than reporting experiences and possibilities.

Edwin Morgan, the Scottish poet, wrote of the search for language in which to explore sexual desire and love, often in heavily furtive circumstances, as an urgently creative process. Creativity takes different forms – from the widely recognized creativity of the writer or artist to the little-c creativity inherent in everyday life (Richards 2007) and finding fulfilment and happiness in life (Kersting 2003) – both of which are important in Morgan's 'coming to terms': with his sexuality, and through his poetry (Morgan 2000). Morgan grew up in early twentieth-century Glasgow, a world in which the same-sex relationships he wanted and found were first illegal, then barely tolerated, and in which it was close to impossible to speak directly or frankly about gay sex. He could not simply resort to scripted and conventional means of storying sexuality, as later generations of gay men have done through their coming-out stories (Plummer 1995). This may not have been healthy or easy, but it was productive for Morgan's poetry. Whereas some other men of his generation resorted to the subcultural language of Polari, or took great risks by speaking openly, Morgan explored less direct, yet more eloquent possibilities of sexual discourse, doing so through poetry.

Similarly, for some Muslims in Britain today, we find that sexual discourse is more heavily constrained than it may be for the mainstream population. However, these constraints are not just limiting; they may also be productive, conducive to creativity and possibility. This is particularly the case with same-sex desire, in which mainstream tolerance has not been embraced by all. Many (but not all) of those who claim to speak for Islam and other religions including Christianity and Judaism continue to insist upon heterosexual marriage for all (Yip 2007). It is possible to say one thing and do another, as some Muslims (and some Christians and Jewish people) do when they enter into same-sex relationships (Yip 2004a). That said, not all are content to remain silent on this subject, as the once loquacious and unclosed Ahad illustrates.

Other forms of sexual discourse are constrained too, of course, particularly within Muslim families, but also among groups of friends and acquaintances. For example, among young British Muslims and their communities there is a widespread understanding that dating should not be mentioned, seen or acknowledged, either within the family or in public. The reasons for this are variously cultural and religious. Culturally, prohibitions on dating and on talking about dating are bound up with tradition and honour (Werbner 2007). Religiously, they are grounded in assumptions and beliefs about what is permissible (halal) or impermissible (haram) within Islam. In some families, these rules remain unwritten, whereas in others they are explicit. In some families, they are more forceful than in others. These prohibitions against speaking about dating coexist with others about the practices of dating. Young Muslims respond to these twofold restrictions in different ways. Some neither date, nor talk about dating. Others date openly. Still others find a middle ground to negotiate either or both of these restrictions. For some, this means finding ways to speak about dating, steering around obstacles against what can be said and how.

By desiring or doing one thing and saying another, it is possible for some people to navigate cultural and religious conventions which prohibit same-sex relationships, dating and other sexual practices. But this silence and secrecy can be damaging and unhealthy. Generations of gay men and lesbians have known the loneliness of the closet; gay and lesbian Muslims are no exception, as we see throughout this book. Others find it a strain to keep heterosexual relationships secret, discovering that this sets up barriers with family members. At twenty-five, Hawa had wanted to tell her parents about the man she was dating, with a view to marriage. However, she was worried about how they might react, fearing they might 'disown' her for bringing 'shame on the family'. Looking back, she reflected that the consequences of this secrecy had compounded over time, 'making it worse' and weakening her family relationships. For some young Muslims, if not for all, it is important to break the silences that surround sexual relationships.

For some, storying relationships is not simply interesting; it is urgent, a matter of life and death even. A fictional figure whose storytelling and stories illustrates the life-saving power of the spoken and written word in the Muslim world is the narrator of the *One Thousand and One Nights*, Scheherazade (also spelled Shahrazad; see Warner 2012). Having married a Sultan whose revenge for his wife's infidelity is to wed and then murder a new bride every day, Scheherazade entertains the Sultan with stories. Every night she tells a new tale, ostensibly to amuse her sister Dunyazad, but making sure her dangerous husband can hear. Every night's storytelling ends with a cliff-hanger of some kind. Always wanting to know what happens next, the Sultan cannot bring himself to order her execution. Eventually he abandons his vengeful plan. The stories have saved Scheherazade; through them, she has also defined herself as a storyteller and a wife. Scheherazade might be seen as a symbol of the power of sexual storying.

'It's kind of cliché'

We hear about Ahad's love of Bollywood from his grieving non-Muslim boyfriend, Tom, and by proxy from Imam Qureshi, the author of *The Funeral Director*, the sad and funny play in which these words are spoken. Tom likes to remember Ahad's love of Bollywood because it reminds him of the sexual love that they shared, happily and openly. Evidently, like the films he delighted in, Ahad was not one for understatement. Although this flamboyance brought joy, there was a darker side too; his family and community rejected him for coming out. Even in death, they refused to have anything to do with him, and the Muslim funeral director – after whom the play is named – refused him an Islamic burial. For Ahad and Tom, the South Asian romantic musicals were not to be taken too literally; they provided points of departure through which a young gay Muslim man could begin to express his experiences of sex and love. There is nothing clichéd about *The Funeral Director* – a play that remains original and surprising throughout – though romantic clichés and the cultural forms in which they circulate are referenced.

Although musical films have a special place in the hearts of many gay men, the appeal of Bollywood is more general, even if not everyone is as enthusiastic as Ahad is said to have been. Faisal, who is sixteen and straight, admits to watching 'these dramas' but distances himself, claiming unconvincingly that 'My sister makes me watch them'. Janan also expresses ambivalent feelings for Bollywood. Having passed the point at which women in her community tend to marry – or the age at which relatives hope to have married them off – she is sceptical about the happy endings and the outward joy of these popular, often simplistic stories, and equally of their counterparts in Western film and TV. Janan has learned to distrust such uncomplicated and idealized narratives, enjoying them, while knowing that real life is harder and that 'real' men fall short of their onscreen counterparts.

Referring to this alluring unreality, a number of women we interviewed for the Storying Sexual Relationships project spoke of 'fairy tales'. They used the term 'fairy tale' loosely, seemingly oblivious to the darkness of many actual fairy tales, pointing instead to prettified fables of love and romance. Nabila spoke in the same breath of 'Bollywood movies, you know movies which are quite heavily emphasized on romance' and the stories from 'English culture' that she had encountered at school: 'stories such as *Cinderella, Snow White, Sleeping Beauty*'. Her references to these stories are unstructured and selective. Only the most sanitized editions of stories such as *Snow White* present a life that one might want to emulate. The heroine is effectively the prisoner of seven male figures, whom she stumbles upon in the forest, a dark and threatening locale in which she is vulnerable and alone. But when Nabila refers to the 'fairy-tale lifestyle', she is really only thinking of handsome princes who save female protagonists from their previously unhappy and insecure lives. Yet Nabila acknowledges that 'these movies don't portray a real context of life', with the latter not progressing towards a 'happy ending'. Janan made a similar point, admitting to enjoying but not believing the sanitized, soft-focus fairy tales she associates with Bollywood and Disney: 'I suppose it is always the same thing, there's a problem in between but everything works out in the end. And it's like the perfect Prince Charming'. Janan sees the handsome prince as a fallacy, not worth waiting or hoping for.

Illustrating the appeal of some popular love stories and relationship dramas, fictional characters like Ahad and his boyfriend Tom, as well as real figures such as our respondents Janan and Nabila, allude to both limitations and possibilities.

II. Coming to Terms

Bollywood is glossy, 'kind of cliché', as Janan put it. A cliché is literally an illustration made for one book, reused in another, often as a cost- or time-saving device. It is thus a kind of clumsy shorthand: always universalizing but something of an awkward fit. The content of Bollywood is South Asian, but Indian rather than Pakistani. Hindi cinema's references to sex and love, sexuality and desire, relationships and marriages are often generic but also uplifting and family-friendly. These musical films are thus capable of touching a wide variety of people (see Gopinath 2000; Kumar 2013; Desai and Dudrah 2008; Bhutto 2019b).

For some, particularly those with literary and artistic affectations, cliché is a mark of failure. Not unpretentiously, Martin Amis defined literary work as a 'campaign against cliché'. He elaborated:

> To idealise: all writing is a campaign against cliché. Not just clichés of the pen but clichés of the mind and clichés of the heart. When I dispraise, I am usually quoting clichés. When I praise, I am usually quoting the opposed qualities of freshness, energy and reverberation of voice.
>
> (2001: 19–20)

But cliché is not so bad when it is handled with self-awareness, as it is when Janan speaks about the films she loves to watch. Such clichés may not only be enjoyable; they may also be useful. Ken Plummer has shown that storying – even in conventional, formulaic, clichéd forms such as coming-out stories – may be personally therapeutic and socially transformative, as it 'provides routes into a life, lays down maps to follow' (1995: 1).

Despite reservations about Bollywood, Janan continues to watch these romantic musicals, and interestingly she does so with family members: 'my dad would watch it, we would watch it and you know, it is that kind of cliché boy meets girl, somebody has an issue with it on either side and then you know but all ends well at the end of the film and the boy and girl live happily ever after'. For all their obvious unreality, these popular love stories seem to resonate and to provide rudimentary conversation starters. Via their implausible plotlines, some young Muslims are able to imagine their own futures and even have some difficult heart-to-hearts with family members. Esha, twenty-seven, admitted to 'really' liking a Bollywood movie, the title of which she cannot be sure, 'based on a true story'. Though melodramatic – involving a happily married man who takes a second wife – Esha felt it spoke to her own unspecified 'psychological issues'. These apparently related to insecurity about her future nuptials: 'When I watched that I was so upset and I thought that is going to happen to me.'

Azeem, who is twenty-six and lives in Newcastle, was one of a number of young gay and lesbian Muslims we spoke to who had been impressed by a character in the popular British TV soap opera, *EastEnders*.

> There was a gay character on there called Syed and so he was … you know grew up in a fairly religious family in the programme and got married to this … you know married to this lady, I can't remember who she is, but she was

obviously, she was a Muslim as well. And but he was gay and he was having this relationship behind the scenes with this guy called Christian. That was when I started following that storyline and seeing how it kind of evolved from getting married to this girl, denying this gay identity of his, to this girl I think having a baby, and ... then evolving to you know the two of them, him telling his family and being in a committed relationship with that Christian guy and ... But that was something interesting as well, because I think my mum is not kind of into *EastEnders* either. But I kind of pretty much, not forced her to watch it but because I was into it then she has been watching it, and she never ... I don't think she ever, going back to making comments, I don't think she ever made a stray comment about that is not right, or that is disgusting or whatever.

Of course, *EastEnders* is some distance from the romantic musicals and so-called fairy tales mentioned by other young people. Nonetheless, it belongs to another form of popular storytelling, the soap, and, as such, it works within established patterns and formulae. Despite its hackneyed form, such a story's content may be substantively groundbreaking. It may even change lives or, more precisely, become a vehicle through which people change their lives.

Chatting with friends and strangers

Conversations about sex and love are not always as formal as they come across in some of the interviews quoted above, nor as searching and serious, nor as culturally literate. Young Muslims, like other young people, also chat about these things. Of course, most of their conversations are only heard by those who are involved. Since private, they may be more candid, more explicit, and often more unconventional and fun than the spoken and written words that dominate this book. These conversations are not entirely free, of course, since they may conform to the expectations and demands of peers, particularly within single-sex friendship groups.

We were reminded of the relative ease with which some young Muslims chat with friends, compared to the ways in which they do so in interviews and write in workshops, on a day when we were attempting to attract participants to a workshop in a school in Sheffield. We were struggling to get the young people, aged sixteen to eighteen, to join us. We worried that the topic – private and sensitive as it perhaps seemed – might be off-putting to some. The workshop was to be held in a glass-walled study space, just outside the school library. Nafhesa, who was running the workshop, noticed that the very same young people who seemed so reluctant to join the workshop seemed to be speaking more freely in the library around many of the same topics. Some were talking intimately in couples, other more audibly with friends. As Nafhesa put it in her field diary:

> The interesting fact is that the library space seems to be a popular space for young Muslims within this age group to meet up with each other and you will find that there are couples (who are obviously in relationships, but when I go up to them act as though they are not) having intimate conversations. An example

of this was a couple in the room talking quite intimately and when I went up to them the girl made no eye contact with me and the boy did all the talking, telling me that 'they were too busy'.

Afshan, a published young Muslim writer who was facilitating the workshop, overheard some fragments of conversation, and observed that young people were not quite as reticent as it might first have appeared. Two girls, who attended one of the workshops, wanted to know if one of the boys would be there. Evidently 'wanting to meet up with him', Afshan concluded, 'they clearly used this time (end of college) to socialize and there are definitely some young people who are in relationships or exploring the opportunity to have a relationship'. In contrast with on-the-record-but-anonymous interviews and writing, Afshan observed that 'these conversations are often hush-hush, but definitely happening in this space'.

We were able to get closer to some of these freely spoken and written words during other workshops. Female participants in a series of writing workshops held at the Glasgow Women's Library were initially shy with each other, and tentative in their first attempts to put pen to paper, or hands to keyboard. Over a period of months, however, they built up a supportive group, using social media to encourage each other to attend, and meeting up socially. Gradually they relaxed into friendships and conversations. They spoke freely and openly about sex and love, relationships and marriage. An outsider, listening in, might have been surprised to hear young Muslim women talking and laughing about everything from premarital chastity to anal sex, and from acceptance of arranged marriage to blow jobs within marriage. Like the stories and plays devised and written in earlier workshops, the women's blogs were then shared with wider audiences. Some of the participants performed their work at a public event, hosted by the Library, which was open to the public, and to men as well as women. Some accepted our invitations to be filmed as they read their work. This process revealed a continuum between informal conversations between friends, and more polished spoken and written words. The vitality and rawness of the former found more eloquent expression in the performances and published works.

Though it would not have been ethical to eavesdrop too closely on conversations between couples or friends in school canteens, we were able to initiate and listen in on those between workshop participants who had given informed consent to this research and had the right to remain anonymous. These conversations, which we followed up with focus groups and one-on-one interviews, revealed sometimes surprisingly outspoken efforts to 'come to terms' with sex and love, finding words equal to these difficult topics.

'Let me try and think about what I am trying to say'

The third fragment of speech, quoted in the introduction to this interlude, is from another Muslim who is still young. To marshal a cliché, he is nonetheless old enough to have been around the block a few times, and is feeling ready to 'get real'. This quotation illustrates a different approach to storying relationships.

Rather than resorting to demonstrably inadequate yet smooth language, Hassan appears to be thinking aloud by way of his broken speech. Rather than glossing over uncertainties, he stops to think, rephrasing and reflecting as he goes:

> When we say dating, the thing is like ... like okay so ... with not just, not just in terms of relationships, just generally speaking like in an ideal world ... it is like ... Islamic ... or you know a proper Islamic way of doing things. So I think for example, just give me a second, let me try and think about what I am trying to say ... It is like okay so I think with myself and a lot of people my age like we all know like there is an Islamic way of doing things, and that is the right way of doing things. But we generally don't, we kind of divert from that a little bit or not a lot but a little bit, do you know what I mean? So dating comes within that as well, because ... so like although I say you shouldn't date, like that is kind of a rule or a guideline to follow, people break it. Does that make sense?

Hassan asks the interviewer if she knows what he means and if what he is saying makes sense. It appears that he is really asking himself, thinking aloud, trying out ideas ... coming to terms. Anshuman Mondal (2008: 68) drew similar conclusions from an equally fractured interview with a young British Muslim woman. He reflected that 'she began to think the question through, aloud, her sentences marked by hesitations, doubts and inconsistencies – symptoms of a mind wrestling with a problem that remains just elusive enough to slip through the established patterns of her thought'.

These struggles were also evident in writing workshops, where some participants dropped out and others gave up on the more challenging pieces of work that they had started, or felt compromised or exposed by, retreating to safer ground. Sometimes, these struggles are productive, as writers and speakers may ultimately break through with creativity and candour. Not all of the fragments of speech and stories collected here are artistically accomplished, though some are creative in other ways. Exploring circumstances that have previously been silenced and obscured, they can be bold, playful and experimental. To borrow Martin Amis's (imperfect) terms, they can grapple with cliché and jump the tramlines of genre.

Expressions of uncertainty include qualifiers and verbal tics, which hint at Salim's uncertainty about his future, manifesting especially in his nervous laughter and repeated use of the word 'like'. He originally intended to 'consider marriage' in his early twenties, but the time had come and he wasn't sure he was ready: 'oh no, like it's too soon like, I want to like maybe enjoy myself single a little bit first. But not in a bad way, like' (a longer version of this quotation appears on p. 18 of the Single chapter). Others betray uncertainties through pauses and 'ums', revealing the things they are uncertain about or still working through, and which they have yet to come to terms with. The fissures in Azeem's interview are most pronounced where he touches on sensitive subjects. These include his description of getting his mum to watch a carefully chosen TV programme with him as a way of hinting at his own sexuality and talking about himself as a gay Muslim. At such moments, he is uncharacteristically and tellingly inarticulate: 'I think *EastEnders*, talking about

EastEnders actually, yeah um … So as I said before I was never actually interested in … *EastEnders* you know stuff like that at fourteen, fifteen … not really interested at all.' And, when talking about his crush on the actor Daniel Radcliffe: 'Yeah, I think … I think when I … in first year of uni in that second semester when I told a few people, I started reading the gay magazine called *Attitude* um. I think at first I picked it up because Daniel Radcliffe was on the cover and I am a big fan of Daniel Radcliffe, I think he is um.'

(Not such) free writing

Broken, stuttering, bitty and fraught conversations, in which people are prepared to think aloud and explore different ways of articulating sexual love, find more sustained counterparts in creative writing. The challenges associated with being creative and with writing, both of which many people find daunting, are magnified when they are applied to subjects that a great number of individuals find difficult to write or speak about, such as sexual love.

To illustrate the challenges of writing about sexual love, we shall turn to some of the least successful workshops we convened. That is to say they were the least successful ones in terms of the commitment demonstrated by participants and the quality of their written work. These workshops revealed some broader challenges experienced by young Muslims when they attempt to speak and write about sexual desire and love. But they also show that speech and writing need not come easy, and need not be smooth, in order to count.

The workshops in question took place in a diverse sixth-form college in Sheffield, where the students are aged sixteen to eighteen. These sessions were open to all, but were advertised as opportunities to explore literature from South Asia and the diaspora and do some creative writing. In this way we hoped to attract students with Asian heritage, most of whom in this locality would be Muslims. We began with a taster session led by Afshan, who identifies as a queer Muslim writer, and a male colleague, who is also a young Muslim writer. Afshan was to lead the workshops that would follow.

Having been encouraged by school administrators to expect at least thirty students to attend the taster event, we set up forty chairs. When only two students turned up, we went out into the college, inviting others to join. A few agreed to do so, but most of the chairs remained empty. At sessions in the following weeks, Nafhesa persuaded between two and five students to join us each time, but none returned. As Nafhesa recorded in her diary, some weeks later, 'The groups have got to the stage (last few sessions) where nobody will attend the group and I go out into the library space (as our room is at the end of the library, with a glass front) and ask [visibly Asian and/or Muslim students] to come and join us.'

This was disappointing, of course, but it also led us to reflect on hurdles. We were interested not only in those perceived barriers coming between young people and successful creative writing but also those that make it hard for young people to express themselves, particularly on the fragile subjects of sex and love.

Of course, not everyone feels the urge to put their desires or relationships into words. Those who do write are motivated in many different ways. Some are looking for recognition, others for understanding; some are spurred on by pressure or incentives; for some, writing is a choice, for others a necessity; some write because they want to make money; to connect with others; to explore possibilities; to unburden themselves (Atwood 2003; Harper 2019). Conversely, there are many reasons for not wanting to write, or not wanting this enough to walk through the doors of a workshop, ready to surrender to whatever the convenor may have in mind. Creative writing is not for everyone, all of the time. Not everyone experiences the urge to 'come to terms', while others resist the confessional or aesthetic impulse.

The apparent indifference of some of those who attended these workshops once, without getting involved or letting their defences down, may also reflect the sensitivity of speaking and writing about sex and love, the risks demanded of those who try to put their desires and feelings into words. Looking back, we may have been in too much of a hurry to get these groups up and running. People are more likely to speak or write openly if they are doing so in a safe space; where there is mutual trust and respect. We may not have done enough to cultivate this sense of safety and trust. Over the course of our workshops in the college, we began to see that students regarded the school administrator who promoted our workshops as a teacher-adjacent figure in an 'us and them' environment. We started to see that some students found him overbearing and were constrained by his presence. On one occasion, he commented audibly on how surprised he was to see a particular student in the room, making it clear he had low expectations of her. She never returned. We reflected that our workshops may have come across as institutional – 'Like a lesson', as Afshan noted in her diary. The sessions might have gone better, she felt, if teachers and administrators had been banished, and if the subject material was more risqué, not 'sanitized or censored'.

Conversely, at some of the other workshops that we organized as part of this wider project, we could not accommodate all those who wanted to participate. At the Glasgow Women's Library, successive workshops on blogging, fiction and playwriting were oversubscribed. This was due in part to the space; not only the building itself but also the safe and welcoming ambience created and nurtured by the staff as well as the women who regularly came to the Library with a sense of ownership and belonging. It was probably also due to the greater maturity of participants, most of whom were in their twenties and significantly older than the students in the sixth-form college.

There are other reasons why some participants in the college workshops struggled. Like other creative writing workshops, these sessions involved writing in real time – 'fast, unpremeditated' free writing (Anderson 2006: 23) – and reading work aloud. Free writing themes chosen by Afshan included 'Time, Home, Love, Death, I Am, Fire, Relationship, I've Never, and This Is'. Unlike some creative writing teachers, Afshan did not force participants to read out, but she did ask if they wanted to. None of this was easy or relaxed. Nafhesa found it 'intense' and wondered if it could be less formal. 'As I am watching the group', she wrote in her diary, 'I can see their discomfort once they start, and their wanting to leave'. Afshan observed that 'the first girl who arrived [...] was very quiet' and 'seemed interested in poetry'. Soon after, 'another three girls arrived', one 'very talkative'. The former was also set apart from the others culturally, as 'a young white girl' in a session with 'three hijabis'. Though she showed real interest in creative writing, she never returned; neither did the three friends. Afshan wondered if the 'quiet' participant had felt awkward and alone in the presence of the friendship group, and uncomfortable in the reading-out exercise. To read creative writing aloud is to risk self-exposure: what am I saying about myself, and is my writing any good? This is particularly true of free writing, fast and unfiltered as it is, taking 'you into your deepest ideas, feelings and memories' (Anderson 2006: 23).

Though the workshops in this college were the least fruitful of those we conducted, they did involve some good conversations and insightful writing exercises. Creative writing instructors stress that 'it takes a long time to master the crafts of writing' (Anderson 2006: 28). That being said, it is also possible to benefit from more fleeting participation. Nafhesa reflected that 'even if the students don't come each week' the workshops had allowed them 'to experience creative writing'. Over the six weeks in which these workshops ran, fifteen young people had attended, all of whom had written something. Some had 'produced some good writing and interaction (sharing their thoughts and pieces)' and some had overcome obstacles of shyness and awkwardness 'in talking about relationships'. All, Nafhesa explained, had 'created characters who were then put into different types of relationships', and through these scenarios they had ventilated some sensitive topics. Though they were not prepared or able to open up directly, these young people were able to do so through the multiple distancing afforded by fiction. One wrote a story of sexual desire whose protagonist he said was based on his friend who, as Nafhesa noted in her diary, 'was sitting next to him!'

Finding a voice

It would be wrong to end this interlude with workshops that didn't quite work. This would paint too negative a picture, and dwell upon instances of not fully coming to terms. In other cases participants persevered and they did find voices in which to speak and write. And so we turn to some participants who have not only gone on to write but have done so very successfully and with evident enjoyment.

All of the other workshops gained some kind of momentum. Those in the Glasgow Women's Library were the best attended, with committed participants who attended successive workshops. Some others were quieter but equally invested in creative work. The six young people who signed up to the animation workshops in Sheffield formed a strong group, with deep and trusting relationships. This was reflected in their regular attendance of sessions that, given the demanding nature of the medium, ran to over five hours. The creative writing sessions in Bradford were quieter, thoughtful events, in which the convenor pushed the participants to real achievements in terms of the quality of their writing. Participants from three different workshops – one man and two women – went on to build careers in creative writing. One began helping her friends to establish blogs, another convened a series of workshops within this project, while the third has recently published her debut novel with HQ/HarperCollins (Hussain 2020).

Some participants who started out as complete beginners and others with slightly more experience went on to contribute to an anthology of Muslim women's short stories entitled *A Match Made in Heaven* (published by HopeRoad in 2020), which forms a sister volume to this more academic book. In the anthology, their writing is placed alongside the work of emerging and more established and well-known authors such as Shelina Janmohamed, Ayisha Malik and Bina Shah. And the new authors' writing easily holds its own among the 'big names'. Excerpts from two of these new writers – Noura and Sareena – illustrate this point.

Noura's story 'Her Trials' tackles the issue of adultery – 'cheating' (Chambers et al. 2020: 26–38) – when protagonist Aliyah's husband of just three years, Gabriel, is found *in flagrante* with a brunette in their living room. The narrative arc traces Aliyah's coming to terms with life as a single woman again after deciding she cannot follow her mother's advice and sit 'down to discuss it like adults […]. Find out why he did what he did' (31). If the tonal palette of this story sometimes seems confined to melodrama, self-pity and bitterness, there are flashes of great humour and assertiveness. In one of the most memorable scenes from 'Her Trials', Aliyah meets Gabriel by a pond in the park to discuss their broken relationship:

> [S]he had decided on what she called a 'power outfit'. Casual, but powerful to her. She had paired indigo skinny jeans with a plain white tank top. Over that, she wore a new cropped black leather jacket. Around her neck was a simple gold necklace, with the Egyptian Ankh as a pendant. On her feet she wore a pair of low-heeled black heels as she hated being too high off the ground. Spiky studs trailed along the back of them and down the heel, looking menacing in this light. She had kept her makeup natural. The only dramatic effect was her eyeliner, with its deadly-looking point that lent her a fierce glare. She needed it. Needed the confidence boost the winged eyeliner gave her. She wore her hair in a high, sleek ponytail. Her favourite black handbag, with its own small sprinkling of metal studs, completed the kick-ass look. She thought her outfit got across the point that she was not to be messed with, but respected and admired.
>
> (32–3)

Rather than following her mother's advice to please her husband and smooth over his infidelities, Aliyah power dresses to confront her ex. The scene culminates with the wronged woman lobbing her wedding ring into the pond.

A very different story from the anthology is 'A Simple Nature' by Sareena, also from the Glasgow workshops. It opens with the protagonist, Mariam, bewailing her mother's inability to find a *rishta* for her, because all the matriarch's attention is on Mariam's older half-sister Hanna. Left to her own devices, Mariam becomes close to a course-mate, whom she is allocated to work with on an assignment. Over cups of coffee and intense chats about his art and her writing, they become closer, and this young man opens up to Mariam:

> 'Lots of things happened to me before I found Islam,' he admitted. 'The truth is, I come from a family who see no pleasure in equality and simplicity. They aren't very religious. My brothers would always come home drunk and encouraged me to do the same, but I knew that wasn't what I wanted. I was searching for peace and freedom, so I ended up spending most of my time drawing. By the time I was twenty-four, I was thinking of marriage, but seeing my brothers' failed marriages put me off. I never considered finding a girlfriend because most girls in my home town were doing all sorts of stuff: smoking weed, getting drunk, partying all night – the list goes on and on.'
>
> (173)

Perhaps somewhat surprisingly for a female-authored narrative, the story ultimately endorses this perspective, judgemental as it is about women's (and men's) behaviour. Mariam declares, 'I want to marry someone who's a pious Muslim, with firm morals and a kind personality. Someone who lives their life to seek Allah's pleasure, and someone who will be a good companion and respect me and my family' (179). The story ends with her happy marriage.

Conclusion

Those who teach creative writing often advise students to write 'what you know' (Neale 2006a: 44). But writing can be more searching, a process of discovery, reaching towards 'what you come to know' (Neale 2006b: 56). The same is true of the spoken word: of thinking aloud and exploring experiences and opportunities by talking about them. This articulation, exploratory and uncertain as it is, cannot afford to remain smooth or assured, and those who attempt it necessarily take risks and confront uncertainties. The rewards of this are significant. The writer can find a voice, and find confidence in that voice (Anderson 2006: 28). For some, this voice may be distinctive and artistically assured. For others, it may be conventional and generic, readily understandable and ordinary. Some people want to tell conventional coming-out stories, or borrow the words through which to say something as unoriginal but personally liberating as 'I love you'.

Whether 'coming to terms' involves the written or spoken word, it involves something both ethereal and powerful: grappling with language; not always being fluent; finding words to express and experience life; using words to explore possibilities. All of this can be a struggle. The real difficulty of coming to terms might have been lost if we had only quoted those who had already found a voice. Complexities would have been diluted if we had only referred to edited and burnished writing, to workshops that seemed to work; and if we only quoted interviewees who had spoken clearly and dexterously. We did not want to do that.

By remembering the writing that was aborted or seemed to fail, and by quoting interviewees who stumbled over their words, we hope to have brought alive the vital, frustrating, sometimes difficult and sometimes productive experiences of coming to terms.

Table I1.1 Interviews quoted in Interlude 1, 'Coming to Terms'

Name	Gender	Age	Relationship Status	Location
Janan	Female	30	Single	Glasgow
Hassan	Male	29	Single	Yorkshire
Hawa	Female	25	Married	Yorkshire
Faisal	Male	16	Single	Glasgow
Nabila	Female	30	Divorced	Newcastle
Esha	Female	27	Married	Yorkshire
Azeem	Male	26	Single	Newcastle
Salim	Male	24	Single	Newcastle

Table I1.2 Workshop participants and convenors in Interlude 1, 'Coming to Terms'

Name	Gender	Age	Workshop Series	Role in Workshop	Title
Noura	Female	28	6. Blogging, Glasgow	Participant	'Finding Your Power'
Afshan	Female	Not stated	3. Creative writing, Sheffield	Facilitator	Research diary notes
Sareena	Female	20	5. Fiction, Glasgow	Participant	'A Simple Nature'
Nafhesa	Female	Not stated	3. Creative writing, Sheffield	Researcher	Research diary notes

Chapter 3

DATING

It's a controversial topic in our generation because less people go towards arranged marriages, which is why they're – putting up quotation marks here – 'dat[ing]'. So people don't speak about it, it's just swept under the rug but we know it's there.

(Zarah, twenty-three, focus group discussion)

Nadia had been seeing a musician for some time. [...] She had, as was by then usual for her, been wearing her black robe, closed to her neck, and he had, as was by then usual for him, been wearing a size-too-small white T-shirt, pinned to his lean chest and stomach, and she had watched him and he had circled her, and they had gone to his place that night, and she had shuffled off the weight of her virginity with some perplexity but not excessive fuss.

(Mohsin Hamid, *Exit West* (2017: 33))

This chapter explores how young Muslims speak and write about dating, and in doing so how they respect and negotiate religious and cultural expectations and make decisions about what is acceptable to talk about and ultimately do within the boundaries of faith and identity. Their experiences and stories range from those who are enjoying casual dates and more serious relationships; those who differentiate between halal and haram dating practices; those who are cautious in speaking on this subject; and those who believe that any form of dating is haram. We look at the dating lives of fictional characters in new creative writing by young Muslims, a medium which can provide a space to question taboos and affirm beliefs. We also consider how dating is portrayed in recent novels, from the chaste, halal version in Ayisha Malik's 'Muslim Dating Book' *Sofia Khan is Not Obliged* (2016/2015) to casual dating in a more intense, sexual context in Mohsin Hamid's *Exit West* (2017).

'What if you get caught?'

Dating is not necessarily an easy topic for young Muslims to discuss openly. Alongside the usual embarrassment that arises for many young people in talking about romance and sex, they must also negotiate religious and cultural expectations concerning the permissibility of relationships before marriage. For many – particularly women and girls – the expectation that they will not date is communicated directly by family members. Janan, single at thirty, said she and her siblings have experienced parental pressure their whole lives not to date:

> My dad, from a religious point of view, didn't want us dating and he's been very vocal about that. And my dad was very clear about that amongst all five of us, that he didn't want us going out and having like pre-marriage relationships with anyone ... The expectation was always there from a very early age.

Such unequivocal direction meant that some young Muslims who took part in this study saw dating as off-limits, not only as a thing to do, but even as a topic of conversation.

Some of the young people we interviewed spoke cautiously and indirectly, recounting the experiences of friends and family members rather than themselves, or framing the discussion hypothetically. Hiba, for example, spoke about her older brother. Since 'my parents wouldn't have approved' if he was dating, she said, 'if he did anything like that it would have been in secret'. Hiba uses the conditional *would have been* to avoid, first, the direct implication that her brother has been dating and, second, that she has any knowledge of it. She suggests that *if* he had dated, her parents wouldn't have approved or known about it – the 'if' speaking to the ways in which dating can be surreptitious. Others were more candid with our interviewer, if not with their families. Aisha, single at the time of her interview though later married, said the 'only easy bit of a relationship' is 'keeping it a secret from your parents':

> In our community it is frowned upon if you have got a boyfriend ... But most of my friends have had boyfriends and it has been like they have had a double life, so they are hiding it from home. And then they are just pretending to meet the girl next door to go to town, but that will be how they meet their boyfriend.

For some young people, some of the time, these assignations can be thrilling. Interviewees described how they can get away with texting their girlfriend or boyfriend without their family noticing, how they arrange to 'accidentally' bump into someone they are seeing while out shopping with friends, or – for proper dates – travel to places where they won't be recognized.

Others, however, are not so comfortable with keeping secrets. Shafiq, now married, admitted to two previous relationships that his family don't know about, and the unease he felt at the time: 'I didn't like – it was challenging, like because of our religion – sometimes, it was proper challenging.' Zainab, younger and single, chose her words carefully when she discussed the reputational risk that dating carries for women and girls:

> Dating is quite hard I would say, in today's generation. It is all about, 'What if you get caught? What is going to happen then?' I think there is that fear in sort

of girls you know if they are seen to be seen doing something wrong, you know you could get taken back to Pakistan and married off. So I think a lot of what we do is sort of kept hush-hush […] you have to be careful who knows what – and what is sort of out there and what you are doing, where you go and who sees you.

For some, dating in secret is no mere diversion or game to test their parents; it requires careful planning and carries a serious risk. Khadija, nineteen, said she avoids dating altogether to avoid the risk of being caught because 'for women especially, that could like knock you back completely like with your future and getting married'. Together, these accounts offer a glimpse into young Muslims' dating practices which are seldom talked about, even between friends. They suggest that there is value in breaking the silences and secrecy around dating in ways that approach the subject with respect and sensitivity, acknowledging young Muslims' lived experiences.

'Going out with girls and stuff'

Dating is more explicitly forbidden in some families than others and, as our discussion above suggests, this is particularly the case where daughters are concerned. The young men we interviewed were more likely to allude to 'don't ask, don't tell' attitudes, and some were relatively open about unchaperoned meetings and sexual encounters. Bilal, in a serious relationship with a view to marriage at the time of his interview, sought to distance his dating practices from his 'wider group of associates', whom he described as 'probably a lot more liberal … like I know a lot of guys who mess about'. Similarly, teenage Farooq, whose comments we revisit in the interlude 'Speaking to Stereotypes', said he would describe some of his friends as 'players': 'They have got – like going out with girls and stuff. But me I just can't be bothered with that, not yet!' While Bilal and Farooq seek to distance themselves from their more promiscuous peers, their comments are nonetheless revealing of ways in which young men are given more freedom to explore premarital sexual possibilities without tarnishing their reputation.

In an untitled play written at a playwriting workshop at Glasgow Women's Library, Farah imagined a conversation on dating between two male characters, Tami and his friend Qayd:

Tami: Fuck you Qayd, I got plenty of girls. Iman was begging for it last night. You should see some of the texts she sent me.

Qayd: Iman has screwed every guy in Glasgow. Even the white breads won't touch her.

Tami: Na, Iman isn't like that. She is a good girl. All these other guys are just *kuttay* [dogs] spreading shit about her. I think she's the real deal. Wifey material.

Qayd: Let's see how round her *rotis* [chapatis] are for you. That's how you pick wifey.

In this scene, Iman's sexuality is juxtaposed with Tami's: for him, having 'plenty of girls' is a badge of honour, whereas for her, even the (alleged) expression of sexual desire leads to slut-shaming. Tami defends Iman as a 'good girl' and 'wifey material', while Qayd evokes the prized quality of domesticity in the cliché of the perfectly round chapati, both characters personifying the author's frustration with dating double standards for women as compared with men.

The stories that most interviewees tend to leave untold – except perhaps in banter with friends – are those that include touching and kissing, especially when no one is thinking about marriage. Azeem was one of the few young Muslims we interviewed who were relatively open about casual sex and dating. He reflected that a previous relationship 'was quite sexual more than – you know kind of emotional or kind of emotional connection or romantic kind of connection'. Azeem's comments were inflected by two things: his age and his sexuality. Being in his mid-twenties, he has some experience in dating, even though he feels that he 'probably came into dating late, probably about nineteen'. Having come out as gay and distanced himself from his religion, Azeem also feels he has less to lose in speaking directly – if anonymously – about sex. Young, gay and out, he is happy to be single, not 'massively bothered' about whether dating should lead to a relationship, or just to sex.

Some spoke of ways of navigating casual dating while hopefully keeping their families on board in the long run. Aisha, who was frank with our interviewer about enjoying secret dates while single, said that you should only introduce your parents to the boyfriend you intend to marry: 'To my friends it is don't tell your parents you have got a boyfriend until you are absolutely sure you are wanting to marry him … it is just best to keep it quiet until you are sure you want to be with that person.' Likewise, Masood felt that clandestine dating means you can get to know someone without things getting too serious, too soon: 'You've got that sort of societal expectation of commitment. Whereas when you're in that sort of relationship, a girlfriend–boyfriend relationship and it's secretive, there's no expectation there.' His strategy was similar to Aisha's: at some point you meet the person you want to marry, and once you know it's serious you go to your families to sort things out. This suggests that, for some young Muslim women as well as men, families are willing to turn a blind eye to dating transgressions if they eventually result in a successful match. This is a particular way, admittedly a sly one, that young Muslims are negotiating terms under which dating is acceptable. Others prefer a more above-board approach. The associated vocabulary of 'halal dating', which we explore below, enables some Muslims to rework religious and cultural expectations about what is and is not permissible.

'Call it halal dating'

Halal, or permissible, dating is defined in contrast to that which is haram, or impermissible within Islam. The idea of halal dating is gaining traction in online

Figure 3.1 'To date or not to date: Halal is the question'. This still from the animated film *Halal Dating*, which was made by the participants in Workshop Series 1, visualizes the conundrum faced by many young Muslims: the question of whether or not dating can ever be religiously permissible.

platforms and imaginative literature, with some young Muslims adopting this vocabulary and bringing it to bear on their own lives. This of course raises the question of who decides what is halal or haram: here, we are interested in how young Muslims judge this for themselves, broaching the taboo subject of premarital relationships without compromising their religious principles.

The first of the storying workshops convened within this project used the medium of animation. Working together, the participants made a single animated film on a topic they agreed together: *Halal Dating*. The script, which they devised through a series of discussions and scriptwriting and editing sessions, states that halal dating is 'dating, but within the boundaries'. For those who embraced it, this term typically meant dating with a chaperone present, avoiding physical intimacy and dating with a view to marriage. Bilal, who contrasted his own dating practices with more 'liberal' friends who 'mess about', said:

> When young Pakistani people date, and from my own experience too, like you would be talking about certain things at a younger age. From my experience I think, like, every relationship that I have been in – I have, it is like – we have spoken about marriage, do you know what I mean? So there has been an end goal.

The animation contrasts halal dating with 'having to meet each other once over tea and biscuits and then having to get married the next week' (Figure 3.2). Explaining how young Muslims can put halal dating into practice, the animation gives examples such as avoiding the temptation of physical intimacy by getting to know someone over the phone or online (Figure 3.3), and it presents dates in which more than two people are present, such as the family dating gameshow shown in the previous chapter, 'Meeting'.

Figure 3.2 Traditional first meetings between potential brides and grooms are symbolized by the tea and biscuits which are typically served by the young woman, with all eyes on her. Tea and biscuits are, of course, also symbols of Britishness, Pakistaniness, and wholesome hospitality. This still image is from the animated film *Halal Dating*, which was made by the participants in Workshop Series 1.

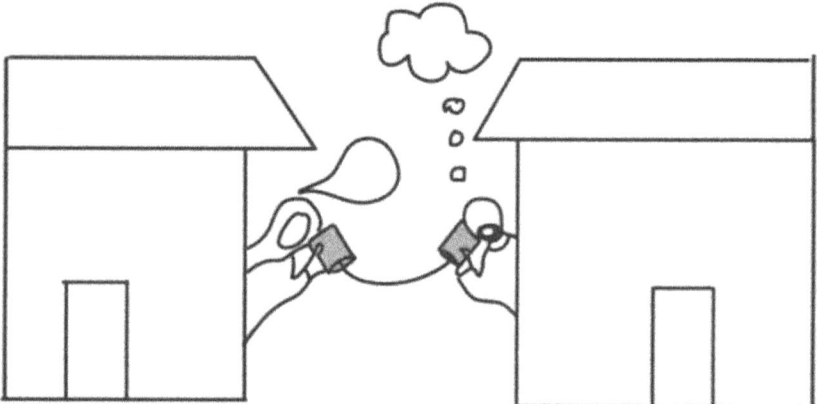

Figure 3.3 Those who entertain the possibility that dating can be religiously permissible tend to agree that it should not involve physical contact and that it should be chaperoned. Given the challenges of the former for two young people who are drawn to each other but find themselves anxious about the awkwardness of being chaperoned, some young Muslims speak of dating over the phone and online. This image, illustrating such virtual dating, is from the animated film *Halal Dating*, which was made by the participants in Workshop Series 1.

Reflecting on why they chose this topic for their animation, the group identified a shared hope of questioning negative assumptions about dating, in particular the idea that it should not be mentioned, seen or acknowledged, and a hope of encouraging intergenerational dialogue. Zarah observed: 'with the older generation, I think when they hear the word dating, they're like "Oh God no, that's a very Western thing, that's completely haram"'. Halal dating provides a vocabulary to think and talk about premarital relationships with peers, families and communities in a way that respects cultural and religious boundaries. At least, that was the perspective of some of the participants in these workshops. Others were more ambivalent about the term, but nonetheless felt that it is important to be able to have these conversations. Safa, whose experience we return to in the chapter on marriage, talked about 'dating' her husband following their arranged marriage. She was on board with the general topic because she felt that other young couples should have the opportunity to get to know one another earlier, saying: 'I quite like the idea of the different perspectives of dating being out there and people's kind of viewpoints being changed.'

Two members of the group had some reservations about the idea of halal dating. Zarah was a little sceptical of how people use and perhaps misapply the term to get their own way, rather than coming from a place of religious conviction: 'Call it halal dating and say that oh, we're not going to touch or be intimate so there's nothing wrong with it.' Yusuf, meanwhile, said he felt it could never apply to him because, as a gay man, his dating would always be considered haram by others. In other words, he thought that halal dating is contingent upon the notion of dating as a precursor to heterosexual marriage. It could therefore be helpful for challenging some taboos about premarital dating but not others.

'She struck gold first time. Or so she thought'

Another way in which silences may be broken is through creative writing. Shortly, we will turn to the work of published authors who have chronicled young Muslim dating life in accounts that are variously comic and sad, disappointing and promising, timid and salacious. First, however, we consider the freedom that this approach allows new writers who, by transposing experiences onto fictional characters and adopting pseudonyms, may feel free to express their thoughts on dating more fully.

Let us turn to the early draft of a short story called 'Rearranged', which was later published in the anthology *A Match Made in Heaven* (see Chambers et al. 2020: 104–105). In this story, Meena, who participated in a fiction writing workshop at Glasgow Women's Library, narrates the experiences of a widowed Muslim woman named Sapna who is online dating for the first time: 'It had started out so well. She struck gold the very first time. Or so she thought. SonaSona was clean and interesting and funny. He was a lawyer. He dressed well. And he seemed to like her. Then, the unthinkable had happened'. In the following extract, Sapna has an unexpected – and ill-timed – encounter with SonaSona, having nipped out on an errand to the local supermarket in her 'lounging around the house jeans':

> Oh God, no!
>   His back was turned. She had to get rid of the sole item in her basket. She picked it up and hurled it into the adjoining aisle. Then Sapna turned to the shelf next to her and dropped something – anything – into her basket.

In that second she realized her prospective rishta was about to turn around. That's when she heard a light thud and a high-pitched scream.

'Hai, meri Rabb!' Pinky exclaimed. 'Somebody just tried to kill me with a TENA box!'

SonaSona turned around to Sapna. He took in the straggly hair escaping her hijab, her jeans–kameez combo, and smiled. 'JaffaCakes! So nice to see –' He stuttered and stopped talking as though someone had pressed an off switch on his back. He was staring at the item that Sapna had grabbed for her basket and his mouth made a wide O.

She looked, and saw only two words. *Ribbed. Flavoured.* Sapna screamed and ran. Only to find she was still clutching her basket as the alarms at the exit began beeping.

She never saw SonaSona again. He never even gave her the chance to explain. Blocked and deleted. All that glitters …

Here, the romcom genre enables Meena to explore some serious themes – disingenuous men; keeping up appearances for dates; the taboo of premarital sex – in a humorous and light tone. Sapna's online suitors are ironically named, from the materialistic and shallow SonaSona (Sona meaning 'gold') to the too-traditional PunjabiPrinceCharming, who shows up to their first date in a curry-stained white shalwar kameez. Charting the love life of an adventurous and resilient older women, 'Rearranged' offers a glimpse of the excitement, disappointment and unexpected turns that online dating can take.

Another scene, drafted in a playwriting workshop at Glasgow Women's Library, offers a very different take on dating. Written by Taibah, this untitled play dramatizes a relationship between two Muslim characters, Harris and Aliza, who meet at university. Early in the play, we witness Aliza's cynicism about Harris's intentions:

Aliza: (Angry) Look Mr, I don't do the whole dating-a-guy thing, okay? I may look like this but I have principles, standards and family values that I adhere to. 'For marriage reasons' (puts up her fingers and makes quotation marks in the air) let's meet up for coffee a few times a week. And get to know one another. For marriage reasons lets have some pointless midnight chats and text exchanges asking each other's favourite colour or favourite biryani. For marriage reasons lets hold hands. For marriage reasons let just kiss and on and on and on. Till one day the guy (pointing at Harris) turns around and says 'Oh I'm sorry, I can't marry you. My mum doesn't approve. She wants me to marry my cousin in Pakistan'. (Crosses her arms in defensive pose)

Harris: Woooo eassssy Aliza. I wasn't asking you to date me. I know you ain't that kind of girl. I'm Muslim as well. I get it.

Aliza: So what are you asking?

Harris: I'm asking you to consider me? As someone you could marry. I'll bring my folks over to your house. I'll do it the right way. I'll do it the Halal way. I will take care of you. I will provide for you and our family. I will Aliza. I promise.

Aliza: Big words kid. Prove it.
Harris: I'll prove it.

In this exchange, Aliza expresses a negative attitude towards dating as something that is against her 'principles, standards and family values'. Echoing Zarah's earlier comments on halal dating, she questions whether Harris's motives are genuine, and moreover expresses her concern that dating can lead to physical intimacy. This scene highlights how some young Muslims may reject the vocabulary of dating, which they associate with casual encounters, and look for other ways to express the idea of getting to know someone with a serious view to marriage.

The 'Muslim dating book': Sofia Khan is Not Obliged

The eponymous heroine of Ayisha Malik's debut novel, *Sofia Khan is Not Obliged* (2016/2015), is working as a publicist in a London-based publishing house, trying to find stories for a book on Muslim dating as solicited by her manager, and navigating her own love life. Sofia, who is thirty years old, Muslim and with Pakistani heritage, has a series of dates – both to find material for her book and also a potential life partner – which are variously promising, disappointing, funny and sad. Though not all of the men she dates are equally religious, she upholds her religious principles, only dating with marriage in mind, and holding back from physical intimacy. Of course, it is not only women who approach dates with marriage rather than sex in mind. Towards the end of the novel, readers see Sofia fall in love with her non-Muslim neighbour, Conall, who ultimately converts to Islam. Over the course of the novel, she has spent considerable time discussing her unique intermingling of personal and professional experience while taking refuge at his house and trying to write her 'Muslim dating book' (57).

The novel starts with Sofia having broken up with her fiancé, Imran, just before Ramadan, due to her aversion to living with his family after marriage. Because of her age, Sofia's family are eager for her to get married soon. However, contrary to received ideas about overbearing parents, this eagerness never amounts to anything more than some light and good-humoured nagging. Sofia emerges as a witty, smart, fun-loving and independent woman for whom faith helps to maintain her life's equilibrium. A practising Muslim who prays five times a day, she jokingly refers to herself as the 'saint-like offspring to my immigrant parents' (10). We see her handling her proposed life partnership and its attendant complications with both seriousness and a certain degree of serenity. When a concerned older sister Maria asks Sofia whether she is all right after the break-up with Imran, Sofia quips: 'Well, thankfully break-ups aren't fatal' (42). This breezy reply indicates her self-contained pragmatism but, beneath a stoical exterior, she nonetheless hides a penchant for romantic gestures.

In the first few lines of her 'Muslim dating book', Sofia writes about how marriage takes centre stage in what she calls '*authentic*' Muslim dating. This sort of dating often involves the chastening presence of a chaperone, but it is noteworthy that Sofia does not take a *mahram* with her on any of her romantic encounters. For Sofia, if first dates involve ordinary small talk about '*the socio-political effects of 9/11 and skinny jeans*', they also include '*discussions about living arrangements, how many times you pray in the day*'. Ultimately, though, '*[t]here is one purpose, and that is marriage. You are diving, head-first, into the fire*' (72; emphasis in original). This not only illustrates issues specific to Muslim dating but also its non-negotiable emphasis on marriage as the end goal. Although Sofia is quite comfortable with her single status and does not want to rush into marriage, she reflects on the religious dimension of her love life: 'getting married is apparently completing half your faith. Does this mean I'm less successful in Islam as well as society?' (27). This arch observation nonetheless registers Sofia's sense that she is negotiating faith and relationship choices at once, a tension that is constitutive of Malik's narrative of Muslim dating.

Faith is indeed an important component in Sofia's own dating stories. As a practising, hijab-wearing Muslim, she faces judgemental and offensive responses from both so-called liberal and conservative men. Even Sofia's mother discourages her daughter from wearing the garment since it might, she suspects, put off potential dates. We are told that Sofia once met a 'beardie' – a staunch Muslim man with a beard – who called her 'disco hijabi', suggesting her 'clothes weren't that bad – they just needed to be painted black' (19). Disgusted with such extreme reactions to her sartorial choices, Sofia complains to one of her friends:

> There are the men who'll marry a hijabi – but then expect her to move in with a hole-in-the-wall, or think she's going to be this weird paragon of traditional values. [...] And then there are the men who are all, '*You're living in the west – what's with the hijab?*' Honestly, I can't help it if I like God. Life would feel so much harder without God, you know?
>
> (43; emphasis in original)

These lines capture the complications that an independent, pious Muslim woman might go through while dating in the hope of finding a husband. On the one hand, a hijab-wearing woman is often assumed to be a compliant person, easily prevailed on to obey conventional cultural diktats. Yet on the other, as we have seen, some potential partners consider her not 'modern' enough, and thereby lightly relegate her to an object of pity and disdain.

It is not only with her dates that Sofia has to negotiate her faith; this is also something that she grapples with on a personal level. In her diary, she writes: 'The other problem with my being alone stance is being celibate and believing in no sex before marriage. Surely never having a shag, ever, will have an adverse effect on my health'. Concerned, she even Googles 'lack of sex in life' (26). As a devout Muslim she is particular about not having sex before marriage, but she also worries about depriving herself of sexual satisfaction. This incident, humorously presented, once again subtly enacts one of the thorny issues that a practising Muslim might confront while (not) dating.

Throughout the experience of dating Sophia asks herself one fundamental question about potential suitors: 'how will he enhance my (Islamic) life?' (181).

She believes that 'sharing the fundamentals [on life and religion] is rather basic' (39). On this basis, she rejects one man, Naim, who is Muslim but, she concludes, not seriously committed to religion or to the idea of marriage. When Conall asks Sofia whether her choice is limited to Muslim men, she answers: 'it hardly makes sense to marry someone with whom I can't share what's essentially the main part of my life' (232). What is evident in this quotation is Sofia's deep attachment to her faith, and her clear understanding of the implications of this. Interestingly, when she falls for the non-Muslim Conall, Sofia holds herself back until she finds the love reciprocated. Crucially, readers learn that Conall has already converted to Islam, as he is attracted to the religion for himself and is well aware of what faith means to Sofia.

Underneath its unashamedly frivolous style, this novel depicts the complexities of Muslim dating with insight and empathy, provoking readers to think differently about the love lives of religious women like Sofia.

'When I say you should come over …' Exploratory dating in Exit West

Not all writers or characters are as pious or chaste as Malik and her protagonist Sofia. As we have already seen in this chapter, some young and single Muslims do not rule out sex outside marriage. Several writers take these themes further, elaborating on the role of sex within both casual and serious premarital relationships. Mohsin Hamid's novel *Exit West*, which was shortlisted for the Man Booker Prize in 2017, presents readers with the development – including the near-consummation – and then the unravelling of the relationship between the novel's only named characters, protagonists Nadia and Saeed. From the outset, Nadia bluntly tells Saeed: 'I don't pray' (M. Hamid 2017: 3). Inverting readers' likely expectations on being first introduced to the on-point designer stubble that Saeed sports, and the conservative black robe worn by Nadia, Saeed is religious but open-minded and Nadia is uninterested in faith. The pair explore sex, begin to cohabit and flee the city of their birth together.

Having ignited their relationship in a municipality which is loosely based on Lahore but could also be Baghdad or Raqqa, Saeed and Nadia grow frightened at the militants' takeover of their country. In a magical realist twist, they escape through a portal to the island of Mykonos, a Greek isle long associated with glamour and pleasure (and more recently with the refugee crisis), then to London, and finally to Marin, California. Their relationship is at once sexual and chaste, described with beautiful ambiguity as follows:

> [T]hey found themselves in those early days of their romance growing hungry, touching each other, but without bodily adjacency, without release. They had begun, each of them, to be penetrated, but they had not yet kissed.
> (37)

At this early stage, the relationship is relatively monastic; the couple are falling for each other and experiencing desire, but not yet acting on it.

On their first date at a Chinese restaurant Nadia and Saeed find they can talk easily to each other. They are so absorbed in this conversation that these tech-savvy millennials switch off from the outside world, placing their phones screen down between them, 'like the weapons of desperadoes at a parley' (16). At the end of the date, having focused on each other to the exclusion of everything else, the two are reluctant to be parted. Nadia invites Saeed back to her upstairs flat, where she is unusual in living on her own as a young, single woman (Saeed resides with his parents, so there would be no privacy at his place). Entering on her own, she throws one of her long, all-enveloping robes out of the window down to him. He puts the garment on to gain access to the property, safely undetected by prying eyes. This subterfuge chimes with interview accounts of how dating is often shrouded in secrecy.

She has already warned him, 'When I say you should come over, I'm not saying I want your hands on me' (22). Without the help of a chaperone, Nadia has therefore been clear about her boundaries. Feeling a little 'traumatized' by her candour (22), Saeed rushes to reassure her of his agreement to her terms. Once alone together, Nadia plays Saeed some soul music and they smoke marijuana. Nothing explicitly sexual happens between the couple on this first date. Rather, dating is presented as a way of getting to know each other, finding out if one wants more. It is also about companionship, intellectual connection and pleasure in the moment.

Yet Nadia and Saeed's process of discovery is more sped up than is usual in dating, because the crisis in their unnamed country 'accelerates and intensifies their relationship' (Hamid, qtd in Leyshon 2016). Nadia experiences the crisis first-hand: her cousin is killed in a bomb-blast, so Saeed's and her unusual second date involves a trip to visit his freshly dug grave, where Saeed says a prayer and Nadia appears lost in thought. Eating together afterwards, Nadia 'felt things change between them, become more solid, in a way' (M. Hamid 2017: 30) because of this shared experience of grief and trauma.

After knowing each other a few weeks, the couple end up in bed together. They find pleasure in sexual activities short of penetration, but when Nadia asks if Saeed has a condom he says, 'I don't think we should have sex until we're married' (53). Initially assuming he is joking, Nadia's mood moves quickly from surprise and anger, to tenderness and acceptance – at least for the time being. Through the process of dating, both Nadia and Saeed are exploring what they want and do not want from each other. Nadia remains wary of commitment, so when Saeed asks her to marry him, her response, once again, is not only loving but contains notes of incredulity, 'galloping terror […] and […] something altogether more complicated, something that struck her as akin to resentment' (62).

Dating, for Muslims as for others, can involve being with someone but not being committed fully to them; that is often the point of dating. In fact, Nadia is seeing a musician when she and Saeed first meet, a man who had helped her to 'shuffle […] off the weight of her virginity with some perplexity but not excessive fuss' (30–1). She even has 'passionate farewell sex' with this musician after deciding to go exclusive with Saeed, and this sex 'was, not unsurprisingly, surprisingly good' (32). Dating can thus be expressed through still having a weather eye to other men or women.

Dating is also about trial and error, and a relationship's termination can be positive as it can be a moment of knowing oneself better. It becomes increasingly clear that Nadia is uncomfortable with intimacy, unsure of her sexual orientation or her ability to reciprocate Saeed's love and desire for her. Matters are complicated further by Saeed's religiosity and respect for his parents, which hold him back sexually in this premarital relationship. Nadia's and Saeed's break-up is inevitable, given their different approaches to sex and religion. Opposites attract, but ultimately her cosmopolitan, liberal worldview and his religious, family-oriented mindset prove incompatible. Nadia has passionate dreams about and memories of a girl she met in hedonistic Mykonos. She is growing into her identity, whereas Saeed's seems more fixed and rooted. Through this story of a young couple coming together and growing apart, *Exit West* explores how dating is a matter of finding out about one's sexuality and what one does or doesn't want from a relationship.

Conclusion

It is fitting that *Exit West* draws this chapter to a close, as the range of dating experiences and views we have explored really coalesce in the tension between this novel's two young lovers. For some young Muslims, as for Nadia and Saeed, the extent to which religion inflects one's love life, and the question of how to handle sex, will be a point of conflict or difference. Despite some things said about halal dating – for example that there should be no physical contact between unmarried couples, they should be chaperoned, and they should move forward quickly towards marriage – this chapter has shown that dating can be about pleasure in the moment, exploring possibilities and sexual attraction. Even Malik's doughty protagonist Sofia thinks about sex, if not acting on it, as she navigates her dating life. Of course, there are also those who do not date at all, some out of religious conviction, others who deem the risk too high. Given the taboo of premarital dating and sex, the experiences of fictional Muslim characters in creative writing and published literature are illuminating, advancing issues that people can be reluctant to discuss in person, breaking silences and challenging stereotypes.

Table 3.1 Interviews quoted in Chapter 3, 'Dating'

Name	Gender	Age	Relationship Status	Location
Janan	Female	30	Single	Glasgow
Hiba	Female	27	Married	Glasgow
Aisha	Female	27	Single, then married	Yorkshire
Shafiq	Male	29	Married	Newcastle
Zainab	Female	20	Single	Yorkshire
Khadija	Female	19	Single	Newcastle
Farooq	Male	17	Single	Yorkshire

(Continued)

Azeem	Male	26	Single		Newcastle
Masood	Male	21	Single		Yorkshire
Saamiya	Female	18	Single		Glasgow

Table 3.2 Workshop participants and convenors quoted in Chapter 3, 'Dating'

Name	Gender	Age	Workshop Series	Role in Workshop	Title
Noura	Female	28	5. Fiction, Glasgow	Participant	'Untitled'
Farah	Female	25	4. Playwriting, Glasgow	Participant	'Untitled'
Meena	Female	35	5. Fiction, Glasgow	Participant	'Rearranged'
Taibah	Female	36	4. Playwriting, Glasgow	Participant	'Untitled'
Zarah	Female	23	1. Animation, Sheffield	Participant	Focus group discussion
Safa	Female	23	1. Animation, Sheffield	Participant	Focus group discussion
Yusuf	Male	22	1. Animation, Sheffield	Participant	Focus group discussion
Bilal	Male	22	1. Animation, Sheffield	Participant	Focus group discussion

Chapter 4

LOVE

I was in love, I thought I was finally getting my cheesy chick flick moment. I remember the butterflies in my stomach, how I couldn't eat or sleep and the way my mind would wander as I imagined our future.

(Farah, twenty-five, creative writing exercise)

Love when you get married, love is not – you can say love a person when you get married on the first day, you know; [but] love will come after four or five years and then you can say.

(Arshad, twenty-nine, interview)

When young Muslims speak and write about romantic love, some of the stories they tell are resonant, if not universal. Stories of desire, first love, uncertainty, hope, conflict, disappointment and fleeting passion – all themes in Farah's creative writing piece – speak of youthful naivety and inexperience in matters of the heart. For some, first love is simple, while for others – like the star-crossed lovers Monty and Layla in Fatima Bhutto's unsettling novel *The Runaways* (2019a) – it is profoundly complicated. Some speak of everyday acts of love in the small things that constitute a loving relationship. Some, like Arshad, believe that love is a growing bond that becomes more meaningful as husband and wife get to know each other properly. Some stories are obviously inflected by religion and culture: telling of love *after* marriage; of 'love marriage' (going against expectations of arranged or selfless marriage); and of loveless marriage (where love does not follow the ceremony). Some are sceptical of 'dream perfect' love as it is portrayed in films and fiction, but not all love stories are guilty of glossing over relationships in this way. One such story is Ayisha Malik's second novel *The Other Half of Happiness* (2017), which explores what happens after 'happily ever after' as her witty protagonist Sofia Khan confronts the realities of married life. The love stories in this chapter – simple and complex, hopeful and cynical – are marked by their diversity.

Love is ...

In a free-writing exercise during a workshop at a Sheffield sixth-form college, pupils were prompted with a series of single words, one of which was 'love'. Their responses were hesitant. 'Love your parents', wrote Afreen. 'Love everyone around you but love who you want to love. Love is love. I don't know what to say. LOL.' Despite the naivety of its writer and her recourse to cliché and shorthand, this nonetheless reveals various thoughts that love conjures up: filial piety, caring for others and the right to choose who you love. Huma likewise reflected on different kinds of love: 'It could be either a romantic love or a caring love [...] it shows we are important and wanted.' Their classmate Fariha, like Afreen, appeared to run out of words: 'Love is a feeling towards someone special who has meaning and who you want in your life. Love, love is amazing.' These brief and faltering extracts reveal the difficulty of putting love into words. Of course, it may be that these teenagers lack the relationship experience to advance their theories on love. Another classmate, Daud, reflected sadly: 'I had a crush in middle school, but I never had the courage to tell her so it never developed into love or a relationship.' Here, romantic love is something of a mystery, for now off-limits.

Some who lacked experience in love, like Saamiya, an interviewee in her late teens, drew on stories for inspiration. When asked if she has been in love, she said 'Uh – not necessarily. I have read a couple of books maybe.' She mentioned a novel given to her by her cousin, in which the young Muslim protagonist has an arranged marriage in Pakistan to a much older man. Saamiya described how, in the story, the protagonist 'ended up escaping, coming back to the UK', where she 'kind of found herself, fell in love with a man [who] she had known her entire life' and lived happily, if not ever after, then at least on her own terms. Saamiya liked this book because it offered reassurance that 'relationships can turn out', with scope for something 'positive'. Her expectations of finding love remain low but, remembering that story, she is able to see some light at the end of what seems like a tunnel. Here, a love story with a Muslim character is a comfort to a young woman who has grown up with strict parents who expect her to have an arranged marriage. As a lesbian who has felt unable to come out to her family, Saamiya's relationship experiences to date have been challenging, but love stories offer hope.

Iman, single and in her late twenties, had a more cynical view of love stories. She felt that their portrayal of romantic love bears little similarity to the trials and tribulations of real life:

> I mean if you find someone that you love and you care about and you're happy together, there's going to be certain things that you don't like about them and vice versa. And there'll be situations that happen where things don't work out and there's arguments. So I think a lot of movies, but I guess that's what sells, that's what people want to see, that kind of dream perfect relationship, so they can kind of have that moment of escape.

Here, Iman offers a more mature perspective – perhaps speaking from experience – on the power of the 'happily ever after' narrative and how this can lead to unrealistic expectations. She suggests that even happy relationships aren't perfect, that the everyday experience of loving someone can be difficult. The illusion of perfection and the disappointment it inevitably leads to is borne out in some of the stories that others told about first love, a subject to which we now turn.

'I was utterly mesmerized': First love

Hamid met his now-wife when attending school in Azad Kashmir as a teenager. They struck up a friendship pretty quickly and he looked forward to seeing her on subsequent visits to Pakistan, but his first thoughts were not of love. Hamid explained: 'I didn't think much of it. I just thought it was – I didn't think it was going to go any further.' Over the years, their relationship matured and Hamid felt that it was 'getting a bit more serious'. When asked what made him think so, he replied, 'Because the bond was getting stronger.' Struggling to put into words the quiet yet palpable affection he feels for his wife, Hamid told a simple, unaffected story of them falling for one another.

For others, first love is not so straightforward or happy. Zohaib described the difficulty he had in moving on from his first girlfriend, and how he found little sympathy among his friends:

> In my first relationship like because I'd never experienced it before, it was really hard for me because I'd never had this feeling before. And I had to kind of deal with it on my own. I told my friends and that but they just like said to man up, there's plenty of other girls and all that stuff. But it took me ages to get over that but I did eventually get over it.

Again, the word 'love' hovers in the background as Zohaib describes a bewildering strength of feeling that lack of experience made him ill-equipped to handle. This relatable story of a first break-up will surely hit a nerve with anyone who has experienced heartbreak. It also particularly underlines the difficulty that adolescent boys may face in expressing and navigating their feelings. When Zohaib reached out to his friends for relationship advice and support, he was bluntly told to 'man up'.

In a creative writing workshop in Bradford, Bilal explored a disconcerting first experience of love from the point of view of an unnamed, ungendered character. In the first-person narrative, he describes love as 'a whole new unexplainable feeling that I couldn't quite grasp or make sense of'. In the following passage, his mystery protagonist reflects on being torn between the dual impulses of longing to share and suppress their feelings:

> What did it mean, I used to always ask myself, that I'm feeling this way? Why was it that I felt like I wanted to avoid every glance – every look – I wanted to avoid him so bad that I subconsciously found myself drawn to finding him in the hallways and the streets – random places where I didn't ever think I'd see him. But he was always there like a thought.

This story describes first love as a fixation and as a personification of latent desire, embodied in an acquaintance whom the narrator is drawn to in spite of themselves. The passage teases with tantalizing moments of possibility and physical connection: 'It had to be broken into a smile – into an ushering moment. A silly grin – the whisper of his voice in my ear.' However, the narrator concedes that '[i]t was never anything more than those looks.' Like Zohaib's real-life example, Bilal's story illustrates how first love can produce mixed emotions – excitement, yes, but also loneliness, fear and frustration.

In a creative writing exercise at Glasgow Women's Library, Farah drafted a story of first love from the contrasting perspectives of a young couple in a relationship. In one version, her female first-person narrator, Orla, gushes with excitement about her 'cheesy chick flick moment' and her future relationship:

> I had already planned the names of our children (two girls, Anna and Sara, and one boy, Leith). I felt insecure around him, he was cool and calm; all the other girls wanted him, but he chose me. I couldn't describe how happy that made me. I was perfect as I was, even with my eye bags and flat arse. I was utterly mesmerized by him. I convinced myself he was the one I would be with forever.

In this passage, Farah captures the overwhelming experience of first love, a rush of emotions that makes Orla feel 'perfect' and desired.

Written in the past tense, there are clues that all is not as wonderful as it seems. Orla confesses that she feels 'insecure' next to her 'cool and calm' boyfriend, while the mention of the 'chick flick moment' hints at a relationship founded in fantasy. In another draft of the story using third-person focalization, we learn more about the object of her affection:

> Girls had always been easy for Issac but something had drawn him to Orla. Orla had an innocence about her that he wanted to explore. At one point, he did think he liked her and blurted it out without thinking. He instantly regretted it, but by then it was too late, she had already fallen for him. Girls fell for Issac all the time and this is where the problem lay; once they were in love it was all too easy. The problem was that when Issac had gotten all that he wanted he wasn't sure if he wanted her any more. He could see it in Orla's eyes, she was completely sucked in and panic began to set in. Issac couldn't breathe, he needed space and he had to get out.

Here, Farah explores the blurring of flirtation and love in the frivolous mind of a young man conscious of his powers of attraction. Although the relationship is one-sided, we learn that Issac was initially intrigued by Orla, a passion that petered out on closer acquaintance. This story of pursuit, passing fancy mistaken for love, and unrequited love underlines the gendered dynamic in their relationship, in the false reassurance that Orla feels when she perceives Issac's lust.

'For Monty, everything began and ended with Layla': Young love in *The Runaways*

Many of the love stories that young Muslims shared with us – both from their own lives and in creative writing – are decidedly ordinary, rooted in everyday settings such as school and university and in finding their way to adulthood. Some love stories in published literature are more dramatic, foregrounding the entanglement of social, religious and sexual identity and speaking to wider political themes. Fatima Bhutto's unsettling novel *The Runaways* (2019a) is set in multiple locations in Pakistan, the UK and the Middle East. This polyvocal novel follows the lives of three young individuals – Anita Rose (also called Layla), Sunny and Monty – who, for various reasons, go to Iraq to join a fictional extremist group known as the Ummah Movement (based on ISIS). The novel probes issues of social inequality, alienation and religious extremism, with a love story grounded in the disastrous reality the characters find themselves in. The names of the lovers – Layla and Monty – function as a clear allusion to the ill-fated lovers Layla and Qays (known as Majnun, or madman) from Arab legend. Meanwhile the novel's catastrophic conclusion suggests the profound irony and subversion of such a resemblance.

In the novel, love is mostly presented through the perspective of Monty, a young boy from a wealthy family in Karachi, who lives a privileged life of luxury and mobility between the UK and Pakistan. While Monty's father is preoccupied with maintaining his wealth and status, and is keen for Monty to embody conventional masculinity, his mother is a blindly devoted follower of a televangelist. Distanced from his parents by their respective obsessions, Monty's affluent existence has everything except meaning and higher purpose. When Monty meets beautiful and fearless Layla, he falls in love. In contradistinction to Monty high's social position, Layla, or Anita Rose, comes from a poverty-stricken Christian family in Karachi. Aspiring for a life of dignity and freedom she, through various means, adopts the identity of Layla and gets admitted to the elite private school where she meets Monty. However, tragedy follows when Layla disappears to become an icon of the Ummah Movement. This leads Monty to frantically search for her in the desert, like the legendary lover Majnun for his lost Layla.

As a consequence of his emotional estrangement from his parents, Monty has an intense yearning for love, coupled with insecurity, self-doubt and fear of intimacy. Through free indirect discourse, he discloses: 'For all his school flirtations, late-night calls with girls in his class and meaningless hook-ups at after-parties, he'd never had a real girlfriend. Maybe it was true what his father said: maybe he didn't know how to be a man, how to command the world around him' (58). When Monty meets Layla in school, he is drawn to her uninhibited attitude. His fascination with Layla is limned with pathos:

> Everyone wanted Layla. Because she was beautiful, because she was a tease, because she flirted absent-mindedly, easily, the way other people dreamed. But Monty wanted her because she was fearless. And he was – and had always been – afraid.
>
> (90)

Layla's indomitable nature compensates for Monty's low self-esteem. His love seems to stem from a sense of insufficiency – a yearning for qualities that he desires but himself lacks.

If Monty is attracted to Layla for her fearless spirit, Layla, who is sexually bold but emotionally controlled, is touched by Monty's honesty and guilelessness. Their love is vividly expressed in the following lines, again from the perspective of the Muslim-heritage-but-secular-minded rich boy: 'Monty thanked whatever God existed for Layla and the impossible, miraculous fate that had brought her into his life' (104). Although Layla's motives are questionable and she is 'always in her own world', an inchoate love is also subtly evident: 'When she saw him, how he looked at her, full of love and trust, Layla's heart swelled with something close to pain. […] It cost Layla so little to make Monty happy' (104–5). For Layla, who has experienced the world's unjustness acutely, Monty's complete surrender of himself induces empathy. She realizes Monty's genuine love for her in an intimate moment between them: 'She looked into his eyes, watching her hopefully, and it occurred to Layla that was why his heart beat so fast. Out of love, not fear' (148). These words bespeak the gentle attentiveness of young love. Love is refracted through the other's gaze, as images of eyes and seeing predominate when Bhutto writes of lovers' encounters.

As the narrative progresses, love becomes at once a prayer and a mission as Monty desperately searches for Layla and joins the Ummah Movement in order to find her. Finally, after discovering his lover, 'Monty sat on his haunches in the cooling desert sand and closed his eyes in gratitude […]. It had only been three months, just about, since he had been out here in this dry, miserable wasteland. He always knew he would find Layla, love of his life' (168). Monty here seems to function as a perpetually lovestruck swain, since for him 'everything began and ended with Layla' (189). The novel's portrayal of love is effectively captured in the following statement that illuminates how love is enmeshed with life's other realities: 'Monty's world was so much simpler before Layla. But it was also empty, that was true. […] Layla pulled all Monty's edifices down. Without her, he would have known nothing – especially what was painful – about the world' (245, 247).

Although we have been focusing on the novel's predominant romantic couple, Monty and Layla, it should not escape our notice that *The Runaways*' third protagonist, Sunny, also experiences love's vicissitudes. Sunny is the novel's British Muslim character, having grown up in Portsmouth with his Indian Muslim father. The teenager is good-looking and popular with the opposite sex, but his success with women quickly gives him ennui: 'He didn't want any of those girls, brown or white. He was done with all that' (41). Instead, he turns to an online world, dabbling with religion and politics. From there he moves on to matchmaking apps such as Tinder or Scruff and, more furtively, a proxy server to access YouPorn. He continues to find his own sexual identity and others' articulation of consent hard to understand. Hamlet-like, he 'lurked and hesitated, swiping left all the time' (52). Yet he forms close bonds with a German fitness trainer named Stefan who works at his gym and later with his own radicalized cousin Oz. More than for either of those men, though, he feels love for a Syrian refugee DJ named Aloush. As ever, this tender affect is expressed through ocular tropes: 'Sunny felt Aloush, he saw him. And in that moment he understood that, for the first time, he too had been seen' (228). Love, in this political novel, assumes many forms. It may be between men and women or members of the same sex; it has a seductive power, but also evinces a spiritual and ethical dimension; it is at once turbulent and placid.

'Love is something you build, like a house'

While some stories speak of young love as passion bordering on obsession, others are more measured, telling of love *after* marriage, grounded in everyday acts of care and intimacy. Madeeha described love as 'something that grows'. In trying to put her feelings into words, she reflected on how, for her, love is evinced through the mundanities of married life. Speaking of her husband, she said:

> [H]e puts up with me, like the small things [laughs]. […] Why the hell is he so patient with me? Like I get stressed with the kids and like I've been stressed with doing other things and he'll be patient. And sometimes I think oh my God, why is he doing that? And then you realize he must really like you; he must really love you to do that.

In this account, love surfaces in a strong relationship founded on empathy, tolerance and support, originating from shared caring responsibilities and a life together.

Arshad similarly felt that love comes through marriage and deep commitment. His perspective was coloured by an unsuccessful arranged marriage in which he had struggled to get to know his wife, but also by a happier second marriage. He said people use the word 'love' far too often and early:

> [Y]ou can't just say you love a person because you don't know what colour she likes, you don't know what food she likes, you don't know what she likes to wear, you know what I mean, and that comes gradually into a marriage, that comes after four years, then you have a rock base there that you can say yeah, I do love that person. You get to know that person really well.

This reflection could be applied to both arranged and love marriages formed on limited acquaintance, and to non-marital relationships that become long-term. Arshad suggests that the 'love' professed to someone you scarcely know may be sincerely felt in the moment, but shallow compared to the love that emerges from prolonged intimacy. In his view, it takes years to build the firm foundations of a loving marriage.

Aisha, in an interview, contrasted her belief in falling in love with her parents' experience of love after marriage:

> My mum always has this thing that love doesn't happen like you meeting somebody going out and getting to know them, and you fall in love with them, like how I was saying in the fairy tales. They meet each other and they fall in love, Mum and Dad don't believe that that exists. They believe that love is something that you build, like a house, you build it over time and you fall in love and that is what love is, not this fairy tale that you meet someone and you can hear like songs in your head and you fall with each other. They don't really believe that, that is how you fall in love. It is built over time, in trust.

While sceptical of her mum's advice that 'all you need is a husband' and love will follow, in this quote we glimpse Aisha's deep respect for her parents' relationship and her certainty of their love for one another. In using the language of 'fairy tales' she acknowledges that her view of love may be naive, but nonetheless she would like to pursue it on her own terms.

'I just would like to meet someone, then fall in love'

Several young Muslims, like Aisha, spoke of love in the context of wanting a 'love marriage' as opposed to an arranged marriage. Tahir, under pressure from his parents to marry as soon as possible, complained: 'I just would like to meet someone, then fall in love with them, then get married to them.' Similarly, Zainab alluded to a conflict of interest between her hopes for a love marriage and the hopes of her family: 'if you fall in love, and you think that is the right person for you, then you should just go ahead with it. But then when it comes to family, that is a completely different story'. These quotes highlight the challenges and contradictions that young Muslims may face in reconciling their views on how love comes about with those of their family. Both Tahir and Zainab present the act of falling in love and getting married as a matter of meeting the right person and trusting your instincts. At the same time, they concede that their romantic notion that you meet someone and 'just go ahead with it' may be complicated by family interference.

In short stories drafted in creative writing workshops in Rochdale, young men imagined falling in love as serendipitous and simple. In a story by Mobeen, two mixed-heritage characters called Adam and Shanice meet in school and start dating. Things move fast between them: 'They were in love through college and stayed together'. In this story, the young couple's love is a constant amid drama and unhappiness in Shanice's home, caused by her drug-dealing father. Another story, written in equally simple language, develops a more sustained and intricate picture of young love. As in Mobeen's writing, love offers comfort and direction to young people whose lives are otherwise unstable. It is something to trust, and be led by. The author, Raheem, imagines a union between reformed 'bad boy' Raja and his friend Farah. Early in the story, we learn that the two developed a bond while in university:

> Raja had managed to undergo a complete makeover; his appearance, mannerisms and mentality had completely changed. Farah got close to Raja during this period, in this process he became her best friend. At the end of the first year Raja had confessed his love for Farah and expressed his desire to marry her. Farah was excited, but scared at the same time because of what her family's reaction to this might be. Raja assured her that, Islamically, this is the correct thing to do.

Raja's love is reciprocated, and the two plan to marry. However, their families present a hindrance. Raja's parents are 'happy for him' but don't want him to get married too young: 'they felt he needed to establish his career and get on the property ladder first'. Farah's siblings, meanwhile, warn her that their dad won't approve of the marriage. The young couple reluctantly hold back despite their love for one another:

> Farah told Raja what happened, and that she believed their relationship was impossible. Farah didn't want to hurt her family. Raja respected her decision and went about his business as normal. During their second year at uni Raja and Farah often interacted. Raja continued to be polite to her and gentle during their interactions. Raja's influence on Farah had grown leaps and bounds, she had witnessed first-hand the growth of Raja from being a troubled boy to a man. During this period Farah had family issues […] her elder brother and sister-in-law were having marital issues and were heading for a divorce, and they had an arranged marriage. This was difficult for Farah; to date she hadn't witnessed family problems of this magnitude. Raja was there to comfort and console her. He advised her and shared his experiences, he quoted the Qur'an to her: 'Allah (swt) is the best of planners', so be patient. Their friendship continued to blossom over the next year and a half.

In the end, Farah tells her 'shocked' parents about Raja, professing her love and commitment: 'Farah said to her parents, whether they accept him or not she will marry Raja and him alone.' She may not have the approval of family, but she acts with religious integrity, signalled in the title of the story: 'We Created You in Pairs'. This refers to the Qur'anic line 'And We created pairs of every thing' (al-Qur'ān, 51:49; Ali 1987/1984: 450), which makes clear that pairs (of animals as well as human souls) meant for each other are divinely ordained.

This story displays many of the characteristics of other, more familiar love stories: attraction and love, whose course is circumvented by obstacles which the protagonists ultimately overcome. Other elements are more specific to the Muslim setting. These include the contrast Raheem draws between Raja and Farah's hopes for a love marriage and her older brother's failed arranged marriage; the way the young couple look to Islam as their guide; and their unwillingness to enter into a premarital relationship, instead growing to love each other through a deepening friendship.

Though many young Muslims dream of love marriage, it does not follow that such marriages are all plain sailing. What happens after 'happily ever after' – the reality of sustaining love beyond an initial attraction and romance – is the subject of the final story in this chapter.

'Happily ever after doesn't exist': Love marriage and loss in The Other Half of Happiness

Love in Ayisha Malik's second novel *The Other Half of Happiness* (2017) is complex, humane and abounding with irony and ambivalence. This sequel to Malik's debut novel depicts the post-marriage ordeals of her sparkling protagonist Sofia Khan, following her dramatic elopement with her Irish, Muslim-convert husband

Conall. Early in the novel, the couple stay in squalor in Karachi, where Conall is working on a documentary. Sofia is blissfully satisfied to have the love of her life by her side. She is, however, a little cautious of this newfound and much longed-for happiness. She says to herself, 'No one really prepares you for it: having to weave this much happiness with this much fear of what could go wrong' (10).

A Londoner born and bred, Sofia misses England's capital city: her friends and family and the convenient life back home. Looking at the shabby room she is currently staying in with her husband, she reflects, 'If I've decided to live in this cesspit, it must be love. More's the pity. Anyway, I did my Isktikhara before marrying him – that foolproof prayer which, once you've decided to do something, makes your path easy if it's good for you, and difficult if it's bad for you' (11). With her usual wit, Sofia tries to make sense of the current state of her life as she stands at the beginning of a new journey. As in Malik's previous novel, faith remains a constant emotional refuge for Sofia; she continues to draw strength from her religiosity as she pursues an unconventional narrative towards love.

As Sofia apprehends, the practical details of married life start revealing themselves soon, sending ripples across the smooth surface of the couple's mutual love. An early, seemingly minor, disagreement concerns when they will return to London. While Sofia wants to be back in London soon, a busy Conall is reluctant and seems unresponsive to her proposal. Noticing his unwillingness to move back to London any time soon, she ponders: 'In the haze of getting on the plane and eloping we didn't quite discuss a timeline. I hadn't thought we needed to. Happiness felt infinite – practicalities were unwanted parameters' (33). A more serious point of contention is Sofia's growing insecurity over the intimacy that exists between Conall and his assistant Hamida. Although Sofia tries to be reasonable about it, she can't shake off the occasional fear that Hamida is a potential threat. The final blow to the marriage, however, comes when Conall's long-hidden secret comes to light. Conall discloses to Sofia his abandonment of an ex-wife and a young son who is now suffering from cancer. The rest of the novel sees the couple trying to reconcile and coming to terms with the choices they have made, with Sofia ultimately deciding to get a divorce.

After her husband's shocking revelation, Sofia becomes disillusioned if not bitter about love and marriage. She tells a journalist interviewing her about her upcoming book on Muslim dating: '*You and I both know that happily ever after doesn't exist*' (188; emphasis in original). The narrative nonetheless foregrounds complexity rather than portraying characters or relationships in black and white. Conall's love for Sofia and his sense of guilt are evident despite his usual reticence, and so is Sofia's love for Conall notwithstanding her deep disappointment and hurt. Although Sofia cooperates with Conall to look after his son, his regular absences from their home back in London as part of his attempt to make up for his desertion of his former family make Sofia painfully aware of their possible future separation. She muses on love and loss: 'It doesn't matter how complete you are before you're married; the person you're with pokes holes into you – one by one – and they replace these scooped-up holes with pieces of themselves. What happens if they leave? Do you walk around as a perforated human form?' (230).

This moving reflection poses as a question about incompleteness stemming from a loved one's departure that is as universal as it is personal. Sofia's thoughts brim with love and bewilderment in the face of life's unpredictable vagaries.

During Conall's absence, we see Sofia struggling to accept her loneliness. When Ramadan comes she is pleased, thinking: 'It'll make me think of higher, spiritual things as opposed to the empty side of my bed. God, I could do with his arms round me' (279). Once again, she turns to her faith and Allah to ease her perturbed mind. The bare side of the bed is a tangible reminder of her husband's absence, evoking a sense of profound longing. Yet Sofia is intelligent enough not to harbour any naive, romantic ideas as she scoffs, 'Thank God I never really believed in the adage, *Love conquers all*. It can barely conquer itself' (304; emphasis in original). However, the latter part of the realization stems from her chequered experience of love and marriage. In spite of this pragmatic view, her despair is poignantly expressed in the following soliloquy: 'That was it. The emotional finishing line in this marathon of a marriage. Me, coming in last and losing spectacularly' (364). This candid confession, with its self-deprecating timbre, is unsentimental yet movingly humane.

The final encounter between the couple in the novel comes as they enter the mosque for a divorce. As life has driven them both to an irresolutely complex situation in which separation might give them some peace, they seem to accept this eventuality gracefully. Conall thanks Sofia for '[g]etting on that plane' (427), a bittersweet reminder of the exciting conclusion of Malik's first novel and the early days of their romance. Even in the moment of separation, love shines through: 'I tightened my arms round his waist, because you hold on to the things you love for as long as possible' (427). The love marriage, its subsequent thorniness and the eventual separation of the couple in many ways provide a refreshing contrast to the conventional romantic love story.

Conclusion

Some love stories are naive; others are clouded by experience. This chapter has shown that, when young Muslims speak and write about love, it surfaces in many different ways. In creative writing workshops, we asked young people to reflect on 'love and relationships', skirting around the project's interest in sexual relationships, both in fear of deterring participants and of imposing a Western cultural conception of romantic love. By circling around the topic, we ended up with early submissions of stories about family members that, while at times stimulating, highlighted the need for a more direct approach – albeit with the risk of idealizing romantic love. Even once we addressed the topic less ambiguously, love sometimes stayed beneath the surface, as a feeling or experience that young people struggled to acknowledge in words. Others – as we have seen in this chapter – hid behind clichés, the 'cheesy chick flick moment', or throwaway platitudes such as 'Love is love'. Yet, where this chapter has scratched the surface, Muslim love stories emerge that are at once culturally distinctive – speaking of love *after* marriage, dreams of love marriage and lovers guided by Islam – and a reflection of the broad appeal of a love story. Fittingly ending on the bittersweet note of a divorce in spite of enduring love, this chapter has also shown that love can be flawed, imperfect and sometimes painful, as well as a source of great joy and comfort.

Table 4.1 Interviews quoted in Chapter 4, 'Love'

Name	Gender	Age	Relationship status	Location
Madeeha	Female	30	Married	Newcastle
Arshad	Male	29	Married	Glasgow
Saamiya	Female	18	Single	Glasgow
Iman	Female	27	Married	Glasgow
Hamid	Male	30	Married	Newcastle
Zohaib	Male	19	Single	Newcastle
Tahir	Male	20	Single	Yorkshire
Zainab	Female	20	Single	Yorkshire
Aisha	Female	27	Single, then married	Yorkshire

Table 4.2 Workshop participants and convenors quoted in Chapter 4, 'Love'

Name	Gender	Age	Workshop Series	Role in Workshop	Title
Afreen	Female	16–18	3. Creative writing, Sheffield	Participant	Writing exercises
Huma				Participant	
Fariha				Participant	
Daud	Male	17	3. Creative writing, Sheffield	Participant	Writing exercises
Bilal	Male	22	2. Creative writing, Bradford	Participant	'Untitled'
Farah	Female	25	5. Fiction, Glasgow	Participant	'Untitled'
Mobeen	Male	26	7. Fiction, Rochdale	Participant	Short story
Raheem	Male	27	7. Fiction, Rochdale	Participant	Short story

Interlude 2

SPEAKING TO STEREOTYPES

When Muslims in Britain (and many other Western countries) speak and write about sex and love, they do so in the shadow of stereotypes. These stereotypes about Muslims and Muslim sexualities are typically negative, often hatefully so, and in many cases Islamophobic and systemically racist too. We did not want to let these prejudices and stereotypes form the launchpad for this book, setting its agenda, because the first and last words belong to the young people themselves. But these stereotypes are at very least elephants in the room, adding to the difficulties that young Muslims experience when they speak about sex and love. Received ideas can prompt them to be defensive and cautious, second guessing and seeking to refute their audiences' expectations.

Though they may not say so explicitly, some Muslims anticipate and implicitly speak against types such as the passive bride, the unhappily married couple, the sexual predator and the homophobe. These stereotypes define Muslims and particular Muslim individuals and communities. They include received ideas of British Pakistani Muslims as sexually repressed, unfulfilled, unhappy and even dangerous – whether to themselves or to others. These embodiments of sexual difference and sexualized embodiments of difference emerge from an overarching imaginative geography. This sexualized Orientalism – a variant of the colonial discourse that sets West against East, and Western majorities against Eastern outsiders and/or minorities – constructs overlapping groups including Arabs, Asians and Muslims as sexually different (Alam and Husband 2006; Kabbani 1986; Massad 2007). While coherent, Orientalist discourse is marked by local variations and apparent contradictions. Its human figures are in some cases sensuous and hypersexualized; in others, sexually repressed (Phillips 2016). Europeans once depicted a world of sensual harem-dwellers and pederasts; now they focus on examples of moral rigidity and homophobia. Still, there is continuity in their attention to ethical and sexual attitudes and customs, and in the identification of sexuality as a marker of difference between self and other, 'mainstream' and Muslim (Krishnadas 2006; Phillips 2007). This discourse is highly conventional and repetitive, but it matters. Its impact, which we explore in this interlude, includes defining figures that seem real to many people, and that are invoked both in times and places of crisis, as well as in everyday life, in the things people think they know about Muslims, and in the need that many Muslims feel to speak and write back to these stereotypes.

Like other phobias, Islamophobia revolves around an irrational and ill-informed fear or hatred. Current understandings of this term can be traced to a report published in 1997 by the Runnymede Trust, which is an independent race equality think tank. *Islamophobia: A Challenge for Us All* (1997) documented an 'unfounded hostility towards Islam' with 'practical consequences' including 'unfair discrimination against Muslim individuals and communities' and their 'exclusion [...] from mainstream political and social affairs' (Runnymede Trust 1997: 4). This 'closed view of Islam' marks Muslims as outsiders, and Islam as an unchanging, undifferentiated monolith (Runnymede Trust 2016: n.p.). Sexual attitudes and practices are prominent in these depictions of 'barbaric, irrational, primitive, sexist' others, whose ways are 'inferior' to those of the West (Runnymede Trust 1997: 5).

Some activists and academics regard Islamophobia as a form of racism. Abdoolkarim Vakil, Claire Alexander and Avtar Brah are among the signatories of a statement, published online, asserting that 'Islamophobia is rooted in racism and is a type of racism that targets expressions of Muslimness or perceived Muslimness' (see Islamophobia Definition 2019). Andrew Shryock (2010: 2) identifies Islamophobia with a range of anti-Muslim sentiments, laws and practices, which range from 'acts of violence against Muslims' to 'legislation averse to certain traditions of Islamic practice'. He adds that 'Islamophobia, as a unifying concept, brings all of these possibilities into a single framework, and the sensibilities nurtured within that framework produce[s] a predictable range of stereotypes'. Anti-Muslim hatred, then, relates to but is not a synonym for racism. Some Islamophobes seeks to draw a distinction between attacking ideas and attacking people. However, this common argument that religion – unlike skin colour, gender and sexuality – consists of private beliefs that one chooses and can equally abandon does not hold. Both religious and secularist beliefs actually tend to be rather fixed, context-specific and inherited. It is not just 'ideas' that anti-Islam zealots are attacking, but people – and in the West these people often belong to vulnerable and impoverished minority groups.

Evidence of Islamophobia in Western countries is plentiful and terrible. As we began to write this chapter, news broke of violent attacks in Christchurch, New Zealand. An Australian terrorist had entered two Islamic places of worship on 15 March 2019, killing fifty Muslims. The gunman previously issued a manifesto, expressing hatred towards Muslims and asserting that they were swamping and overpowering white people. Soon after the Christchurch attacks, a Muslim teenager in Surrey, southern England, was stabbed and badly injured by a man who claimed to be inspired by the bloodshed in New Zealand. Tell MAMA, the group which monitors and counters anti-Muslim hatred, reported that these events were connected with hatred and racism swirling in multiple directions (Chambers and White 2019). The Christchurch attacker not only inspired a wave of violence in Britain and other countries but also took inspiration from events like the Finsbury Park mosque attack in North London in June 2017, and the murder of seventy-seven young people by a far-right killer in Norway in 2011.

Islamophobia matters in other, less dramatic ways too. Islamophobic stereotypes shape the everyday experiences of Muslims and particular Muslim communities. In 2019, Shelina Janmohamed argued that stereotypes make it 'harder for Muslim women to get jobs'. In the meantime, she added, 'verbal abuse and physical assault are on the rise. All of us should be deeply alarmed' (Janmohamed 2019: n.p.).

These stereotypical figures haunt the stories that young Muslims tell about sex and love. When they do not contradict these expectations outright, young Muslims tend to use them as points of departure from which to explain themselves, working from reductive and often unflattering pictures and prejudices. So, for reasons ranging from how young Muslims see and story their sexual lives, to the ways in which their sexual lives are storied and impacted by others, it is important to elaborate on these representations of Muslims, which run through politics, the media and other public discourse.

Oversexed men: Sexual predators

> They are like, they are players, innit? They have got – like going out with girls and stuff. But me I just can't be bothered with that, not yet!

Speaking about women, seventeen-year-old Farooq – whom we met in the 'Dating' chapter – was careful to distance himself from other young men. He alluded to unnamed peers, presumably including members of his community, who might be more frivolous and promiscuous in their sexual relationships. His expression is youthful, but with an underlying gravity: his slangy tag question 'innit' translating statements into enquiries, appealing for the approval or understanding of the interviewer; his claim not to 'be bothered … yet' affecting a casual swagger but revealing that he does not feel ready for sex.

Others spoke in similar ways. Bilal, in his early twenties, distinguished himself from men who treat women badly. He spoke of friends 'who will be in relationships with a girl and not take it serious, and have no intention of it ending in like a serious relationship'. Both Farooq and Bilal differentiate themselves from other Muslim boys and men, British Pakistani Muslims in particular, whom they present as sexually promiscuous in one way or another.

Farooq, speaking more directly, is paying lip service to stereotypes: things that are said about young men who might be seen as being like him. No longer easily dismissed as the racism of the gutter – the insults of the openly racist – these stereotypes have been endorsed by informed and authoritative mainstream commentators. Jack Straw, a former Labour Home Secretary, spoke of young Pakistani-heritage men 'fizzing and popping with testosterone' (BBC 2011). As a long-serving Member of Parliament for Blackburn, a northern English town with a large Muslim minority and Pakistani-heritage community, Straw presented himself as well informed. He spoke of specific communities. Though 'they act like any other young men' and though 'they want some outlet' for their sexual desires, he stated, these men are frustrated because 'Pakistani heritage girls are off-limits and they are expected to marry a Pakistani girl from Pakistan, typically'. But 'these young men are in a western society' (BBC 2011) and they have other options, if they are prepared to look outside their communities for pre- and extra-marital sex. However, in doing so, Straw opined, they exchange the restrictive moral codes of their own families and communities for an anything-goes attitude, as well as amoral or even immoral sexual activity.

These comments are not isolated. They speak of broader patterns, ways of seeing and speaking about Muslim men, some of whom are also identified as Asian, Arab and/or Oriental, as oversexed, dangerously or perversely sexed, sexually threatening and predatory. Ibrahim Abraham traces the 'notion of the Muslim Other as a sexual predator' from its recent mobilizations – in the 'stereotype of the Muslim terrorist' in Western countries from Australia to Britain – through some much earlier iterations, 'as far back as the Crusades' (Abraham 2009: 83). During that medieval conflict, he argues, Muslim men were depicted as 'sodomitical' and 'bloodthirsty homosexual predators'. Meanwhile, returned Crusaders were portrayed as 'feminised and perverted – that is, queered – by their tours in the Muslim world' (83; see also: Boswell 1980). Muslim men are widely stereotyped in this way: as a corrupting sexual danger, especially to women and girls. In Australia, for example, journalists have portrayed Muslim men as 'gang rapists targeting "Aussie" women', and a local politician portrayed violent attacks on Lebanese-Australian Muslims as 'revenge' for sexual assaults in other countries (Gleeson 2004; Puar and Rai 2002; Poynting, Noble, Tabar and Collins 2004; Abraham 2009: 84).

This generic discourse also has some culturally, historically and geographically specific variants. Examples include the stereotype of the British Muslim with South Asian and specifically Pakistani heritage as a sexual predator, a dangerous and threatening figure. This grotesque caricature has emerged in the context of public debate about the apparently disproportional involvement of overlapping groups of Asian, Pakistani and Muslim men in incidents of sexual exploitation and abuse in England in the 2010s. Straw, quoted above, was commenting on the case of two British Pakistani men who had been found guilty of rape. Debates about Child Sexual Exploitation (CSE) and Child Sexual Abuse (CSA) have taken some similar turns, since the scale of this problem was first acknowledged by the Independent Inquiry into Child Sexual Exploitation in Rotherham (1997–2013). Presiding, Baroness Alexis Jay reported that '[b]y far the majority of perpetrators were described as "Asian" by victims, yet throughout the entire period, councillors did not engage directly with the Pakistani-heritage community to discuss how best they could jointly address the issue' (Jay 2014: 2, 91–7; see also Britton 2018; Tufail 2015). Some other commentators went further, accusing public figures of failing to face up to the involvement of Asian, Pakistani and Muslim men in CSE, for fear of acknowledging the race, religion and culture of those who they said were disproportionately involved. Dame Lowell Goddard, who chaired the Independent Inquiry into Child Sexual Abuse, reportedly speculated that Britain has so many paedophiles 'because it has so many Asian men' (qtd in Norfolk

2016; see also Norfolk 2012). These arguments were contested by Children's Commissioner Sue Berelowitz, who pointed out that the racial profiles of those convicted for CSE/A mirrored the profiles of the areas in which these crimes took place (Berelowitz et al. 2012b). She joined a number of politicians who argued that – as Keith Vaz (then Chair of the Home Affairs Select Committee) put it – it 'is wrong to stereotype an entire community' (BBC 2011). Researchers have come to similar conclusions. Ella Cockbain finds that, while 'Asians have been overrepresented, relative to the general population, among suspected child sex exploiters', CSE is a wider issue, and there is 'thinly veiled racism' in its representation as 'racial crime' (Cockbain 2013: 22).

But 'an entire community' *was* being stereotyped. Although women, families and traditions were all presented as complicit in grooming cases, the men within this community were especially singled out. In October 2018, another British Home Secretary, the Conservative MP Sajid Javid, commented on the conviction of twenty members of a sexual grooming gang in Huddersfield. He drew attention to the ethnicity of those convicted, calling the men 'sick Asian paedophiles' (qtd in Mohdin 2018). Jasbir Puar and Amit Rai argue that Muslim men are widely depicted as 'racial and sexual monsters', figures of 'sexual perversity' and 'failed heterosexuality' (Puar and Rai 2002: 117; see also Mattu and Maznavi 2012).

None of the men we encountered in this project referenced quite such monstrous stereotypes when speaking about their own lives. But these stereotypes matter to them because they cast long shadows over communities and the places with which they are associated. They present extreme forms of insidious racial stereotypes. When Farooq says that he is not a player – an oversexed and sexually opportunistic young man, and a relative of the stereotypical sexual predator – he distances himself from some of the things that others say about Muslim men. He has been pushed into a particular kind of defensiveness.

Undersexed women: Passive wives

Behind every sexually aggressive young Muslim man – or so the doxa goes – is a young woman whose premarital chastity drives him crazy. If this sounds overstated, it is helpful to revisit the words of Jack Straw, when he commented on the conviction of the two rapists in 2011. Straw placed blame upon 'the Pakistani community' – not just the individual perpetrators – and seemed to blame the women for refusing to provide unmarried men with a sexual 'outlet', remaining passively but culpably 'off-limits' until marriage (BBC 2011).

Straw's allegations about the toxic codependency of out-of-control men and their excessively chaste female counterparts were not original. We see similar tropes in other times and places. Writing in *The New York Times*, the French-Algerian writer Kamel Daoud blamed a series of sexual attacks that took place in German cities in January 2016 on the religion and ethnicity of some of the perpetrators. Generalizing from individuals to groups, and spreading the blame, he asserted that a 'sick relationship with women' was common throughout the

Arab and Muslim world (Daoud 2016). Daoud portrayed Arab and Muslim men as sexually dangerous, Muslim women as downtrodden or exploited and the wider world of Islam as culpable.

The figure of the passive bride, who simply gives in to the marriage that others have planned for her or cannot find a way of refusing, is another stereotype with which younger Muslim women have to contend. Within this stereotype, arranged marriages are confused with forced marriages. In articles promoting a radio documentary, broadcast in 2019, Muslim-identified journalist and broadcaster Yasmin Alibhai-Brown looked back on a time when '[m]ost marriages were arranged, not forced' – without acknowledging that the same is true today. Alibhai-Brown portrayed Muslim brides as passive and powerless, ground down by an increasingly puritanical and 'grey' Muslim culture, citing an unlikely exception to prove this rule. Venturing the kind of topical argument favoured by editors, she connected this broad generalization with the news story of the moment: the flight of fifteen-year-old Shamima Begum from London to join ISIS in Syria. Alibhai-Brown presented Begum's actions as a clumsy escape from the claustrophobia and constraint of her Muslim family and community in Britain – rather than from Britain itself – and an assertion of her own will, culminating in her decision to marry an ISIS fighter in Syria. Begum was back in the news at the time this documentary went out, following the fall of ISIS, the death of the young woman's first two babies and her attempt to return to Britain, where she hoped to give birth to her third (BBC 2019a). (Her baby was born in the refugee camp and died soon after, in April 2019.) According to this twisted logic, Begum is the exception that proves the lassitude of other British Muslim girls and women, who simply accept the fate that is decided for them.

Such representations of women who passively or fatalistically accept their own oppression are subtended by broader stereotypes of Muslim women, which present the headscarf as evidence and a symbol of oppression. This stereotype has been widely contested, for example by Katherine Bullock, a Muslim woman who argues against 'the popular Western notion that the veil is a symbol of Muslim women's oppression' (Bullock 2010: 3). She argues that Muslim women who cover their heads are widely regarded – not only by the public but also in academic literature – as 'at best as silly, duped, or bizarre, and at worst, as Islamist ideologues equally responsible and culpable as men' (Bullock 2010: 13).

Liberation from such arrangements, it is often said, comes from without: from white saviours and secular culture, and from state agencies and legal protections. Freedom is rarely seen as coming from within, from manifold ways of being Muslim. British media have run stories about individuals affected by forced marriage, in the context of moves to protect women and men suffering from this practice and campaigns to legislate against it. Examples include the story of a forced marriage, told in the *Daily Mail* in 2006, in which 'a terrified and unworldly 16-year-old' called Inshana was forced to marry 'a middle-aged cousin 33 years her senior'. 'Incredibly, in the eyes of the Muslim community', according to the *Mail*, 'this appalling union was going to bring honour to my family' (qtd in Cable and Connolly 2006). Inshana's eventual liberation from unhappy marriage begins with renunciation of Islam. She 'tore off [her] hijab and flung it down', converted to Christianity, and went about becoming 'a thoroughly modern Englishwoman' complete with a 'designer wardrobe of must-have designs' (qtd in Cable and Connolly 2006). It is difficult to read these supposedly factual reports without being reminded of the fundamentals of Islamophobia, identified by the Runnymede Trust (1997, 2016), in which Islam is identified 'as inferior to the West – barbaric, irrational, primitive, sexist' and in which this comes into particular focus when it comes to sex and marriage (Runnymede Trust 1997: 5).

Not all mainstream depictions of Muslim women, their sexual relationships and marriages are quite so negative, nor so despairing of the possibilities of liberation within Islam. Another article, published in the *Daily Mirror*, that begins within an unhappy Muslim family – Ayesha is 'beaten, raped and then twice almost murdered by her own family', who force her to marry a 'stranger' during a 'family holiday in Pakistan' – ends without recourse to white saviours or dramatic renunciation of faith of family. Ayesha, who eventually manages to escape, goes on to work with Karma Nirvana, 'a charity which helps victims like herself' (Owens and Wilkinson 2013). Acknowledging this 'charity supporting victims of honour-based abuse and forced marriage', which stresses that such 'crimes are not determined by age, faith, gender or sexuality' (Karma Nirvana 2019), this article acknowledges that Muslim families are not all the same, and that some young Muslim women can find liberty within their faith.

The stereotype of the passive bride – the Muslim woman with little or no agency – is contradicted throughout this book, through a wide range of stories. These counter-stereotypical stories include novels such as *Love in a Headscarf*, which present different ways of being, loving and eventually marrying as Muslim women. The authorial persona of this novel is anything but passive, and if she submits to anything, it is to spiritual satisfaction and the adventure of love. Explaining some of her broader motives for writing, within a newspaper article, Shelina Janmohamed explains how she writes against the stereotyping of Muslim women:

> On our streets, on our front pages and across much of our media, in the mouths of our politicians, at the dinner table and in even the most genteel of establishments, the stereotypes of Muslim women over the last decade persist, in fact I'd say have become more entrenched. These stereotypes include: being at once both victim and terrorist, oppressed, 'traditionally submissive', unable to speak English, brainwashed, waiting to be saved by feminists among others, lacking in agency (but also at the same time blamed for bringing up young jihadis).
>
> (2019)

Janmohamed concludes that 'these stereotypes are incredibly resistant to change'. Though a decade has passed since the publication of *Love in a Headscarf*, it 'could be written today, and would still run up against the same stereotypical thinking' (2019: np.).

These observations chime with the ways in which some young Muslim women speak about their own lives, and about the ways in which they are not only not oppressed by their religion, but liberated by it. Esha, whose experiences and words are discussed in more detail in the chapter on Pressure, might surprise a *Daily Mail* reader when she explains how her religion has helped her to stand up for herself:

> When I started practising more when I was about 17, I learned that marriage isn't supposed to be, you are not, you shouldn't be treated badly. That is where I learned it. And I think that is where I got the guts, because I became stronger in my religion. I felt that 'they are wrong!' and even if I die trying to do the right thing, I would rather be dead than be a sheep. I felt, I feel really strongly about that [...]. I became more practising and I knew what was right and what was wrong, and I just wasn't having any of it. So I became quite rebellious.

Other Muslim women speak or hint of sexual fulfilment, making it clear that their marriages are not just for their husbands' pleasure or their families' convenience. In this spirit, Sabrina Mahfouz has brought together essays and stories that promise to 'blow away the narrow image of the "Muslim Woman"' in a collection entitled *The Things I Would Tell You: British Muslim Women Write* (2017). Here, stereotypes are not simply challenged; they are ridiculed and playfully exploded. The publisher's blurb (Saqi 2019) invites readers to:

> Follow the career of an actress with Middle-Eastern heritage whose dreams of playing a ghostbuster spiral into repeat castings as a jihadi bride. Among stories of honour killings and ill-fated love in besieged locations, we also find heart-warming connections and powerful challenges to the status quo.

Contrasting the drama of Inshana's 'escape' sensationalized in the British media, the Muslim women we have heard from in this book speak of marriages and relationships that are ordinary in many ways: they speak of routine, affection, intimacy, conflict, good sex, boring sex and everything in between.

Overbearing parents

When Muslim women assert their autonomy and agency in relationships, they also contest stereotypes about overbearing parents. Young Muslims of both sexes implicitly challenge this hoary image when they describe and write about their own romantic experiences, insisting that they have not simply complied with decisions that others have made for them. Maryam insists that cousin marriage was her own choice. When her 'dad just pops out the question so, like do you want to get married?' she replied that she 'was ready' and then spoke to her mum about it. She found that her 'mum was looking for … potential spouses here, and my dad was like potential spouses from Pakistan':

> And then I was asked whether I wanted to get married in the family or not, and I said that I didn't mind, but it has to be distant, because I just didn't want that connection. And I don't really like family from back home [laughs]. So it was one of those ones. And then it just got to the point where, and then I knew some of

my cousins that came from Pakistan. So like it was just one of those things where your parents said well these are your options, you can choose. And I ended up getting married to my distant cousin. But it was out of choice, but my parents had told me that you know this is the choices that you have and you can tell us if you want to get married to one of them or whether we will look elsewhere.

Though she comes across as a little defensive in her repeated assertion that she has made her own 'choice', Maryam challenges her own depiction as a passive woman, and that of her parents as dictatorial family strategists. When her father suggests she marry a man from Pakistan, she agrees in principle but expresses her own preferences: for a more 'distant' cousin who is not from 'back home'. In this way, she feels able to make a traditional route more acceptable to herself. Challenging the usual storyline of the overbearing parent and compliant daughter, Maryam makes it clear – to her father and to this interviewer – that she is not taking orders and that her parents are not making important decisions for her.

Tolerant and flexible parents who allow their sons and daughters space to arrive at their own decisions are acknowledged in other ways too. In a *Guardian* article, 'Single Muslim Women on Dating', an interviewee who identifies as Esma insists on making her own decisions about men and marriage and refuses to 'be the submissive wife' (Ahmed 2013). Other Muslim women, whose search for love has been featured in the mainstream media, describe their experiences of dating websites and apps such as Muzmatch, Minder and Salaam Swipe (T. Hamid 2017). Parents sometimes assume comic bit parts in these stories, for example as participants in speed-dating events that feature entire families rather than potential couples alone.

Precisely because they are peripheral to many of the stories that young Muslim women and men tell about their sexual relationships, these minor or absent characters implicitly contest their representations as overbearing figures, who straightforwardly decree the terms on which their offspring will marry. Counter-stereotypical parents appear in many of the interviews and stories that run through this book. Like other young Muslims discussed in this interlude, twenty-one-year-old Waheed acknowledges a stereotype, only to distance himself from it. He said that although some families are strict, his own relatives are more malleable and responsive: 'My parents said if you find someone that's fine. If you want us find someone for you that's fine as well [...] Some people are a lot more strict but my parents, they know how to handle stuff like that'. Waheed acknowledged that some Muslim parents are strict, and others confirm this. Farooq feels pressure from his mother: 'she wants me to get married in Pakistan. And like find a girl from there.' Farooq resists: 'I don't know if I want to get married from here', he says, adding more defiantly, 'I am not getting married to my cousin!' But, while such overbearing parents are a reality for some, this is not the case for all. When all Muslim parents are portrayed as demagogues, many are misrepresented and the whole group is stereotyped.

A final story – from one of the creative workshops we convened – explores the power of stereotype in this context. Haris, who is twenty-five, chose to write from the perspective of a young woman who chooses her own husband and is initially delighted when her father agrees. His story – entitled 'Qabool: The Happily Never After' – provides another example of a Muslim who is conscious of stereotypes and actively decides to go against them:

> Dad simply said 'yes'. I couldn't believe my ears. I was over the moon that I squealed like a pig. The joy in my mother's eyes were priceless. But why was it so easy? In hindsight and within my bitterness, why did my dad not protect me from taking such a stupid decision? We are Chaudhurys! [...] It dictated my father's choice that day. He'd heard about all the 'oppressive' fathers preventing their daughters from love marriages. He didn't want to be the next prominent, villainous face of BBC propaganda.

The father, like so many of the real and fictitious characters we have met in this interlude, is a victim of negative stereotyping. Wanting to distance himself from 'villainous' and dictatorial parents – the stereotypes seen on TV – he reacts with a 'stupid' decision which his daughter lives to regret. Comparing her own cry with that of a beast which embodies the religiously impermissible and grotesque, the daughter is portrayed in animalistic terms, her behaviour haram. She is incapable of making sound decisions for herself, and her mother's uncritical delight is not much help either. This is a twisted story – speaking primarily of its male author's conservative views about who should make decisions for whom – but it adds another dimension to understandings of the seductive power of stereotypes. Here, the parent overcompensates when attempting to prove the stereotype wrong.

Homophobic and intolerant

Another thing that many non-Muslims assume they know about Muslims is that they are intolerant of homosexuality, and that they do not share mainstream Western society's supposedly liberal attitudes on this subject. The assumption is that Muslims are automatically homophobic – exhibiting an irrational fear of homosexuality and 'the dread of being in close quarters with homosexuals' (Siraj 2009: 42) – or more generally illiberal in outlook.

It is true that some more conservative Muslims express difficulties with homosexuality, as we explain in the third interlude, '(Not so) Different'. But, of course, not all Muslims can be described as either homophobic or homonegative, and some express liberal views on this subject. And some Muslims experience and act on same-sex attraction or identify as gay or lesbian, reconciling their religion and homosexuality (Yip 2004a, 2004b; Rouhani 2007). But these attitudes and accommodations are often dismissed as exceptions that do little to destabilize the rule. The stereotype of the homophobic and anti-progressive Muslim persists.

Mainstream British and Western attitudes towards homosexuality are contradictory. Those who were only recently condemning and marginalizing gay men and lesbians are now turning their fire on those who have not been so quick to change, asserting that the latter do not share 'core European values' of tolerance and respect for personal choice (Fekete 2006: 2). They find individuals who supposedly speak not only for their communities and cultures but for all Muslims, who are represented in the characteristically broad brushstrokes of Islamophobia: as 'a single monolithic bloc, static and unresponsive to new realities' (Runnymede Trust 2016: n.p.). Thus, when parents demonstrated against anti-homophobia lessons in their children's schools – resisting a 'No Outsiders' programme at a primary school in Birmingham in 2019 – the media portrayed the protesters as Muslims (they were actually more diverse and included Jewish and Christian parents) and the issue as a clash of cultures (in which the Muslim parents are portrayed as out of step with apparently woke mainstream culture). For example, the *Daily Mail* ran a story on 5 March 2019, reporting that 'Primary School AXES Anti-homophobia Lessons After Protests from Muslim Parents Who Withdrew 600 Children from Lessons' (Harding 2019). This illustrates how establishment media and commentators embroidered pictures of Muslims as outsiders.

Tabloid newspapers are not alone in portraying Muslims in this way, though some others are more careful to make it clear that they are speaking specifically about individuals and circumstances rather than generalizing about Muslims. In this spirit, human rights campaigner Peter Tatchell has made a series of sharp, specific criticisms of named individuals such as Dr Iqbal Sacranie, leader of the Muslim Council of Britain, when the latter asserted that homosexuality was 'immoral […] and spread disease' (Morris 2006). And, in her (much-contested) report on social integration, commissioned by the Home Office, Dame Louise Casey blamed British Pakistani transnational marriages for the 'perpetuation of foreign cultural practices' that undermine social integration and threaten liberal causes such as the recognition of lesbian and gay rights (Casey 2016: 1.21, 1.58). This fits a broader pattern, observed by Joseph Massad, in which liberals construct Islam as the other of liberalism (Massad 2015; see also Phillips 2016).

Paradoxically, stereotypes of the homophobic and intolerant Muslim coexist with others, in which Muslim men are represented as 'sodomitical' and as 'homosexual predators' (Abraham 2009: 83). These contradictory but consistently negative stereotypes are variously acknowledged, explored and challenged in the things that Muslims say and write about homosexuality. These sexual stories speak both of being gay and Muslim – in books such as Shanon Shah's *The Making of a Gay Muslim* (2017) and Mohsin Zaidi's *A Dutiful Boy* (2020) – and also of being straight and Muslim: whether this means being emphatically and anxiously not gay, or being straight but liberal.

Such stereotypes are damaging. Ibrahim Abraham stresses that many 'queer Muslims' are adversely affected by heteronormativity within their families and communities, but he explains that not all Muslims are homonegative. The assumption that they are reactionary in this way helps to undermine the acceptance of gay and lesbian Muslims within queer communities. As he puts it, 'whereas for conservative Muslims a *queer* Muslim becomes the unviable subject, for some in the queer community, a queer *Muslim* is an impossible – or at least dubious – subject' (Abraham 2009: 88–9; emphasis in original; see also Jamal 2001: 1). So, while this form of stereotyping is harmful to Muslim communities as a whole, it is doubly damaging to those most directly affected: young queer Muslims.

Unhappy stereotypes, counter-stereotypes and real people

The stereotypical gay Muslim is not alone in his 'sexual misery' (Chambers et al. 2018). He is joined by lesbians, of course, but by others too. The figures of the sexual tyrant and the passive bride which we have met are miserable in their own ways, and they also bring misery to others. *The New York Times* articles about sexual assaults that had taken place in Cologne, Hamburg and Stuttgart in 2016, which we have mentioned, painted a much bigger picture of 'sexual misery of the Arab world' (Daoud 2016). The story of the forced marriage, discussed earlier, conveys the same emotion. Inshana's parents endured lives of 'silent misery' and 'drudgery', which the writers blame on their religion (Cable and Connolly 2006). Hegemonic British politicians and journalists are not alone in their unflattering depiction of British Pakistani and Pakistani men. Some similar, and similarly negative, stereotypes have also been found circulating within British Pakistani communities. British Pakistani women have been known to see and describe Pakistani migrant grooms as 'perverts' (Bolognani 2014: 108), sexually deviant and even revolting figures, who are bothersome as strangers and undesirable as husbands. These men are not only portrayed as repellent to their wives (Bolognani 2014: 115); they are also portrayed as 'unhappy' in themselves, due to the emasculating experience of living, against tradition, as dependants in the extended families of their British-born wives (Charsley 2005a).

All this misery is pathologized, identified with Muslims (and with others including Arabs, who are automatically assumed to be Muslims), who are blamed for the unhappiness that is ascribed to them (to adapt Cvetkovich 2012). Yasmin Alibhai-Brown illustrates some assertions that are often made about how unhappy Muslims are in love, and how unfulfilled they are said to be in the bedroom. 'I mourn the closing of the Muslim mind and heart', she writes in an article about her radio documentary, *From Sensuality to Puritanism: How Muslim Cultures Turned Grey*. In this article, she identifies the Iranian Revolution as a turning point, a time when Muslims lost their happiness:

> In the 17th and 18th centuries, puritan attitudes to sex and art were found in the West. Those escaping Christian injunctions against homosexuality and erotica went to Arabia, India and the Ottoman lands (there is no original sin in Islam). […] After 1979, shadowy puritanism fell across the Muslim world and the West became relaxed, open and receptive, and immensely successful.
>
> (Alibhai-Brown 2019: 15)

Looking back on happier times within her own living memory, Alibhai-Brown reflects that '[b]eing a young Muslim then was easy and, mostly, joyful'. She recalls a mythical golden age when '[m]ost marriages were arranged, not forced' – without acknowledging that the same is true today. Her message is not that Islam is intrinsically joyless – she stresses that it has been and can be the opposite – but that it has become this way, descending into a kind of misery through the 'social conservatism that has spread across the Muslim world in the past 40 years' (Alibhai-Brown 2019: 15.).

Sara Ahmed argues that unhappiness is a racialized category, identified with 'melancholy migrants' (Ahmed 2010: 121–59). Ann Cvetkovich quietly concurs that such emotions are 'not so much a medical or biochemical dysfunction as a very rational response to global conditions' (Cvetkovich 2012: 5). These theorists challenge the widespread identification of happiness with the reductive concept of 'good' and misery with 'bad'. Whether or not it is really feasible to change these broader attitudes towards happiness and misery, it is possible to see how they impact upon stereotypes surrounding Muslims and Muslim sexualities, in the form of a series of pictures of unhappiness. Again, when Muslims story their sexual relationships, these neat pigeonholes tend to lurk in the background. It is against such narrow assumptions that many young people find it necessary to define and distinguish themselves.

As we have seen through this chapter, one way of responding to the stereotypes – one form of which is the sexually miserable Muslim – is to contradict them. Referring specifically to stereotypes of Muslim women, Shelina Janmohamed argues that 'we need to keep destroying the stereotypes' and the 'systemic problem' of which they are symptoms (Janmohamed 2019). Unfortunately, contradicting stereotypes does not make them go away. When young Muslims speak about their sexual relationships and when they stress how happy they are, they are also saying how miserable they are not and how sexually unfulfilled and unhappy they are not. They are defining themselves through double negatives. Presenting themselves as happy and well-adjusted, they implicitly contest expectations and assumptions. Take, for example, the following interview with twenty-four-year-old Shahid, who repeats the word happy at least once in all but one sentence:

> I said one day I wasn't going to get married in Pakistan but next thing you know I did and it was my own choice, so I'm happy […] It wasn't forced upon me or anything. So it was actually my own choice and like looking back on it, I'm actually happy. […] [W]hen it comes to marriage, it's not about trying to make somebody else happy, it's about obviously you need to make yourself happy obviously with the partner you're choosing. Not just to make your dad happy or make your grandad happy …

Responding to the pervasive pictures of misery described above, happier images of Muslims and their sexual relationships are gaining traction and attention. To begin with the mainstream media, the *Herald Scotland* (Duffy 2014), BBC (2003) and *The Guardian* (Ahmed 2013) have run stories about the popularity of speed dating and modern matchmaking experiences in Muslim communities. The very act of publishing these stories serves to depict Muslims as rounded human beings who engage in diverse dating and relationship norms, thus unsettling commonplace perceptions of Muslim relationship practices. Stereotypes of sexually repressed and joyless Muslims are also contested online, for example through the YouTube video *Happy British Muslims*, posted by an incognito group of British Muslims known as Honesty Policy (2014), which has been watched more than two million times. Alluding to sexuality through its inclusion of music and dance, which includes interaction between male and female dancers, *Happy British Muslims* was a joyous antidote to many of the assumptions and stereotypes surrounding Muslim sexuality.

And yet, it is unusual to be happy all the time, and exhausting to feel compelled always to present oneself in sunlit uplands. In challenging stereotypes, there is a danger of countering unhappy Muslims with happy Muslims. In *Islamophobia/Islamophilia*, Andrew Shryock (2010: 10) argues that variously well-meaning and defensive reactions to Islamophobia can reproduce problematic binaries and stereotypes:

> The 'good Muslim,' as a stereotype, has common features: he tends to be a Sufi (ideally, one who reads Rumi); he is peaceful (and assures us that jihad is an inner, spiritual contest, not a struggle to 'enjoin the good and forbid the wrong' through force of arms); he treats women as equals, and is committed to choice in matters of hijab wearing (and never advocates the covering of a woman's face); if he is a she, then she is highly educated, works outside the home, is her husband's only wife, chose her husband freely, and wears hijab (if at all) only because she wants to.

Shryock argues that Islamophilia limits Muslims to monochrome saintly categories out of 'wishful thinking and a politics of fear' (2010: 10).

There is a danger that, with so many stereotypes in circulation, Muslims (and others who share their struggle against Islamophobia) might end up matching negatives with equally one-dimensional positives, and speaking about sex and love in ways that are reactive and defensive. Imen Neffati argues that writing back to stereotypes can be counter-productive, leading to Muslims being portrayed simplistically as 'angelic' and 'innocent'. Too much attention to happiness flattens out the texture of real life, burying experiences of love and lust that are neither terrible nor wonderful, neither stereotypical nor counter-stereotypical. This demands less sensational, less adversarial attention to the sexual lives of young Muslims. It is fortunate, then, that so many of those whose voices and writings appear in this book have resisted the temptation to simply assert that all is well with Muslims. Their words are strongest where they explore the more complex realities of life, rejecting the attractive but misleading simplicities of good and bad, happy and miserable.

Table I2.1 Interviews quoted in Interlude 2, 'Speaking to Stereotypes'

Name	Gender	Age	Relationship Status	Location
Farooq	Male	17	Single	Yorkshire
Bilal	Male	22	In a relationship, then married	Yorkshire
Zohaib	Male	19	Single	Newcastle
Esha	Female	27	Married	Yorkshire

Maryam	Female	23	Single		Yorkshire
Shahid	Male	24	Engaged		Yorkshire
Waheed	Male	21	Single		Glasgow
Saamiya	Female	18	Single		Glasgow
Yusuf	Male	22	Single		Yorkshire

Table I2.2 Workshop participants and convenors quoted in Interlude 2, 'Speaking to Stereotypes'

Name	Gender	Age	Workshop Series	Role in Workshop	Title
Haris	Male	25	7. Fiction, Rochdale	Participant	'"Qabool" – The Happily Never After'

Chapter 5

PRESSURE

> I think it is to do with the culture, my parents are very strict on everything. Like if I go out, I have to call them every hour. So there, the problem [is] them constantly calling me, always asking me to come home.
>
> (Saamiya, eighteen, interview)

> My father wants me to marry the same background as me ... Aye, my dad, he wants me to get married straight away ... He said that he got married when he was 18 and stuff like that. He always goes on about it ... It is my mum too. She wants me to get married, she wants me to start a family.
>
> (Tahir, twenty, interview)

Things that young Muslims can say about sexual relationships, as well as the things they can do, are informed and bound by religious understandings and cultural norms. Young Muslim women and men in novels such as Muhammad Khan's *I Am Thunder* (2018) and Nadeem Aslam's *Maps for Lost Lovers* (2004) are often represented as struggling to reconcile their own desires with the expectations of their parents and wider community. These expectations can include, as Saamiya and Tahir delineate above, family pressure not to date or socialize, and pressure about when and whom to marry. Underpinning both dating and marriage considerations is the pressure to understand and respect conventions of honour, or *izzat*, and shame (*sharam*). These pressures relate to other expectations and assumptions, often unspoken but nonetheless compelling, about gender expression and heteronormativity. In this chapter, young Muslims tell stories about the ways in which they variously internalize and resist such pressures, sometimes by keeping secrets, sometimes by rebelling, and otherwise findings ways to assert their agency in choices about sex, love and marriage.

'Why were you with those boys?'

For Saamiya, a lesbian who has not come out to her family, the pressure to be chaste has been explicit from a very young age. She has felt pressured by her 'traditional' parents not to socialize with the opposite sex, and indeed not to socialize very much at all beyond going to school. According to Saamiya, her father 'would always say just like stay home [...] Like go to school, come home'. She expressed frustration with these strict boundaries, and in particular with being treated differently from male peers and relatives:

> Boys can go outside and hang out with other boys and they won't necessarily be penalized for that. And even if they are hanging out with girls, they are not necessarily going to get yelled at. Like if it was a girl hanging out with a boy and a bunch of girls, they would probably get some disappointed looks from a passerby and even parents that, 'Why were you with those boys?' even though there were girls present.

Here, pressure is not only about parental disapproval, but community gossip and fear of risking one's reputation. Saamiya felt that this pressure was 'common amongst a lot of girls' in her peer group, often leading to secrecy. She described how a former classmate 'would sneak out of school to see her boyfriend, because her parents would, like they would react similarly like mine'. Saamiya concluded from her own and others' experiences that '[w]ith relationships now, with Muslims especially, they hide them so that others don't find out about them'.

Similar themes were explored in a fictional setting by Heena, in a playwriting workshop at Glasgow Women's Library. Her untitled play focuses on two older female characters, Samira and Bushra, who are on their daily walk and conversing about a neighbour's daughter:

> Samira: You know, these girls bring so much shame to their parents.
> *Silence. They continue their walk.*
> Samira: I did not want to say but I've heard she is dating a boy.
> Bushra: If you did not want to say, you should not have said. Although now that you have, are you sure?
> Samira: Well my sister-in-law saw her walking in the town with a Pakistani boy. And in any case, Shaista has not got her married yet. She is probably telling her mother she is not ready because she has a boyfriend. [...]
> *Both observe a young couple in the distance.*
> Samira: Do you think that's Shaista's daughter?
> Bushra: It could be anyone ...
> *Walking closer to couple.*
> Samira: Same tight clothes on. It's probably her. I should tell her mother she is still sneaking off to meet this guy. They are holding hands. What next? Kissing?
> Bushra: Oh.
> Samira: What?
> Bushra: I don't think that's Shaista's daughter.
> Samira: Well she's someone's daughter.
> Bushra: You're right. She's yours.

In this scene, Heena highlights how young Muslim women's sartorial choices, marriage status and meetings with the opposite sex are pored over by others, putting pressure on these young women and their families through prescriptive notions of honour. Samira pointedly comments that 'these girls bring so much shame to their parents' and believes it is her duty to inform the mother if she sees a Muslim girl 'sneaking off', illustrating the real threat of community surveillance. The twist at the end of the scene – that it is Samira's own daughter in tight-fitting clothes holding hands with a guy – holds out both the danger of repercussions and a teachable moment.

Esha, another interviewee, had first-hand experience of the kind of pressure that such gossip can lead to. While dating a man she met at college, she became the focus of exaggerated rumours and family 'drama'. According to her, once the relationship was found out, 'things got really messy, really quickly'. Her father was furious and her brother threatened violence. Despite these extreme pressures, she recalled how she was able to use the situation to her advantage when her father asked if she would marry against his wishes:

> I said, 'No. I won't marry him if you don't want me to. But if I don't marry him, is anybody going to marry me now because of these things that my sisters-in-law have been saying?', so I played that card on him, because I knew that would work. So he said, 'Yeah, that is true.' So he was like, 'Okay, so do you want to get married next week or do you want to get married at the end of uni?' And I was like, 'If those are my two options, I will get married next week.' So within one week I was married, after all this drama.

This story speaks of different kinds of pressure: to be chaste, to involve your parents in matchmaking, to marry or break off a relationship if you are caught dating without their consent. While with the benefit of hindsight Esha could add flippancy to her words, she recalled her fear as the situation unfolded and the careful balancing act she had to perform in managing pressure from different quarters.

'I don't like, go out, mess about, do anything'

Pressure from elders can take many forms, from the more explicit and/or coercive examples discussed above, to behavioural standards that are tacitly understood or gently encouraged. Fatima described how, in her household, there are some unspoken rules. In reference to her older sister, she said: 'Before my sister was married I don't think my dad would talk about it, but I don't think he would let her go out with someone. Because she was like, she is good at school and my dad didn't want her to mess it up.' Here, she highlights the pressure of parental aspirations for their children. Fatima felt that she gets off lightly in comparison with her sister. Although her parents sometimes give 'lectures' and have suggested that she 'cut down on going out every day', they offer her guidance rather than enforcing strict rules.

Faisal, who is still in school, said that his dad has no problem with him socializing, but does expect that he will take his education seriously before his thoughts turn to dating:

My dad says 'You can go out with anyone as long as you don't mess about' [...] because my dad is like 'You are only sixteen, you have got your life to think about it. [...] You can go out and get a job, earn more money and then do what you want [...]. There is no point going out with someone, you fail your studies.'

He contrasted his experience with his dad's upbringing, and felt that his dad has a relatively permissive attitude to relationships because his own mother 'wouldn't let him go out with anyone [...] I think that was just the way it was before'. Despite this observation, it is interesting to note that dating is gently discouraged by his father's emphasis on education and Faisal's eagerness to comply: 'I am pretty much like, I don't like go out, mess about, do anything. He knows I want to make something of my life.'

Both of these examples couple a parent's wish that their children will get a good education with hopes that, while still studying, they won't get distracted by dating. Fatima and Faisal acknowledge these expectations, while also feeling free to make their own decisions. Yet, as we have already seen, in some households rules are more explicitly enforced, and this can give rise to conflict between parents and children. This is the central theme of the young adult novel *I Am Thunder*, to which we now turn.

'*Izzat is everything*': Honour and rebellion in I Am Thunder

Muhammad Khan's debut novel *I Am Thunder* (2018) is about a teenager, Muzna, who cannot reconcile her parents' expectations with her own desires. Pressure starts mounting for the fifteen-year-old girl early in the novel, manifesting in her father's assumption that Muzna will have a medical career. Muzna wants to be a writer and struggles to square their opposing aspirations: 'Me becoming a doctor meant the world to him. How could I break his heart after all the sacrifices he'd made?' (15). As the story progresses, parental pressure overspills into other spheres: socializing, sartorial choices and the edict against finding a boyfriend. Her parents are 'dead against' their daughter getting into any relationship before marriage. Muzna by contrast does not think 'having a boyfriend had to get all X-rated and haram' (39), and she is open to the possibility of romance.

On the one hand Muzna longs for a boyfriend, while on the other her conservative upbringing means she is hesitant about viewing premarital relationships in a favourable light. Furthermore, she dreads the consequences if her parents were to find out. During a conversation with her best friend, Salma, Salma says of Muzna's parents: 'all they care about is you not embarrassing them in front of the bitchy-arse Pakistani community. Meanwhile you're so damaged, you think dating is *perverted*' (39; emphasis in original). This indicates the prominent role of cultural norms in shaping parents' expectations, and the fear of embarrassment that often prompts parents to impose various dictates on their children.

When Salma gets caught having sex with her boyfriend, it blows up as a big scandal, leading to the community ostracizing Salma and her mother. Muzna's parents tell her to end her friendship with Salma, fearing Muzna might end up doing something similar. Moreover, associating with someone who has committed such a 'shameful' act would risk her family's reputation. Muzna's father warns: 'Her poor mother [...]. Tomorrow, everyone from London to Lahore will know about it. They will say, "[Your] daughter was her best friend, so she must be like that too." You cut all ties with that wicked child right now, Muzna! Do I make myself clear?' (47). Muzna's mother echoes this order, saying: 'You listen to your father! [...] No daughter of mine will bring shame on this family as long as I live!' (47). Their main concern is to retain honour and respectability in the community. Under pressure from her parents, Muzna reluctantly stops communicating with Salma, writing: 'If I speak to you, some snitch is going to snap a pic and show it to my parents. Then I'll get shipped off to Pakistan and probably have to marry one of my cousins!' (48). The pressure for conformity is thus maintained through estrangement from friends in Britain and the threat of an early marriage.

We also see pressure being exerted on seemingly trivial issues such as makeup. Impressing on Muzna not to wear cosmetics while attending a wedding ceremony, her mother says, 'I'm not about to let my only daughter make her daddy the laughing stock of the community. We are respectable Muslims, Muchi! *Izzat* is everything.' Muzna reacts with suppressed anger, expressed in the following passage: 'I hated the way "Honour" was always chucked in my face to stop me from having any fun. [...] I wanted to tell Ami exactly what I thought of their stupid *izzat*. But though my confidence was definitely on the rise at school, it wasn't happening at home' (126–7). This mother–daughter squabble intimates how pressure can build through everyday tensions and lead to low self-esteem in the domestic sphere.

Despite her qualms about relationships before marriage, Muzna feels increasingly drawn to Arif, one of the most attractive boys at her school, and the two begin dating. In this relationship she seems emboldened and speaks of feeling free:

> Dad had pulled out all the stops to segregate me. And now here I was, with my very own boyfriend, determined to have the time of my life. [...] Hiding my feelings under a self-conscious act had passed from habit into DNA. Maybe being with Arif would help me become a normal person. I *really* wanted that.
>
> (173–4; emphasis in original)

However, even amid these precious times with her boyfriend, Muzna apprehends the consequences if her father spotted them together: 'I was trying to enjoy the moment, but I just couldn't help thinking about what would happen [...] [i]f he caught me [...]. He'd lost it over Salma. This would be terminal' (175). Reflecting on her lack of agency, she states: '[A]s long as I lived under his roof, Dad would always be my judge, jury and executioner' (234). This situational analysis sums up the authoritarian, even violent nature of honour-based pressure.

The more her parents exert their control over the course of the novel, the more Muzna craves to break free. She secretly marries her extremist boyfriend, Arif, according to religious law, since a legal marriage is not possible because of her minor status. Consummating her marriage through 'messy and painful' first-time sex (235), she arrives home anticipating her parents' fury because of her prolonged absence. Her mother hurls abusive remarks at her: '[W]hat will you tell your father when your belly grows fat with your bastard?' (235). Muzna's response is captured in the following passage that shadows forth her revolt, as well as a sense of isolation that she has been unable to articulate until now:

> I glared back at Ami. For one self-righteous moment, I felt like breaking it down for her. How my stupid parents with their stupid rules had driven me to desperate measures. How their controlling attitudes meant I could never bring stuff like boyfriends or sex or marriage to them without being threatened with getting shipped off to Pakistan. How my life and my body were my own, and I had every right to do with them as I pleased.
> But – most of all – I wanted to tell her how scared and lonely I was feeling. I needed Ami to hug me, not shout at me.
>
> (235)

This passage, incorporating both indignant and poignant tonal shades, illustrates the extent to which parental control can affect the young individual, and the repercussions that might ensue from a suffocating parent–child relationship.

'Get married!'

In *I Am Thunder*, Muzna's marriage is an act of defiance against her parents. Others rebel against parental pressure to marry young, staking a claim to singlehood. Tahir said his parents have been nagging him about marriage since his late teens. He observed: 'I think that for people in the Muslim community, their parents expect them to get married soon after they leave school.' Tahir's experience so far has been one of gentle resistance of this pressure, aided by his unmarried older brothers bearing the brunt of it:

> They are really, they get heavy, my dad is heavy telling them off to get married and stuff, because my dad is trying to tell me to get married, but I cannae get married before my older brothers. So they, so my dad is telling them off to get married. But they get it, they get it way more than me, they get it every single day. Get married!

This story highlights profitless parental pressure rather than coercive control, with Tahir and his siblings steadfastly resistant of matrimony. At the time of our interview, Tahir was not seriously thinking of marriage and felt that pressure to marry young is 'wrong'.

Waheed also benefited from his sibling being the main focus for his parents' matchmaking, in this case aimed at his younger sister. He observed: 'I don't know why but in our culture it's the case where girls get married at a younger age. I've spoken with my parents and they say she'll probably get married before I get married. So I think there's definitely a case for different expectations for girls.' This emphasizes that the extent of marriage pressure varies not only between families, but within families, with male children sometimes granted more freedom.

Saamiya, eighteen at the time of our interview, was increasingly aware of her family's expectation that she will marry soon. She spoke of a number of family members recently 'asking about like marriage and what my thoughts on it were, and when I was hoping to get married. What kind of man I would want to be getting married to.' She also suspected that her father was actively trying to matchmake for her:

> My dad has been doing it a lot, like he is always saying, 'Send me pictures of you wearing this pretty dress, I want to send it to a friend.' And I am pretty sure he is just trying to get me hooked up and married. And I think when you hit a certain age, if say if I am eighteen, it is a more of a thought of: Oh, who is the possibility she is going to get married to, and bringing people round to like – this is my daughter, look at her, she is old enough now for getting married.

Here, pressure to marry manifests through a conventional expectation that Saamiya is now the right age for her family to start making enquiries. For Saamiya, this situation is doubly awkward as it concerns not only the (wrong) idea that she desires to marry young but also the assumption that she is straight. Her experience illustrates how young Muslims may be placed in situations that make it difficult to speak or act in accordance with their own wishes.

'You can't afford to be fussy any more': Marry soon!

Marriage pressure was also a common theme in creative writing workshops, with short fiction by young Muslim women focusing on moments of family conflict and self-doubt. In a creative writing workshop in Glasgow, Farah developed a storyline about an unmarried woman in her mid-twenties. This story's protagonist, Sara, is under pressure from her mother and extended family to marry as soon as possible, for they fear she is already past the most marriageable age. When Sara's mother suggests a trip to Pakistan to find a *rishta*, Sara – who eagerly wishes to please her family – feels 'unable to say no'. This story deals with both family pressure and the internalized pressure of feeling inadequate, at fault, and that time is running out. Having always been told that marriage 'is what needs to happen in order for her to be happy', Sara consents to various humiliating matchmaking attempts.

A more light-hearted conflict between mother and daughter is the focus of a play entitled 'Life As We Know It', written by Sofia. The central character, Maryam, is a 'thirty-seven-year-old Scottish-Pakistani Muslim' who 'wants to know happiness again'. Her 'Ma' is 'late sixties, strong, matriarchal. While Ma '[j]ust wants her daughter to be happy', she is also 'getting old and doesn't understand what [Maryam] wants'. In the play's opening scene, they speak on the phone and Ma gets straight to the point:

Ma: You're listening aren't you?

Maryam: Turmeric. Coriander. Garam masala. Hmm? Yes, Ma.

Maryam adds a splash of water to the pot and the spices hiss and sizzle.

Ma: You don't get good rishtay easily these days beta. You must learn to compromise. Adjust. *Sab kuch nahi milta.* ['You don't get everything.']

Maryam: Salt. I forgot to add the salt.

Ma: Maryam!

Maryam sighs.

Maryam: Yes Ma, I'm listening. You said you don't get everything in a partner. You said they're coming tomorrow. You said I just need to say yes to any Tom, Dick or Haroon that walks through the door.

Ma: Hai Allah! What am I going to do with this girl!

Maryam: I'm a woman, Ma, I'm nearly forty years old.

Ma: Forty! See. You're getting too old. You can't afford to be fussy any more. What was even wrong with the last boy? He was tall, he had a good job and he had hair.

Maryam: *Boy.* What does being tall have to do with anything, Ma? Look, I will be there tomorrow. I need to go now, I'm in the middle of cooking. Allah hafiz.

This fictional encounter evokes with humour the pressure family members impose upon their daughters: to marry while still of childbearing age, to say yes, to put doubts aside. Sofia is riffing on a stereotype, but also exploring truths about how young people are pushed towards marriage. Maryam is a confident character who makes her own decisions, but still has to contend with her mother's misplaced efforts to secure her happiness.

'It was through the marriage process that I learned what caste is': Marry well!

Faisal confidently claimed, 'My dad, he would let me get married to whoever I want.' Then, after a pause, he added: 'So long as she has got a good background as well. There is that.' As with Tahir's comment at the opening of this chapter, it is unclear whether 'background' is a euphemism for religion, culture, economic status or caste, or simply a reference to good upbringing. Whatever coded meaning the term holds, Faisal is conscious that he will have parental expectations to contend with in his choice of future spouse.

Pressure to marry someone of a 'good background' can, for some, include specific considerations of class and caste. Fatima reflected that while this has not been a source of pressure within her own family, she has encountered others from her parents' generation who feel caste or *jati* is important:

> It seems to be – which is very surprising for me because in my family we never really knew what caste we were, we never talked about it, it's just such a non-issue. But it was really through the marriage process that I learned what caste is

and that people are really insistent on it. And there is a big Arain community that only wants to marry other Arains and like various other groups that only want to marry the same group. And it's just, I find it really baffling because it just doesn't make any sense to me but it seems to be just this perpetual issue. And my mum gets very annoyed by it. So whenever somebody would say on the phone to her, 'Oh you know, we're only looking for I don't know, Jat or whatever', then my mum would turn round to them and say 'Well, why is that? Do you think that that's going to get your son into heaven faster if he marries someone who's the same caste? Is that why you're doing it?' [Laughs]. Like just turning it round to Islam.

This example illuminates how Fatima and her family have experienced pressure from others within their community to observe a cultural tradition of marrying within their own caste: a tradition that seems wholly irrelevant to Fatima. Luckily for her, her mother is an ally in resisting this pressure. The way Fatima describes her mum's response demonstrates how Muslim families may variously emphasize cultural and/or religious identity. By insisting that caste is irrelevant to Islam, Fatima's family trump traditions with religion.

In Farah's story about Sara, reluctantly single in her twenties, caste and race are impediments to marriage. Farah describes her protagonist as 'smart, educated and dark-skinned. Her skin tone and her mother's caste issues are the reasons she is not married.' Farah emphasizes the pressure Sara feels under to alter her appearance. In an early scene, Sara is introduced to an older woman as a potential bride for her son. The older woman's response follows a familiar pattern for Sara, where people 'take one look at her dark skin and say no. The potential match and her do not even meet.' Sara's mother attempts to remedy the situation with 'constant commentary on her colour' and purchases whitening cream. This 'causes Sara to suffer from crippling insecurity'. Desperately unhappy, she begins self-harming to experience a 'sense of escape', feeling that this is 'the one thing she has control of'. It is common for fair skin to be revered as a colourist beauty standard within South Asian (and other brown and black) communities as a legacy of colonialism and an example of what Anne McClintock calls '*commodity racism*' (1995: 32; emphasis in original). This story highlights the impact this can have on young women for whom light skin is unattainable, the pressure to be other than what you are provoking frustration and self-loathing.

Sara's unhappiness is a result of external pressure, in the form of comments and rejection. It also stems from internalized pressure: she has come to believe that she must marry in order to be happy, and that her failure to attract a husband is her own fault. Harbouring ideals that she knows to be at odds with her self-image proves, ultimately, unsustainable. Farah chooses to end her story on a cautiously optimistic note. At the final call, Sara refuses to get on a flight to Pakistan for what would have been her family's last-ditch attempt to find her a husband. She resolves that she 'does not want another boy's mother to tell her she isn't pretty enough to marry their son', coming to the realization that '[s]he is beautiful but has been made to feel worthless by those around her'. It has been a difficult journey to self-acceptance, but Sara is finally able to resist the pressure that has dominated her life for so long.

'A fear had been breathed into the house': Gendered pressures in Maps for Lost Lovers

In Nadeem Aslam's novel *Maps for Lost Lovers* (2004) relationship pressures figure both explicitly and in subtler ways. The novel centres on a horrific 'honour' killing. This murder takes place before the novel's opening but haunts the narrative. Readers' knowledge of this act from the outset imparts a sense of foreboding even among Aslam's lushest descriptions of the scenery of a fictitious northern English town. Lovers Jugnu and Chanda, readers learn, were murdered by Chanda's brothers because they lived together without being married. This violent event is indicative of a regressive, claustrophobic migrant community in which, Aslam believes, pressure can transform into obsession and violence. Chanda had bowed to pressure twice and married husbands approved by her family, but both those marriages ended unhappily. The fact that she is not yet divorced from her second husband causes Chanda to live 'in sin' (a term used several times, for example, 15) when she forms a third, happy, relationship with Jugnu. Despite themselves being debauchers whose sexual lives are much more questionable than Chanda's, her brothers exhibit a double standard when it comes to the disgust and shame they feel about their sister's living arrangements.

Depictions of pressure are also found in the tense and layered relationship between Jugnu's sister-in-law Kaukab and her children Charag, Ujala and Mah-Jabin. A devout believer in a narrow version of Islam with unbending views of gender and sexuality, Kaukab exerts oppressive demands on her children that irrevocably rupture their filial ties. At just sixteen, her daughter Mah-Jabin capitulates to an arranged marriage in Pakistan. Despite the fact that the husband proves violent and the marriage ends in divorce, Kaukab is unrepentant about the pressure she had exerted on her young daughter. She makes it clear that she too was subjected to outside pressures around the family's social standing: 'We had given our word, the wedding arrangements were ready over there, and [...] I would have *tied* you up and taken you there had it come to that' (111–12; emphasis in original). This incident demonstrates the intensity of the strictures around marriage-related matters. Since marriage involves familial and cultural reputations, a change of heart or contravention of custom is unconscionable.

Although women bear the brunt of reputational and relationship pressure, the novel also captures the burdens that male children shoulder for the family around bread-winning and career choice. Kaukab's elder son, Charag, feels that the onus of the family's 'betterment' has mostly rested on him: 'Nothing was ever made verbal but this expectation had been inhaled by him with each breath he had taken during those early years' (122). A talented artist, Charag, like Muzna in *I Am Thunder*, is expected to pursue a medical career. This career expectation for the eldest son infiltrates other familial relationships. For example, when Charag decides to pursue fine art, having been unable to achieve good grades in science at A-level, he hears her mother slapping his sister, Mah-Jabin, saying, 'who would marry you now'? (123). This implies that Charag's medical career and its attendant honour is inextricably intertwined with Mah-Jabin's marriage prospects.

Having grown up under his mother's stiflingly rigid rule, Charag remains distant from girls and relatively inexperienced in relationship matters. When he moves away and starts seeing a girl named Stella (whom he later marries), Charag comes under conflicting psychological pressures, and hesitates to enter into a sexual relationship. On arriving in London, with its multitudinous anonymity freeing him from his northern town's gossip, he nonetheless feels far from liberated: '[H]e was inhibited by incompetence and inexperience, by a profound sense of shame regarding his virginal state' (125). There is an intimidation, probably unwitting, exerted by his white, non-Muslim peers for a boy to lose his virginity as a teenager and be sexually competent by his early twenties. There are also other compulsions and worries: 'The anxieties had been many. The sense passed on to him during his upbringing was that the differences between the whites and the Pakistanis were too many for interaction to successfully take place; many marriages ended' (126). This betokens a struggle to reconcile expectations with long-held prohibitions against love matches and mixed marriages.

In the initial years of his relationship with Stella, Charag is too scared to tell his parents, especially his mother, about her. Whenever he visits home, he tries not to contact his girlfriend. In the following passage, Aslam creates the impression of a household devoid of flexibility or sensitivity:

> He could not have given Stella his phone number, and longed to talk to her, to touch her. A fear had been breathed into the house once when a girl from school had telephoned Charag about homework: he hardly ever left the house after school but his mother had suspected a girlfriend behind that *one* phone call. She didn't know (nor would he himself for a while yet) what it meant to have a girlfriend, that a relationship was replete with subtleties through which intimacy and commitment were demanded and demonstrated, that you were supposed to meet regularly, even daily, introduce each other to the parents.
>
> (127–8; emphasis in original)

This passage not only sheds light on how pressure is exerted but also the cultural and generational chasm which creates and stokes such pressure. Coercion appears to have been present for as long as Charag can remember, dating back to the innocent phone call from a platonic friend at school. This fuels Charag's present-day distress over the impossibility of reconciling his longing to be with his girlfriend with his mother's expectations that he will marry a woman of her choice. Stella's assumption that their relationship will develop through regular dates and introductions to family members clashes with Charag's mother's desire that he will have no intimate contact with white women and will ultimately marry someone of Pakistani Muslim heritage chosen by his elders.

Elements of Charag's experience in *Maps for Lost Lovers* are echoed in some of the interviews we conducted. Yusuf, reflecting on the 'torturously long process' of becoming comfortable in his sexuality as a gay Muslim, spoke of internalized pressures that are contextual, coming in and out of focus in different settings. He described how he was mostly able to ignore his attraction to men until university, where he was suddenly confronted with a more multicultural peer group including 'the rugby team and the football team and you know, [those] kind of sexual stereotypes':

> [E]verything just starts getting worse because people are a lot more freer in the way that they're dressing and the way that they're behaving and stuff like that. I'm not going to go down the whole 'university is where you find yourself' and all that kind of white hippie bullshit but you know, people do – university is a time for them to kind of behave in slightly different ways that they might not do at home.

Yusuf felt less under scrutiny during his time at university, surrounded by peers who were experimenting with their adult identities. This enabled him to question his previously held belief that same-sex desire was something he needed to 'get over'. This pressure, though internalized, was neither absolute nor irresistible. Resisting the pressures he faced, Yusuf's story highlights the limited power of pressures in the sexual lives of young Muslims.

Conclusion

This chapter has explored various ways in which young Muslims experience pressure, how it feels, how it affects their lives and the choices they make. Many of these experiences concern marital pressures: the pressure to get married, to do so at a young and fertile age, to marry within caste and class, and to marry a person of the opposite sex. As is shown by the contrasting fates of the male and female characters in *Maps for Lost Lovers*, and by some of the stories told to us by young Muslim men and women, pressure has a gendered dimension. Young women seem to be more explicitly bound by patriarchal notions of *izzat*, pressure to marry young and while of childbearing age; though young men too often shoulder the weight of family expectations and internalize dictates about appropriate relationships.

It is important to recognize that not all young Muslims experience such pressures. By focusing on this subject, this chapter has inevitably drawn on the experiences of those for whom pressure is a reality. Our book would be incomplete without giving voice to these experiences alongside joyful, less complicated accounts of Muslim dating, love and marriage. The persistence of negative stereotypes and a desire to rebut them should not blind us to the facts that, in some families, such issues are a source of consternation, and that this affects the way young Muslims live their lives. We have traced different forms of pressure. Explicit instructions sometimes come from family members and others in the community about what a young person must or must not do. More subtly, individuals pick up on unwritten rules about what is acceptable and unacceptable. And young people put pressure on themselves, whether through internalizing norms or in less direct ways because of a lack of self-confidence. Thus, some pressures are external and overt, even coercive; others are more intangible. Even when pressures are severe, stories in this chapter – such as Esha's story of marrying a man of her choosing and Yusuf's story of eventually embracing his sexuality – prove that they are resistible, at a personal cost and with perseverance and skill.

Table 5.1 Interviews quoted in Chapter 5, 'Pressure'

Name	Gender	Age	Relationship Status	Location
Saamiya	Female	18	Single	Glasgow
Tahir	Male	20	Single	Glasgow
Esha	Female	27	Married	Yorkshire
Fatima	Female	21	In a relationship	Glasgow
Faisal	Male	16	Single	Glasgow
Waheed	Male	21	Single	Glasgow
Yusuf	Male	22	Single	Yorkshire

Table 5.2 Workshop participants and convenors quoted in Chapter 5, 'Pressure'

Name	Gender	Age	Workshop Series	Role in Workshop	Title
Heena	Female	25	4. Playwriting Glasgow	Participant	'Untitled'
Farah	Female	25	5. Fiction, Glasgow	Participant	'Untitled'
Sofia	Female	37	4. Playwriting, Glasgow	Participant	'Life As We Know It'

Chapter 6

MARRIED

I remember when we first sat down after we were married, and we went for our first meal out, and we had nothing to talk about: like, we were just silent and really shy.

(Safa, twenty-two, interview)

'Aren't you going to pray? It's almost time for Maghrib.' Amina replied. 'And would you please take off that rucksack? It's driving me nuts seeing you like a turtle.'

'Why? It's got almost all your stuff in it. Including that beard grooming kit you thought was necessary to buy at the petrol station.'

(Aleeha, twenty-two, short story fragment, 'The Last Paragraph of a Romantic Novel')

Muslim marriages include unions commonly labelled as 'arranged', 'love' and 'transnational' marriages, though these are not necessarily the terms that young people themselves choose in discussing their relationships. This chapter explores how young British Muslims talk and write about marriage – their own and others' – through love stories, cautionary tales and bittersweet reminiscences. In the first extract above, Safa recalls her shyness with her new husband following an arranged marriage, speaking to a particular experience of Muslim married life. The second extract is a snapshot of married life that many readers will recognize. It is at once ordinary, with its everyday bickering, and specific to its Muslim setting – complete with a carefully groomed beard. This seems a happy if prosaically imperfect marriage, brought to life on the page by Aleeha, who participated in a creative writing workshop in Bradford. Other stories explore the fragility of marriage, such as Roopa Farooki's novels *Bitter Sweets* (2007) and *The Flying Man* (2012), both of which narrate love marriages that ultimately fall apart. Stories from real and fictional settings serve to explore, warn, endorse, celebrate and document marriages that Muslims variously enjoy and endure. This chapter therefore moves between stories which present positive images of married life, and others which are darker.

'We say that we are boyfriend and girlfriend':
Experiences of arranged marriage

Safa, in her early twenties, had an arranged marriage with a distant cousin originally from Pakistan. She spoke of her changing relationship with her husband in cautiously affectionate terms, explaining how – despite some initial awkwardness – she is enjoying getting to know him:

> We knew each other and we were cousins, and we used to have banter and stuff. But I didn't really see him in that light until it was actually like certain this is what I wanted to do. So it is quite different, and I think we are still at, even though I am married I think it is still that thing that it has not actually hit me in the head I am actually married. So it is just one of those things where you just get to know each other [...]. Because quite often in like the British culture, parents give their children the time to go out and stuff. Whereas I wasn't allowed to do that, like dates and stuff like that. So I think it makes a difference. So I felt like he was a complete stranger but it is just getting easier now. I feel like I know him. But at the same time I feel like it was for the best – I think [...]. We always say that we are not husband and wife, we always say that we are boyfriend and girlfriend, it is just something that we have between us. Because it is getting to know. And he will always say, 'Well, why didn't you come out before marriage?' and stuff, but I am kind of like liking it because you like, it is kind of like we are in that phase of being good friends and actually just getting to know each other and it is nice, I think, because I am enjoying it.

This story captures a particular moment in the early days of marriage, when a young couple are finding their feet in their new roles of husband and wife. Safa's experience of transnational marriage is a positive example of two young people negotiating differences between British and Pakistani culture, parental expectations and their own sense of what they want. It exemplifies the often rehearsed idea of getting to know one another and falling in love *after* rather than before marriage.

Speaking from personal experience of arranged marriage, young Muslims sometimes appear conscious of speaking to stereotypes that they wish to rebut. Shahid explained that he hoped to have an arranged marriage, but for a long time this had not seemed likely. His parents 'couldn't settle on someone to even approach' and told Shahid he would 'just have to find someone himself'. Disappointed, Shahid countered: 'I don't really have the time to find anyone, I'm quite busy with stuff.' Eventually, his sister suggested a match that everyone was happy with. Shahid recalled his first impression of his now-wife in a matter-of-fact way, telling his parents: 'Yeah, yeah, a good family, good girl. Yeah, it's fine.' For Shahid, marriage – at least in its initial stages – is not about being about swept off your feet in love, but rather a practical choice to make a lifelong commitment 'the biggest thing is that personal preference and just knowing that you are ready [...]. You want it to progress to something serious.' This suggests an optimistic (if rather unromantic) view of moving forward to the next chapter in his life.

'Marriage was, after all, a bloody compromise': Fictional depictions of marriage

We now turn to portrayals of marriage in A Match Made in Heaven (Chambers et al. 2020), a collection of stories about love and desire by South Asian-heritage British Muslim women authors edited by three of the editors of this volume, namely Claire Chambers, Nafhesa Ali and Richard Phillips. These stories include work completed within the creative writing workshops we convened. They also go beyond these workshops, including the work of published authors who have literary reputations and growing audiences. Together, the new, emerging and established authors, all of whom are younger women from South Asian Muslim backgrounds, present varied pictures of married life.

In one story from the anthology, Sarvat Hasin's 'The Cat That Came in with the Dark', a teenage girl named Uzma feels unsettled and even usurped when her mother adopts a mysterious cat. Although Uzma herself is too young to be contemplating marriage, her mother's unhappy experience of this institution shadows the narrative. The woman was married, apparently at a young age, to a man whose defining characteristic was his anger. This 'quiet and breathless' rage turned their home into a 'mausoleum' (88). There are intimations of his domestic violence against the mother and possible sexual abuse of his daughter. Unsurprisingly, when Uzma was very young her mother removed her from this toxic environment. The two of them fled to a series of temporary havens, each one being abandoned the moment the abusive father got wind of where they were staying. In Hasin's story, then, marriage is a fearful thing, and security is found in intergenerational female relationships – not only between Uzma and her mother but also the girl and her mother's mother, the outspoken, cigarette-smoking Nani. This security is shattered by the incursions, first, of the stray tomcat who charms the mother and, second, of Daniel Mayberry, a boy from Uzma's school who enchants her with a first kiss. The story takes a fantastical turn with Daniel's sudden violent death, apparently linked to the cat. However, the suggestion put forward is that women's companionship and solidarity represents safety, while male intrusion brings danger.

Marriage is portrayed almost as negatively in the story that opens the anthology, Sabyn Javeri's 'Marriage of Convenience'. To avoid an arranged marriage, Javeri's protagonist Saira contemplates getting married in name only to a gay man she meets on a Muslim matrimonial site. Saira regards her parents' union as offering unalloyed misery to all concerned. These parents had an arranged marriage and

> went on to spend their lives in Britain fighting each other to death but never ever contemplating divorce because marriage was, after all, a bloody compromise that had to be struggled through for the sake of the children. So the children, in turn, had to suffer through it for the sake of their parents.
>
> (1)

It is understandable, then, that rather than associating marriage with love or happiness, Saira thinks it is about contempt and suffering. Despite the disappointments of their own relationship, her parents try to coerce Saira into marriage. She resists for as long as she can but, when pressure is becoming unavoidable, enters into the titular 'marriage of convenience' with Saeed. The latter is on paper a 'suitable boy', being young, good-looking and working as a 'high-earning lawyer' (6). But unbeknown to the community, Saeed identifies as gay. He and Saira each realize that by marrying they can get 'the old mother hen off [their] backs' (9). They draw up a legal agreement prohibiting sexual activity or the sharing of assets and go ahead with a wedding. Yet after marriage, Saira finds herself falling in love with her unreachable husband, getting frustrated at his busy social life and especially his close friendship with a male colleague. When she confronts him about this, Saeed grows angry and drags her out of their house, slapping her and making her fall to the ground, lip bleeding. Overcome with remorse, he has a flashback to his own parents' abusive marriage, and realizes, '*I had turned into the man I never wanted to be*' (12; emphasis in original). For both Saira and Saeed, their parents' unhappy marriage contributes to the failure of their own. The story ends with the couple undergoing intensive therapy to understand what has brought them to this point and to dissolve their marriage of convenience on amicable terms.

In Bina Shah's 'Peter Pochmann Goes to Dinner' an intercultural dinner between a Muslim patriarch, his son Mohammed and the son's white British colleague Peter Pochmann leads to tension when Mohammed's wife Rabeea makes an outspoken appearance. Mohammed and Rabeea's marriage is again far from idyllic, but this time it is the woman who has the upper hand. Peter is taken aback that Rabeea wears the niqab and refuses to eat with the men after serving them their food. Despite these markers of alleged subservience, Mohammed's wife is assertive and uncompromising. She makes several sweeping criticisms of the West that offend Peter, who remains silent at first but increasingly tries to argue with her. When Mohammed chastises her for one of her generalizations, Rabeea 'shot a volley back, the double of Mohammed's in both firepower and velocity. Mohammed shrank, visibly cowed' (119–20). She is even unfazed by her father-in-law's magisterial presence. After thwarted remonstrations, her two male relatives 'watch […] her in furtive, frightened silence' (120), adumbrating her largely unchallenged dominance within this household. The dinner table discussion becomes exponentially more fraught, and ends with her fulminating about the War on Terror and departing the room to smash a plate in the kitchen. On her departure, the father-in-law bewails her behaviour and her ambition (which he had quashed) to take a job educating Pakistani women in family planning. He blames his son for his wife's disrespect, saying that when he asks Mohammed why he puts up with Rabeea's attitude the young man talks of love. Mohammed Senior spits out the word 'like an errant pomegranate seed', and tells Pochmann: 'This boy is more English than Pakistani […], no offence. But I hope you will understand. We call that being *angraiz*. For us, it is not a compliment' (129). While Hasin's and Javeri's stories focus on arranged marriage as a source of violence and misery, Shah's story shows that the love marriage can also lead to unhappiness, humorously portrayed, and to verbal lacerations.

Ayisha Malik's 'Heartbeat', a black comedy about a black widow, sketches another empowered woman who has agency in her marriage(s). In part narrated in epistolary style, the forty-something protagonist Beenish writes letters to her dead husbands, Rahim and Tariq, in between dealing with their interfering mothers and trying to return to the dating scene. Beenish's first marriage, to Rahim, seems to have been mundanely unhappy. He would splurge money on himself and criticize her weight, encouraging her to regularly spend a punishing forty-five minutes running on the treadmill. Her second husband, Tariq, comes across as gentler and more romantic than Rahim, but Beenish is dismissive about his lack of a personality, and appears to have been bored in the marriage. These bad experiences and the tragedy of their apparently accidental deaths have not diminished Beenish's faith in marriage. After meeting a younger man, Asif, on a dating app and then in person, she quickly gets engaged for the third time. Her former mothers-in-law react to this decision with incredulity, and start to express their suspicions about the circumstances surrounding their sons' deaths. Beenish ignores them, pressing ahead with her wedding preparations, but the story ends on these comically sinister lines: 'Her smile faltered. She recalled the giving way of Rahim's heart, the crack of Tariq's neck. The necessity of both. Just as with them, only time would tell how long the rest of any life might be' (236).

Compared to this exuberant satire, a happier or even an over-idealized argument about marriage is advanced in Shelina Janmohamed's generically indeterminate 'Love Letter'. In the piece, a mother (based on Janmohamed's own authorial persona) gives advice about marriage from within a Muslim ethical framework to her pre-pubescent daughter. Janmohamed positions love as being one component of a triptych aspired to by Muslims, alongside justice and compassion. She encourages her daughter to search for a partner like her own husband, the girl's father:

> a husband who will bask in how exquisite you are, a husband who will help you sparkle. [...] The soft embrace of a man, his warmth and safety. His belief and encouragement. His companionship and his gentle correction of your mistakes so you can do better. His support in facing head-on the difficulties life will inevitably bring, so you can emerge through the storms rather than be crushed by them.
>
> (212)

Notwithstanding her protest against the imagined response to 'Love Letter' from some readers that she is 'oppressing' her daughter, Janmohamed's persona does indicate a certain subordination on the woman's part when it comes to the sentence about the husband's 'gentle correction' of his wife's errors. However, marriage is also envisioned as supportive and companionate. Janmohamed goes on to write that this kind of love is 'rarely' discussed and goes against the Hollywood or Bollywood depictions of love at first sight: 'I don't mean falling in love, I don't mean being Layla and finding your Majnun. I mean a kind of love in which your innermost self can emerge, and its prickly edges can be smoothed and its shine polished' (212). Here Janmohamed alludes to the same star-crossed lovers referenced in Fatima Bhutto's *The Runaways* (see Chapter 4, 'Love'), but rejects the legend to cast marital love as quietly nurturing and burnishing, rather than dealing in Layla and Majnun's extravagant passion.

Finally, online fetishes, Islamophobia and erotica are pored over in Shaista Sadick's racy and funny satire 'Boneland'. Sania, the main character, is in her forties and married to Jamie, a white history teacher, with whom she has two daughters. When Jamie loses his job, Sania becomes the family's main breadwinner through an increasingly lucrative role writing stories for the website 'Boneland.net: The World's Number One Halal Erotica' (42). Jamie mildly expresses objections to the site because of what Sania herself acknowledges are its 'Fifty Shades of Terrorism' tendencies (42). Sania dismisses his concerns as 'politically correct' (43). However, on the day in which the story unfolds, Sania is contacted by a Boneland executive based in the United States. He requests: 'Can you throw in some American GIs? I mean, the girls have to be Mozlems, of course. But the guys, they could be saving 'em from wherever they're from, and the girls could be showing 'em how grateful they are' (49). Horrified at his stereotypical saviour discourse (Abu-Lughod 2013), Sania Googles the executive, only to find a picture of him wearing a Make America Great Again cap. Her realization that Jamie was right about the website's racism tessellates with the broader image of their marriage. Although the two sometimes bicker, there is warmth and care between them, as well as shared irreverent humour. Sania appreciates Jamie's old-fashioned courtesy and geeky enthusiasm for Plantagenet kings and queens. Equally important, to her, is his distance from and lack of interest in the gossip of London's close-knit British Pakistani circles:

> [He] didn't seem to care how many men she might or might not have slept with [...] It didn't matter to him whether her parents were active in the community, or whether she said her prayers. It didn't matter that she drank, or smoked, or intended to live off Heinz Baked Beans for the rest of her life instead of learning how to cook.
>
> (46–7)

At one point in the story, Sania comes home from buying groceries to find that Jamie has cleaned the kitchen and left an undemonstratively romantic surprise: 'On the counter was a roll of toilet paper. And in the middle of the roll, a single red rose' (47). Moreover, the story's denouement pithily conveys the supportive nature of their marriage. Discomfited by her phone conversation with the Trump-supporting website manager, Sania calls Jamie to ask him to come home. The story ends with him reassuring her, 'Already here, darling', as he turns the key in the latch. This story reminds readers that marriages are not always endogamous and, regardless of background, that they can be grounded on humour, equality and kindness.

'Now she has probably messed her life up': Cautionary tales of how not to marry

Some of the young Muslims who took part in this research were not yet married themselves, and drew on the experiences of friends to express their views of married life. Some of the stories they told were cautionary tales. Hiba, for example, recalled a friend's marriage that ended in divorce:

> [S]he was so determined that she wanted her own place after marriage, which is a bit unusual in the Pakistani culture anyway for a husband and wife to get their own place immediately after marriage. So she wanted her own place and then she did not want to do anything for her in-laws, which again was quite unusual. Like you don't come in with that kind of expectation of not doing anything for anybody. So I think that kind of caused problems within their marriage because he felt he'd given up a lot and she hadn't. And I think that fell apart within a year, actually.

This story highlights a culturally distinctive aspect of newly married life in British Asian Muslim households, in which newlyweds are often expected to cohabit with the husband's parents. Hiba's lightly judgemental tone suggests that she disapproves of her friend's 'unusual' refusal to make this concession to her new husband and in-laws, blaming this contravention of custom for causing marital tension and ultimately separation. We can infer that Hiba herself envisages living with extended family as an essential and inevitable part of early married life.

Others who had been married took a different view of familial cohabitation. Aisha, single when interviewed but later married, had 'a lot to say about getting used to in-laws' while taking part in animation workshops. Workshop facilitator Stacy Bias recorded in her field diary that 'in the down-times between activities', Aisha talked of the 'double-stress' of having a pregnancy, a new husband and his family to contend with. She shared funny anecdotes such as 'fantasizing about chasing her mother-in-law out of the kitchen with a rolling pin!'. This signals the young woman's frustration with her new role and place in the family hierarchy. Arshad, now happily married, felt that his starter marriage had failed because his first wife – a cousin with whom he had an arranged marriage, and whom he only knew 'at face value' – had had to sacrifice a lot more than he had:

> she married into my house and we came home and I found out that she was very, very – because she was only eighteen years of age, she was very close to her family and she was finding it very hard to let her family go and move on. I don't think she was actually ready for marriage … And obviously it's different for a boy in the Muslim culture because we actually bring the girl – the girl marries into the boy's family, so it's harder for her because she has to settle into a life that her husband chooses or her husband has you know, mapped out.

In contradistinction to Hiba's story, Arshad expresses empathy with the wife's perspective in shared living arrangements, ruminating on the inequality between husband and wife and the greater sacrifice being asked of his 'very, very' young wife on entering into marriage. Whilst 'devastated' by his divorce, Arshad said it taught him that 'you both have to compromise ... to make a marriage work'.

Other such parables are starker and more unpropitious. Seventeen-year-old Farooq recalled a former classmate whom he believed had been subject to an arranged – perhaps forced – marriage in Pakistan:

> She was sixteen. I think her mum and dad told her they found someone for you, you know like a strict family. So she went and got married, an arranged marriage I think. But now – she is married and I don't think she went to college; she has gone back to Pakistan ... I think that was a bit wrong though, it is a bit wrong because – she wanted to study, she was like good in class, she was getting like As and stuff. And now she has probably messed her life up.

Here, early marriage looms as a threat to the enjoyment of teenage years, educational opportunities and even residency in the UK: something to be feared rather than looked forward to.

Similarly, some published fiction by Muslim authors explores the spectre of forced marriages devoid of choice and agency, largely operating under parental – and especially male – control. In Almas Khan's *Chapati and Chips* (1993), a young woman named Sameena is described as 'merely a pawn' in her father's 'schemes' (22). She is married off to a relative in Pakistan against her wishes. Sameena then suffers violence at the hands of her new husband. Written in the first person, the plot barrels along and does not allow enough room for development, sometimes resting on stereotypes. Although only a secondary character, Sameena feeds into the stale image of the Asian woman who is silent and victimized. The young woman had appeared to acquiesce with her arranged marriage, but quickly sees that her husband is insufferable. She writes a letter to her parents about wanting to leave him. Her husband hides their reply, so she thinks her parents haven't written back. In that intercepted letter her mother is more sympathetic than the father, but neither of them are uncaring or abusive. Sameena eventually manages to escape back to Britain alone when her husband's visa is refused. Although she is pregnant, readers are given the impression that she will split up with this cruel patriarchal figure. *Chapati and Chips* was published by a small publishing house in the early 1990s, when British Asian writing by authors of Muslim heritage was still in its infancy. From it, we now move to two recent examples from more established publishers – two novels by Roopa Farooki – where doxas or received ideas about Muslim marriage are questioned and complicated.

'Instantly, instinctively comfortable with each other': Love marriage in Bitter Sweets

Roopa Farooki's debut novel *Bitter Sweets* (2007) is an ambivalent portrayal of love marriage. It centres on a young couple from Karachi, Pervez and Shona, who fall deeply in love and elope to London to escape their families' disapproval. Pervez's family are suspicious of Shona, 'an arriviste from Bangladesh' (26) and Shona's father, an Oxford graduate, is resentful of a son-in-law who is not university-educated and therefore not his daughter's 'intellectual equal' (27). Despite financial hardships, the beginning of Pervez's and Shona's married life is full of mutual warmth and affection. As newlyweds, they often express their intimacy through physical acts with 'an intense sexual compatibility', which is depicted vividly by the narrator:

> Any arguments, disappointment and frustrations were put aside, resolved, absolved in the bedroom, crushed with the salty-sweetness of their lovemaking, and melted away in the early hours of the morning, evaporating like discharged ghosts with the sticky heat of their bodies. These bodies were instantly, instinctively comfortable with each other, hand fitting hand, mouth fitting mouth, curve fitting hollow.
>
> (44–5)

Passionate scenes such as these evoke a sexually satisfying and emotionally fulfilling conjugal relationship, but the opening sentence also offers a glimpse of the fault lines of their marriage: fault lines that will later become unbridgeable chasms.

The marriage retains its love and warmth for a decent period, during which Pervez and Shona desperately try for a child and finally have twin boys through IVF. As the boys grow, the strong attachment between the couple starts to dwindle. As a mature couple in their forties, they reflect what went wrong in their initially glorious twenty years of marriage, speculating as to whether it was the increasing demands of life and the hardship of parental duty that made them drift apart. The couple trace the gradual loss of love in their marriage to the need to present a united front against their families and their urgent desire to have children: 'But the more their children grew, the less they needed them, until eventually they had nothing against which to unite' (142). In *Bitter Sweets*, what begins as a hopeful tale of young love defying parental resistance becomes a cautionary one of love ebbing amid the stasis of life, problematizing love marriage as a fragile and ultimately fungible state.

'Magnificent, ridiculous': Flawed marriage in The Flying Man

Roopa Farooki's 2012 novel *The Flying Man* offers another bittersweet take on marriage, this time from the perspective of a Pakistani man who is always on the move. A passionate gambler and 'a man of trivial concerns' (106), Maqil is too restless to be tied down by any attachments – be these filial, marital or parental. The setting of the novel spans continents, as the titular 'Flying Man' Maqil embarks upon various adventures in money-making, from gambling to forgery. He abandons his family – a wife and children – to satisfy his hedonistic caprices. Finally, far away from everyone and reflecting on his rather unusual life, the old Maqil dies alone in his flat in Paris.

Although Maqil gets married three times, it is his second wife, Samira, with whom he settles down for the longest period of time. The chapter focusing on Maqil's married life in London portrays his relationship with Samira with both humour and empathy. Religious and ethnic identity play a significant role when Maqil's family refuses to accept Samira, who is from a family of Christian converts originally belonging to the Indian side of Bengal, making her an 'infiltrator' or 'spy' in their eyes (92). Maqil's love for Samira is viewed as an act of 'treachery' by his family, who warn him not to 'darken their door again' (90). Maqil has a more cosmopolitan outlook, thanks to his 'melting-pot education and frequent travels' (91). He refuses to pay heed to his family and the couple stick together in the face of opposition. Yet Maqil has other anxieties about the match, often feeling insecure next to his pretty, young and well-educated wife: the age gap between him and Samira is described as 'suspiciously close to a sit-com cliché' (88–9). Despite this, Maqil's love and admiration for Samira are evident throughout their time together: 'Love has not been the cage with a keeper he had once feared – as it turns out, he loves someone, and she has set him free' (90). Their relationship is tinged with vivacity too: Samira jokingly describes Maqil as her 'kept man', although, we are told, her words are 'blurred by affection' (96, 97).

In the initial days of their marriage, Samira remains unperturbed by Maqil's addictive passion for gambling. Her willingness to give him space verges on unconcern, but there are clues that it actually amounts to quiet resignation. Despite her apparent indifference, we see Samira coming close to hysteria when Maqil suffers a heart attack, as she sits by his bedside panicking and waiting for him to regain consciousness. However, with her customary sarcastic and arch tone she later scolds Maqil for waking up when she was out of the house getting a coffee. Maqil is 'both touched and impressed by her lack of surprise, by her apparent certainty that he would wake up [...] that he was coming back – today, tomorrow, or the day after – and was waiting for him' (101). This implies the existence of a trusting love between the couple despite their petty jealousies and banal squabbles.

The contradictory dynamics of their relationship are brought to the fore when Maqil expresses his desire to have children. Samira vehemently opposes this idea, mocking it as part of Maqil's characteristic whimsy. Maqil realizes that Samira is choosing him over motherhood, as she knows that he would make an unreliable father. His wish to have a child, he contemplates, is culturally determined: 'like any good Pakistani male, [he wants] to leave another Maqil for his family, to carry on the overbestowed and underused name' (104). Beneath Samira's layers of ironic comments about Maqil's potential incompetence as a parent lies solicitude for her husband, whom she knows too well to burden with the responsibility of parenthood. In a moment of revelation, Maqil is deeply moved by her selfless love, 'a gift he lacks':

> He has never been more aware of her love, as complicated and compromised as they both were already. But still, love, after all. That men and women should be so comically [*sic*] connected, that their breath and blood should be shared

like this, that love should be expressed and reproduced by these trivial physical acts, the softness of a tongue in a mouth, the hardness of a prick seeking its own introduction, seeking to make life, to found a dynasty. That their love might leave an enduring legacy on the earth, or else just a stain on the sheets. Magnificent, ridiculous.

(104–5)

These concluding lines of the chapter deftly capture the sedimented nature of their relationship, as they reveal the oxymorons – the seriousness and absurdity, indifference and attachment, depth and shallowness, and carnality and purity – that underpin a flawed but frequently happy union.

'You look like a turtle': Everyday togetherness

Aleeha's fictional excerpt 'The Last Paragraph of a Romantic Novel', quoted at the beginning of this chapter, presents a more optimistic, if not romanticized picture of marriage for a young British Muslim couple. This story provides an eloquent end to this chapter, charting a husband and wife's quarrelling and everyday togetherness. As its title suggests, the story takes the reader past the early stages of a relationship – when the sight of each other made the young couple's 'heart beat faster' – to the mundane realities of quotidian married life. The following scene, narrated from the husband's perspective, is entitled 'Scarborough Seaside: End of April':

'There's a football match on right now,' I said as we walked into the room. The sun was setting outside and the gulls screeched as they soared in the sky.
   'Aren't you going to pray? It's almost time for Maghrib,' Amina replied. 'And would you please take off that rucksack? It's driving me nuts seeing you look like a turtle.'
   'Why? It's got almost all your stuff in it. Including that beard grooming kit you thought was necessary to buy at that petrol station.'
   Amina huffed and put her hand on her hip. 'I thought you liked it.'
   'How could I say otherwise? You kept going on and on about how cheap it was and I was trying to listen to the radio. I didn't even hear if De Gea saved that goal. I just said I liked it so you would shush.'
   'Honestly! You and that football team.'
   'What's wrong with having an interest?'
   'Those people don't even know you exist!'
   'Yes, they do. I'm the fan leader of the Red Devils.'
   'You set up one web page dedicated to how much you thought Ander Herrera was an underrated player and you honestly think that people care about it?'
   'They care! If they didn't why do you think that it hit almost a hundred views?'
   'I was responsible for nearly half those views.' Amina muttered.
   'What did you say?'

Figure 6.1 In this light-hearted depiction of marital conflict, a woman throws a shoe at her husband for his smoking habit. This scene is taken from the animated film *Halal Dating*, which was made by the participants in Workshop Series 1. This image, and the storyline accompanying it, express realistic rather than idealistic ideas about marriage. The young animators acknowledge the existence of conflict and exasperation, even in marriages that generally work.

> 'I said that I was the reason that you got a hundred views!' she yelled.
> My eyes widened. 'What? What do you mean? I thought ... I was sure ...'
> 'Can we not argue about this? We're here on this lovely holiday and all you can talk about is your affection for Manchester United.'
> 'I thought you liked them.'
> 'I did. But you're obsessed. You need to let it go. Let's just pray and then we can go down and find a nice halal place to eat.'

While the young married couple's low-key irritation at one another is palpable, so is their mutual affection. It is also apparent how well they know each other and feel comfortable in their relationship by the way they openly express their feelings. Amina gently mocks her football-obsessed husband, yet takes an interest and discreetly supports him by boosting the viewing figures on his fan page. The seaside backdrop hints at a longing for adventure and excitement, while the observance of familiar routines reminds the reader that this is a couple who have by now settled into their marriage.

Conclusion

Marriage is of great significance in Islam, and as such cuts across all of the chapters in this book about young Muslims' intimate relationships and sexual lives. In this chapter, we have focused primarily on experiences of *being* married, rather than related and cross-cutting themes such as the search for a spouse. Aleeha's closing story speaks to the ordinariness of Muslim married life, in which religion plays an unobtrusive part in everyday routines and affectionate arguments. Other stories in this chapter highlight distinctively Muslim marriage experiences, such as halal dating before getting to know one another as husband and wife, falling in love (or not) after an arranged marriage, marrying into an extended family household, and dealing with disappointment when love does not follow the marriage ceremony.

Muslim marriages are genuinely diverse, as illustrated by the range of stories from the anthology *A Match Made in Heaven*, whose only common feature is that they touch on younger (British Asian) Muslim women's experiences of marriage. If Sarvat Hasin's 'The Cat That Came in with the Dark' and Sabyn Javeri's 'Marriage of Convenience' portray wives as unhappy victims, the downtrodden partners are husbands in Bina Shah's 'Peter Pochmann Goes to Dinner' and Ayisha Malik's 'Heartbeat'. Sunnier portrayals of marriage can be found in Shelina Janmohamed's sweet, even saccharine 'Love Letter', and in Shaista Sadick's bravura cross-cultural satire 'Boneland'. One notable absence from this chapter (though not from the anthology), however, are stories from lesbian and gay young Muslims, a silence that highlights the typically exclusionary and heteronormative framing of marriage. Janmohamed's letter to her daughter, for example, rests on the implicit premise that love and happiness will stem from marrying a man. This remains a blind spot of many of the stories explored throughout this chapter. That said, most of these tales interrogate simplistic assumptions and chocolate-box optimism, gently confronting questions about what marriage is and can be, why it doesn't always work, and how young Muslims can shape it in their own interests and images.

Table 6.1 Interviews quoted in Chapter 6, 'Married'

Name	Gender	Age	Relationship Status	Location
Safa	Female	22	Married	Yorkshire
Shahid	Male	24	Engaged	Yorkshire
Maryam	Female	23	Not stated	Yorkshire
Mumtaz	Female	23	Divorced	Glasgow
Hiba	Female	27	Married	Glasgow
Farooq	Male	17	Single	Yorkshire

Table 6.2 Workshop participants and convenors quoted in Chapter 6, 'Married'

Name	Gender	Age	Workshop Series	Role in Workshop	Title
Aleeha	Female	22	2. Creative writing, Bradford	Participant	'The Last Paragraph of a Romantic Novel'
Meena	Female	35	5. Fiction, Glasgow	Participant	'Rearranged'
Farah	Female	25	5. Fiction, Glasgow	Participant	'Moments in Time'

Interlude 3

(NOT SO) DIFFERENT

When it comes to sex and love, Muslims are not so different to other people: not as different as they are often made out to be. They bear little relation to the caricatured homophobes, sexual predators, unhappy spouses, and domineering and self-interested matchmakers, all of whom will be familiar to newspaper readers and television audiences in Britain and other Western countries. In some ways, though, Muslims *are* different, with distinctive approaches to sexuality, sexual relationships and sexual love, which stand out from cultural majorities and from other religious groups too.

Young Muslims negotiate certain norms and expectations that others do not. These begin with understandings of which sexual acts and relationships are halal, and which are haram. These understandings spring from a number of sources including readings of the Qur'an and *ahadith*,* and scholarly and theological commentaries on these texts. These texts reach across cultural, historical and geographical contexts, though they assume different forms and emphases in different settings. Because Islamic texts can be interpreted and used in more than one way, and because there is no single Islamic position on sexual matters, it is appropriate to refer to things Muslims say and do in the name of their faith, sometimes with reference to Islamic texts, rather than to speak of the 'Islamic position' on a given subject. Of course not everyone is an Islamic scholar, and many individuals' knowledge and understandings are second-hand, taken from hearsay and teachings, from conversations in families and communities and from material in print and online such as marriage guidance booklets and websites.

Three norms stand out in the things young British Muslims say and write about sex and love, and the things they do. All three revolve around marriage: the

---

* This interlude draws upon the Qur'an (also spelled Quran and Koran) and *ahadith*, the plural of *hadith*. The Qur'an quoted in this interlude is the 1985 translation by Muhammad Taqî-ud-Din Al-Hilâlî and Muhammad Muhsin Khân. The Qur'an is divided into thirty parts (usually referred to by the Arabic term as *juz'*) and 114 Sûrah, each with a number and a name, which are further divided into verses (*ayat*). Quotations typically cite just the Sûrah number and name and the verse number, such as Sûrah 24 An-Nûr 30–31. *Ahadith* quoted in this interlude are taken from the website http://hadithcollection.com/about-hadith-books.html.

fundamental principle that every adult who can get married to a member of the opposite sex should do so; further, that they should consummate this marriage and enjoy sex within it – but only within it. This principle has three key dimensions: heteronormativity, homonegativity and premarital virginity. Surrounding and springing from these fundamental norms are a series of others, which are more specific. They include pressure to marry and have children at an early age; a communitarian approach to marriage; an emphasis on arranged marriage, typically within family and kinship groups and across transnational networks.

It would be wrong to generalize about norms that govern Muslims' sexual lives, even with the caveat that not all Muslims respect these norms all the time. There are two main reasons why the reality is more complicated. First, distinctions between permissible and impermissible sex and love are not set in stone; they vary. While Muslims tend to agree on the status of some acts and things – such as consuming pork and alcohol: both haram – many are less sure about other activities, including a variety of sexual and relationship practices. This leaves space for exegesis by individuals, peers, family and community members, as well as religious authority figures (Hasan 2002). Different people come to different conclusions about the relationship practices that are or are not permissible in their own lives, the lives of others around them as well as in wider Muslim communities.

A second reason not to overgeneralize or overstate the norms surrounding Muslims' sexual relationships is that religion does not exist in a vacuum, but is inflected with the culture and ethnicity of the different groups that practise it. Most British Muslims have heritage and some have personal and family histories that reach overseas, particularly to Pakistan and other South Asian nations and regions including Bangladesh and India, Mirpur and wider Azad Kashmir (Change Institute 2009; Office for National Statistics 2015; Peach 2006). Muslims who live in Britain and other Western countries also engage with the national cultures in which they form a minority (Savage 2004; Bakht 2008; Kabir 2005; Ramadan 2004). Their lives are inflected, albeit reactively and critically in some cases, by those wider societies. All this means that it can be difficult or impossible to disentangle religious from cultural attitudes and practices, such as arrangements for marriage and attitudes to dating and homosexuality. The point at which religion ends and culture begins is not always clear, and nor could it ever be since there is no single, unchanging Islamic culture. Rather, different cultures are Islamic in a panoply of ways. The same is true of individual Muslims, men and women who come to their own decisions about how to live their lives within the Islamic faith.

While British Muslims are culturally and geographically diverse, they are also religiously diverse, with further implications for the ways in which they approach sex and love. The largest single cultural grouping of British Muslims – those with Pakistani heritage – illustrates this religious diversity. The overwhelming majority of British Pakistani Muslims identify as Sunnis, though some others are Shias and Ahmadis (Change Institute 2009; Peach 2006). Sunni Muslims are also further striated, with Deobandi and Barelwi traditions (Peach 2006) and numerous movements including the Tablighi Jamaat, the Jamaat-e Islami and the Ahl-e-Hadith (Change Institute 2009: 39). Some of these internal distinctions have bearings upon marriage discourses and practices. For example, Marzia Balzani (2006) argues that Ahmadi Muslims are characterized by an unusually flexible approach to marriage, with distinctively high levels of tolerance towards exogamous and interethnic matches. These differences illustrate the broader point that there is no single Islamic approach to any aspect of sex or love, relationships or marriage.

Young Muslims are also changing their positions on the place of religion in their lives. In contrast with their parents' generation, who tended to identify with countries and places of origin (Calhoun 2005; Alexander 2000), many young Muslims are increasingly identifying *as Muslims* (Lewis 2007; Mondal 2008), or adopting hybrid identities in which religion is important (Dwyer 2000; Ahmad 2012). Through these actions and identifications, they are finding and asserting forms of agency (Franceschelli and O'Brien 2015: 696). Philip Lewis (2007) and Anshuman Mondal (2008) have both shown how, by embracing Islam, young people have been able to make and assert choices, in some cases rejecting cultural traditions and norms, in others managing to challenge parents while maintaining goodwill and respectability. Distancing themselves from cultural traditions and family expectations, these young people are clearing a space to make their own choices about sex and relationships (Mohammad 2015; Charsley 2005a, 2005b; Charsley and Bolognani 2017). As Pnina Werbner (2007: 171) puts it, 'Being observant Muslims empowers these young men and women with the right to choose their own marriage partners, even against the will of their parents.'

All this means that norms laid down through other people's definitions of the permissible and impermissible do not determine the beliefs and actions of all young Muslims. Only a tiny minority are unequivocally forced into particular sexual relationships and out of others. The vast majority have some say over what they do; they have, find and express agency in their sexual lives. In other words, to borrow a phrase from Sara Ahmed (2014), they have 'wiggle room'. Some manage to postpone or refuse marriage, finding methods for shaping decisions about whom and when to marry. Some – men more than women – get around prohibitions on premarital and extra-marital sex. In other cases, bending and breaking rules may compromise an individual's sense of themselves as Muslims or their ability to present themselves as such within their family or community. This is the case for some individuals who resist heteronormativity and homonegativity, entering into same-sex relationships; and others who explore sex outside marriage. But it would be a mistake to downplay these norms. They still have real power in the lives of young British Muslims.

Heteronormativity

'Compulsory heterosexuality', a term coined by the poet and feminist critic Adrienne Rich (1980), has two components: the affirmation of heterosexuality and the othering and prohibition of homosexuality. In the four decades that have passed since Rich's intervention, heteronormativity and homonegativity have been resisted on many fronts, not unsuccessfully. In Britain, mainstream politicians and establishment figures have belatedly acceded to demands that they recognize LGBTQ+ rights in almost everything from marriage to the military, with the effect that heterosexuality has become a little less compulsory in British society as a whole. Within Muslim communities, less has changed. As we saw in the interlude on stereotypes, variously liberal-identified and/or Islamophobic critics including journalists and politicians, many of whom are recent and probably insincere converts to the cause of minority sexuality rights, have seized upon this. They take the opportunity to portray Islam in a negative light and to advance sweeping generalizations about Muslims. Still, in the interests of a balanced picture, and in order to understand where young British Muslims are coming from when they speak about their sexual lives, it is important to acknowledge that heterosexuality is still effectively compulsory for many Muslims.

Heterosexuality is advocated largely through the proclamation of rules about straight marriage. These are rules that implicitly preclude homosexuality, which is also explicitly condemned. Asifa Siraj generalizes that 'with the exception of those who are physically or financially unable to get married, marriage is obligatory for all Muslims' (Siraj 2009: 43). Some Muslims stress the importance of implicitly heterosexual marriage in their lives and for their faith, and they explain and justify this position by quoting Islamic texts. Perhaps the most commonly quoted *hadith* on the subject teaches that '[w]hen a servant marries he fulfils half the religion; so let him be conscious of God regarding the other half' (Eaton 2008: 84). Others are familiar with Islamic teaching that prescribes marriage for all who can afford it: 'O young men, those among you who can support a wife should marry' (Sahih Muslim 2009). Men are advised that 'He created for you wives from among yourselves, that you may find repose in them, and He has put between you affection and mercy' (Sûrah Ar-Rûm 30: 21).

The marriage referred to here is fundamentally heterosexual and sexual. Islamic texts – quoted in marriage guidance literature that is given to young couples when they marry, as well as in books and articles that they may encounter elsewhere, including online and in face-to-face discussions – do not skim over this. Marriage is recommended because 'it restrains eyes (from casting evil glances) and preserves one from immorality' (Sahih Muslim 2009). In other words, it provides an approved channel for sexual desire.

These are just a few examples of the many references to heterosexual marriage that appear within Islamic texts. These texts are used in different ways and with different emphases, reflecting the understandings and priorities of those who are reading and citing them. Some present marriage as a religious obligation, some as a source of tranquillity, others as a source of legitimate sexual pleasure and still others as protection against the temptations of infidelity or homosexuality (Dialmy 2010). These teachings and sayings vary in important ways, which reveal the agency and priorities of those who express them. That said, they converge around a common position – advocating heterosexual marriage – that young Muslims in a wide variety of social, cultural and geographical settings will recognize. This pressure to marry is reflected in marriage statistics. Muslims in Britain have high rates of marriage and tend to marry young. Yet they are not simply conforming to religiously informed norms and ideals. Angela Dale and Sameera Ahmed (2010) argue that they are also responding to the pressure applied by family members, whose interests are not purely religious but are also social and economic, bound up with livelihood (in which strategic marriages are seen to strengthen family ties and economic allegiances) and the control of family members (Hélie and Hoodfar 2012).

The pressure to marry a member of the opposite sex is reflected across the stories we have collected, elicited and explored in this book, so much so that the book we planned to write about sexual relationships turned out to be largely a book about marriage and the ostensibly religious obligation to marry. Saamiya speaks of the life mapped out for her by her parents. This imagined future involved marriage in early adulthood – her mother suggested the mid-twenties as the best age for a wedding – followed by domestic work and child bearing: 'the things that come with it would be learning how to cook and clean and do the house chores, look after kids'. Saamiya is conscious of the expectations which family members heap upon her, but she does not see these as essentially or narrowly religious expectations. She also recognizes the power of family members and cultural traditions in mediating and enforcing marriage norms. When she ventures a criticism of marriage customs, her reference points are cultural rather than religious. She is turned off by 'how in Pakistan men have always been seen above women'. But it is not just the housework that concerns Saamiya, or the particular suitors at her door. Identifying as a lesbian, she does not want to marry a man at all.

Saamiya's reflexivity – her ability to see these demands for what they are and to respond to them on her own terms – indicates that at least some young Muslim individuals are trying to negotiate the pressures and expectations they face. Others are more transgressive. Given the intensity of the pressure to marry and have children, there is limited wiggle room here. For many young Muslims, this is restricted to postponing marriage, doing so on their own terms, and choosing to have children later on.

This could be changing, for some. Hassan observed 'a massive shift in attitudes' over the past generation, sensing that 'culturally eyebrows are raised when somebody is not getting married … but not as much as before'. For other individuals – but not very many – wiggle room means refusing to marry or pursuing pre- or non-marital relationships, which may or may not be heterosexual. In the course of this book, we have heard many stories by and about young Muslims who are finding ways to negotiate the timing and details of their otherwise orthodox marriages.

Navigating the principle that all those whose circumstances allow them to marry should do so, increasing numbers of young Muslims are seeking out ways to ensure that their circumstances do not allow them to marry, or not yet. Muslims of both sexes are extending their education and throwing themselves into demanding careers, which offer breathing room to live single lives (Bhopal 2009; Ahmad 2012). Parents have an economic interest in their sons' and daughters' education and careers (Ijaz and Abbas 2010: 318). They also tend to be aware of the freedom this avails, a freedom that may involve mixing with members of the opposite sex and perhaps experimenting sexually. In their research involving Mirpuri-heritage Muslims in the West Midlands, Aisha Ijaz and Tahir Abbas (2010: 319) found that many parents worry that, should they allow them to stay in education, their daughters might be 'corrupted by Western values' including (tolerance of) 'extramarital sex' and 'devaluation of the institution of marriage'.

Parents also know, and some come to accept, that single twenty-something sons and daughters are increasingly likely to find their own marriage partners. Even the most conventional among them – those who stay single and chaste before seeking to marry relatively young – find themselves negotiating the ways in which they marry, if not the fundamental parameters of marriage. Studying away from home, twenty-one-year-old Ifrah said that she wanted to move to 'the next stage' of her life. Ready to get married but living away from home, surrounded by her own circle of friends, she alluded to the possibility of finding her own husband. Speaking rather cautiously – switching to the second person – she continued: 'in this place where there is … so many different people, you might find someone'. Many parents are accepting or even welcoming these developments, conscious that the matchmaking customs that worked for them are no longer as effective (Ahmad 2012; Ouis 2007). Looking back on her own experiences, Aqeelah said she had found the *rishta* process had become 'inefficient in terms of meeting someone'. But she added that parents are becoming increasingly adaptable about the ways in which their daughters and sons meet and court prospective husbands and wives. She added that 'modern' arrangements can relieve parents of some of the onerous responsibility of making a match. Young people who play a proactive part, however small, in their own courtship practices do so for different reasons. Some women, many of whom are overtly and increasingly religious, have prolonged their education and started careers. They are taking greater responsibility for finding their own husbands, but many are finding it hard (Afshar, Aitken and Franks 2006: 180). Others, having rejected many of the men presented by their families earlier in life, are also having to take responsibility for finding their own husbands. Still-single men, who have been unwilling or unlucky in *rishtas*, are doing the same.

These young Muslims are interrogating the boundaries between religion and culture, claiming to revere marriage customs that are genuinely religious, and jettisoning those they see as cultural. Janan identified lazy assumptions about the age of marriage with 'the Asian community' rather than Muslims per se. Others alluded to customs that are common among British Muslims without being fundamentally Islamic, such as the tendency for entire families to get involved in decisions about who should marry whom. Recall the fictional dating gameshow in the *Halal Dating* animated film, discussed in the 'Meeting' chapter, in which suitors appeared with their whole families. Bilal, who designed this scene, explained that 'it's applicable to a lot of people, particularly, you know, Pakistani and Indian people'. His observation resonates with research showing that marriages, decided by extended families rather than couples alone, advance 'kinship connections and […] familial interests' rather than purely religious principles (Afshar, Aitken and Franks 2006: 180; see also Dale and Ahmed 2008). Though common among British Muslims, particularly those with South Asian heritage (Shaw 2000, 2001; Mohammad 2015; Qureshi, Charsley and Shaw 2014), these business-like marriages are not exclusive to Muslims, nor are they intrinsically Islamic; other British South Asians and South Asians practise them too (Charsley and Shaw 2006; Wood 2018). Here, at the very least, are grey areas in which religion and culture blur; opportunities for young Muslims to ascertain which norms they are prepared to accept and which they are not. Talking and speaking about – storying – marriage is a crucial part of this negotiation.

Young Muslims have the scope to negotiate their marriages because, although they are often pressed to marry, they are not forced, except in the rarest of cases. Most Muslim parents play a part in the arranged marriages of their sons and daughters. This takes different forms, but typically leaves the potential spouses with degrees of leeway to accept or reject a match. Researchers have identified at least four types of arranged marriage among British Muslims, in addition to other forms of marriage (Charsley and Shaw 2006; Shaw 2006). These range from the traditional arranged marriage whereby bride and groom have barely met before the wedding, to something akin to a love match where the prospective couple have met without supervision and the parents' role is confined to arranging the wedding festivities. Between these poles lie two other forms: semi-arranged marriages and love-cum-arranged marriages (Pande 2014). Young Muslims are increasingly finding their own husbands and wives and getting to know them before making a commitment, some through 'halal dating' (Ali et al. 2019), others through clandestine conventional dating (Bacchus 2017).

Not everyone who looks for a partner finds one; not everyone who looks is earnest about actually getting married; and not everyone is seriously looking, or open to marriage. While most Muslims marry members of the opposite sex, not all do. Some can't and others won't. Some form relationships with members of the same sex, of course, and like other same-sex couples in Britain, some of these get married – though sufficiently few for this to be treated as a headline-grabbing novelty in national newspapers (Dearden 2017). Still, for many or most if not quite all British Muslims, heterosexual marriage is all but compulsory. This is justified religiously, even though its drivers are also cultural, social and wrapped up in the financial wellbeing and power relations of families and kinship groups.

Homonegativity

The corollary of compulsory heterosexuality (in the form of marriage) is the marginalization of or negativity towards homosexuality. Some Muslims express difficulties with homosexuality, and many of those who hold such views provide religious reasons for this, some citing Islamic teachings and texts (Jamal 2001; Siraj 2009). Asifa Siraj (2009) found that there were still 'homonegative and heterosexist views' among the Muslims who participated in research that she conducted. She contextualizes these findings, stating that homosexuality is still understood to be sinful and not accepted where heterosexuality is promoted as 'normal' (51).

Similarly, Ibrahim Abraham stresses that 'queer Muslims' are adversely affected by heteronormativity within their families and communities (as well as within queer communities), arguing that 'for conservative Muslims a *queer* Muslim becomes the unviable subject' (Abraham 2009: 88–9; emphasis in original). All of this resonates with the ways in which the young people we interviewed, and those who participated in the storying workshops we ran, spoke about same-sex desire and relationships.

It may be more accurate to describe these positions as homonegative rather than homophobic, since they are sometimes justified with reference to religious texts, and with some attempt to engage their subject. The Qur'an, like the Old Testament of the Judeo-Christian tradition with which it shares so much, raises the issue of male homosexuality through the city of Sodom. The residents of Sodom – Sodomites – are condemned for their same-sex desire, which they express openly. Lot (or Lūt), the nephew of Abraham, warns the Sodomites (those who 'dwelt in the towns of Sodom in Palestine') (Sûrah 26 Ash-Shu'arâ 26: 160) as follows: 'Go you in unto the males of the 'Âlamîn (mankind), And leave those whom Allah has created for you to be your wives? Nay, you are a trespassing people!' (Sûrah Ash-Shu'arâ 26: 165–6). Whether or not individual Muslims know these particular verses, they underpin Islamic understandings of the morality of homosexuality (Jamal 2001; Habib 2009). These attitudes are echoed in various *ahadith* in which same-sex relationships are condemned, and in modern Islamic teachings in which they are forbidden (Jamal 2001). One *hadith* states that: 'If a man who is not married is seized committing sodomy, he will be stoned to death' (Abu Dawud 2009). Some Islamic scholars have made similar pronouncements, and these have been taken at face value by zealots, as for example in April 2019, when the Sultan of Brunei attempted to introduce what he presented as Islamic justice, in the form of stoning to death for homosexual acts (Tan 2019). The move was met with international condemnation, and the Sultan soon changed his mind (BBC 2019b).

Like other texts, these Qur'anic verses and chapters are read in more than one way, as are the *ahadith* that speak to the same subject. Religious texts do not speak for themselves; they must be read and mobilized. There are 'different understandings about the way Islam should be practiced' with a range of positions on homosexuality (Siraj 2009: 45). For example, each of the four Sunni schools of law come to their own conclusions (Siraj 2009). Whether for theological reasons or through personal judgements and values, some Muslims are more conservative than others, while some are more tolerant. Amreen Jamal observes that 'the morality of same-sex sexuality […] is a controversial topic that evokes differing views in Islam' (2001: 1).

Though contested, condemnations of homosexuality weigh heavily upon some young Muslims. Jamal (2001) identifies directives, widespread within Muslim communities, to resist same-sex desire, should it arise. He argues that abstinence is seen as a 'step in the right direction', leading to the rejection of homosexual identity (70). This disavowal of sex and ultimately sexual identity resonates with some of the stories young Muslims are telling and sharing. In the introduction to this book, we heard from Saamiya, an eighteen-year-old who identifies as a lesbian and lives in Glasgow, who has been spooked since childhood by a story she heard about 'two girls who are both Muslim got like caught holding hands, or just like kissing each other's cheek'. They were forcibly separated, one being 'sent off to Pakistan with her family'. Whether or not this actually happened, the tale had an undeniable impact upon Saamiya, illustrating the homonegativity bearing down upon her. The story also reminded us that Muslims do not have a monopoly over intolerance of sexual diversity. The two girls were attending a Catholic school, and their same-sex desire was punished and reported in the first instance by Christian rather than Muslim school authorities.

Not all Muslims take an equally hard line on this subject (Shannahan 2009). If some attempt to follow 'Islam's explicit condemnation of homosexuality' (Siraj 2009: 41) and harbour negative attitudes towards homosexuality and homosexuals, these tend to be the more 'conservative' individuals and traditions (Siraj 2009: 41). Not all Muslims can be described as either homophobic or homonegative. Many individuals express less conservative views on this subject, or demonstrate a pragmatic approach which involves living with desires, practices and relationships that may fall outside the ideals and teachings set out in religious texts. Siraj (2009) argues that same-sex relationships are more likely to be tolerated when they are discreet, kept out of the public eye. Those who would otherwise wish to identify as gay or lesbian may go along with this, finding ways to juggle seemingly contradictory dimensions of their lives (Yip 2004a, 2004b). This can mean saying one thing and doing another, or perhaps saying nothing at all, keeping their same-sex desires and relationships out of sight. (In this respect, as we go on to say, they have something in common with heterosexual Muslims, who also have to keep non-marital relationships in the closet and often struggle to do so.) As Andrew Yip (2004a) has shown, it may be possible to seal off contradictions between cultural and religious conventions on the one hand, and desires and lived experiences on the other. But this silence and secrecy can be experienced as damaging or compromising, so some other young Muslims are more open about their homosexuality. Some come out as gay or lesbian and introduce their partners to friends and family. These can prove difficult experiences, damaging to some and alienating to others. The range of experiences conveyed in conversations, creative writing and literature illustrate the very real if not universally insurmountable homonegativity that Muslims encounter. They come across this homonegativity variously in their communities, families and, perhaps most challenging of all, their own religiously informed consciences. An increasing number of young people are open and political, identifying as queer Muslims, asserting both their sexuality and their religion (Rouhani 2007).

It would be remiss of us to ignore condemnations of homosexuality put forward by those who claim to speak in the name of Islam, or to fail to acknowledge the effects of these censorious words and deeds. That said, it is also important to recognize the ways in which many young Muslims are picking their own paths through thorny ground. Having expressed her anxieties about coming out as a lesbian, Saamiya was pleasantly surprised by the ways in which some of her Muslims friends reacted:

But at first when I realized it, I didn't really know that there was an actual label for it, until one of my best friends came out as bisexual. And I came out in fourth year, so I think I was roughly fifteen maybe at that time. And all my friends were really supportive of me, and there were some Muslim friends that didn't quite agree with it, they did give me a lot of hate, but I had some other Muslim friends that did stick up for me.

Similarly, when Yusuf confided in an Imam, 'a guy who was at the heart of the kind of Muslim establishment', he felt supported rather than judged. 'He was far more understanding of it' than Yusuf had expected. 'He's never going to accept all the sexuality', Yusuf reflected, but he showed compassion and understanding: 'he didn't turn round' and judge or condemn.

Alongside these examples are many others: of happy, sexually and emotionally fulfilled gay and lesbian Muslims; of others, rejected by their families and communities; and others still, who have not reconciled their faith with their desires and relationships. Some repress their sexuality or attempt abstinence, whereas others embrace their sexuality but move away from their faith (Jaspal and Cinnirella 2010). These realities make the broader point that homonegativity is a fact of life for many but not all young Muslims.

Virginity and premarital chastity

Most Muslims attach great importance to chastity (linked to modesty) before marriage, and to fidelity within marriage. This precludes sexual encounters outside marriage: homosexuality, as discussed above, and pre-, extra- and non-marital sex of any form, gay or straight.

Most young Muslims understand that, as nineteen-year-old Khadija put it to us, 'sex before marriage is forbidden in Islam'. This principle is set out in numerous verses and *ahadith*, which elaborate on the fundamental precept, introduced above, that sex should take place exclusively within heterosexual marriage. As one *hadith* on marriage puts it, 'sexual intercourse' outside of marriage is 'illegal' (Sahih Bukhari 2009).

Despite its religious undergirding, the virginity principle takes different forms in specific times and places. Perhaps the most important social and cultural twist is in its differential application to men and women. Though this religious principle applies to both men and women, in practice it is directed more forcefully at the latter in many Muslim families and communities (Ahmad 2001, 2012; Ouis 2007; Eşsizoğlu et al. 2011). Nazia puts this succinctly: 'Good girls bleed'. She elaborates in her blog piece:

> The bride knows her responsibility; it's been drummed into her as long as she can remember: blood. Good girls bleed. They avoided horse riding, gymnastics and tampons their whole life. Blood is proof of their honour, validation that their family raised them well.

In this context Deniz Kandiyoti's notion of the patriarchal bargain is useful for understanding the heightened pressure experienced by women. Kandiyoti argues in her essay 'Bargaining with Patriarchy' that what she calls classic patriarchy relies on an agreement of 'protection in exchange for submissiveness and propriety' (1988: 283). This pressure is social and cultural rather than specifically religious, though it does intersect with religions including Islam. Young Muslim women speak of the compulsions they are under, not only to refrain from premarital intercourse, but to perform premarital virginity. This involves a delicate balancing act between innocence, interest (in marriage with a man, but not in men generally and nor with women) and readiness (despite a complete lack of preparation) for the sex she is expected to engage in on her wedding night. Contributing to a discussion in a blogging workshop, Nazia spoke of the 'Oscar-worthy performance' she was expected to deliver throughout her premarital period as an assumed virgin and ultimately on her wedding night. Whereas Nazia gives the impression of putting on a display of sexual innocence, others are more genuinely demure about this subject, reluctant even to allude to it. Aliya, twenty-four, cannot quite bring herself to mention what it is she is not talking about:

> I find that a lot of Muslims might shy away from certain elements, talking about certain elements when it comes to explaining your standing on Muslims. I think maybe with time – but that's what you can say with any issue I think.

It is not only women who dance around subjects and project themselves as virginal ingénues. Hassan speaks of a 'taboo discussing relationships: you are not meant to have them, so why should you talk about them'. Therefore if women have to become adept at amateur dramatics, men labour under more reticent rules, summed up by the phrase 'don't ask, don't tell'.

Though young Muslim men are also taught to save sex for marriage, they are under less pressure to do so, as Janan explained. She told us that while her 'dad, from a religious point of view, didn't want' any of his offspring having 'pre-marriage relationships', he exerted greater pressure on his daughters because of the potential impact on their chances of getting married if they lost their virginity before the wedding day. This resonates with Margaret Abraham's conclusion that some Muslim men are merely 'discouraged from being sexually active prior to marriage' (1999: 597) and Shaw's observation that British Pakistani Muslim men have more freedom than their female counterparts do to 'socialize before marriage' (2001: 330), exposing them to sexual opportunities.

The emphasis upon the premarital chastity of women and the relative indifference to that of men is cultural rather than religious. Tellingly, when these young British Muslims speak about this, they speak more about family and culture than religion. Saamiya alluded to the multiple and sometimes conflicting expectations about whether and how she should maintain her virginity until her wedding night, speaking of 'expectations from our friends, from our family, from our neighbours, from pretty much anyone you meet'. The virginity of unmarried women is fundamental to the 'honour' and fundamental respectability of the family (Khan 2012: 4). Establishing the purity of bodies and bloodlines, virginity underpins the status and livelihood of the family (Abboud, Jemmott and Sommers 2015; see also Amer, Howarth and Sen 2015; Buitelaar 2002; El Feki 2013). Honour is not simply a matter of enforcing religious principles; it revolves around the 'control of female sexuality' in the interests of 'patriarchal authority' (Abraham 1999: 596). In such systemic arrangements, men typically act as the 'protectors' of family honour (Khan 2012: 83; see also Charsley and Liversage 2015). The regulation of women's sexuality within honour cultures, diverse and complex as they are, is beyond the scope of this chapter. The important point about honour to establish here is that the sexual attitudes and practices of young Muslims – including their premarital virginity – are not purely religious matters. They are also embedded within social and cultural contexts, and vary across place and time. As such, honour is also subject to the judgement of individuals, who may arrive at different understandings of and positions on the importance and meaning of premarital virginity for Muslim men and women.

Thus, rather than unquestioningly or blindly following religious rules about premarital virginity, Muslim men and women are making their own assessments of what is right for themselves and others. For some women, the 'Oscar-worthy performance' of virginity is just that: a way of keeping up appearances. Single Muslim women who are sexually active tend to be circumspect, cultivating a virginal image within the family and community (Bacchus 2017). Meanwhile some men, recognizing that they might be more able to get away with premarital liaisons and experiments than their female counterparts, are making decisions about whether doing so would be right for them. Haris, in a discussion during a creative writing workshop, acknowledged that he was not expected to prove his sexual innocence when he married. He admitted that he had had a sexual relationship before he got married, though he said he would not advise others to do the same. His reason, expressed hypothetically, was that sex within marriage might not be so good, and this dissatisfaction might undermine the marriage itself.

Most young Muslims recognize the religious principle that, whether or not they live up to this ideal themselves, sex should be saved for marriage. But many find ways to work with and around this principle by exploring the age-old question: how far can you go? In other words, they seek to explore sexual possibilities within the bounds of the religiously permissible. Some are questioning assumptions about what is and is not permissible. As we have underscored throughout this interlude, there is no single way of being a Muslim and, like any other religious texts, the Qur'an and the *ahadith* can be interpreted in different ways. These young people are coming up with different answers to the question of how far a Muslim can go. In so doing, they are coming to their own conclusions, if not about premarital intercourse, which most see as haram, then about the question of what if any premarital relationships may be permissible.

Conclusion: *Constrained* and *enabled*

Focusing upon things that Muslims learn they must do, and others that they must not, this interlude might appear to tell a story of coercion and compulsion. This would be a deceptive assumption, though, for many if not all of the participants in this project. The norms described here – heteronormativity, homonegativity and virginity before marriage – present formidable stumbling blocks to some people, to be sure. But, for those who can be happy within a heterosexual marriage, they are not so forbidding. On the contrary, they open doors to sexual expression and fulfilment.

Verses and *ahadith* on sex within marriage do not simply instruct couples to have sex; they offer guidance on the joys of sexual experimentation and of being a heterosexual man or woman. Numerous *ahadith* present sex within marriage as a source of pleasure, and one that comes with rights and responsibilities, which include a husband's duty to ensure his wife's satisfaction before his own, her duty to reciprocate and guidance for both to be faithful (Maqsood 1994; see also Dialmy 2010: 4). Many Muslims are taught to channel rather than suppress their sexuality, such that they present a modest face in public and among strangers, being sure to avoid sending out sexually suggestive messages. Both men and women are guided towards appropriate ways of seeing and being seen:

> Tell the believing men to lower their gaze (from looking at forbidden things), and protect their private parts (from illegal sexual acts, etc.). That is purer for them. Verily, Allah is All-Aware of what they do. And tell the believing women to lower their gaze (from looking at forbidden things), and protect their private parts (from illegal sexual acts, etc.) and not to show off their adornment except only that which is apparent (like palms of hands or one eye or both eyes for necessity to see the way, or outer dress like veil, gloves, head-cover, apron, etc.), and to draw their veils all over Juyubihinna (i.e. their bodies, faces, necks and bosoms, etc.).
>
> (Sûrah An-Nûr 24: 30–1)

This is not to say that Muslims should never present themselves sexually, only that they should be vigilant about where and when they do so. This leaves quite a large circle including extended family among whom it is acceptable to present a more revealing face. Women are guided 'not to reveal their adornment except to their husbands, their fathers, their husband's fathers, their sons, their husbands' sons, their brothers or brother's sons, or their sisters' sons, or their (Muslim) women (i.e. their sisters in Islâm)' (Sûrah An-Nûr 24: 31).

The joys of (heterosexual, marital) sex and sexuality, as they are described here, clash with the stereotypes described in the previous interlude, in which Muslims are portrayed as unhappy in marriage and unfulfilled in the bedroom. Moreover, these joys are real, according to some recent writing by and about Muslim women and men (Mattu and Maznavi 2012). And while the sexual norms experienced by young Muslims should not simply be seen as constraints, nor should they be seen as absolutes, inflexible rules they must simply follow. In this chapter, we have seen that young Muslims are finding and making choices about how to live their sexual lives, while remaining true to their religious principles and largely respecting the norms of their religious communities. Though elements of the norms discussed here are powerful and far-reaching – above all the pressure to marry and to refrain from pre-, extra- and non-marital sex, gay and straight – young people are also finding 'wiggle room' in which to make choices and decide how they wish to live. They are exploring different ways of getting and being married and of postponing and rejecting marriage (Daneshpour and Fathi 2016; Ouis 2007).

So, while young British Muslim women and men do some things differently – compared with others in society: those of other faiths and none – their stories are not dominated by restraint or compulsion. They do experience pressures that others do not – the pressures of heteronormativity, homonegativity and premarital virginity – and alongside these pressures they also experience exhilaration and contentment and make important choices.

Table I3.1 Interviews quoted in Interlude 3, '(Not so) different'

Name	Gender	Age	Relationship Status	Location
Saamiya	Female	18	Single	Glasgow
Ifrah	Female	21	Single	Yorkshire
Janan	Female	30	Married	Glasgow
Hiba	Female	27	Married	Glasgow
Aqeelah	Female	29	Single	Glasgow
Yusuf	Male	22	Single	Yorkshire
Aliya	Female	24	Married	Newcastle
Hassan	Male	29	Single	Yorkshire
Zarah	Female	23	Single	Yorkshire

Table I3.2 Workshop participants and convenors quoted in Interlude 3, '(Not so) different'

Name	Gender	Age	Workshop Series	Role in Workshop	Title
Bilal	Male	22	1. Animation, Sheffield	Participant	Focus group discussion
Haris	Male	25	7. Fiction, Rochdale	Participant	Post-workshop interview
Nazia	Female	Not stated	6. Blogging, Glasgow	Participant	'The First Time'

Chapter 7

SEX

The dream man, the dream proposal, the dream dress. Expectations look and feel different for every couple around the globe but one expectation rings true for each couple: sex.
(Nazia, age not given, blog post, 'The First Time')

I'm talking about sex. When was the last time? Do you even remember?
(Taibah, thirty-six, untitled play)

Sex is a topic that many people find difficult to speak and write about, provoking feelings of shyness, awkwardness and embarrassment. For young Muslims, speaking and writing about sex means not only overcoming their own self-consciousness but also – as discussed in the previous interludes – challenging assumptions about sexual otherness, explicitly or implicitly. While some speak of sex as strictly off-limits until marriage, others are more candid about sexual desires, frustrations and experiences with partners and spouses. Some young Muslims feel ill-prepared for and intimidated by thoughts of their first time, while others are more open to claims that sex need not be a taboo. High-profile published novels such as Hanif Kureishi's *The Black Album* (1996/1995) offer detailed accounts of sex, some inflected with quintessentially Muslim experiences. Similarly, Kamila Shamsie's *Home Fire* (2017) contains a memorable scene in which nineteen-year-old Londoner Aneeka has sex with Eamonn, a Pakistani-Irish-American Londoner she has just met. Controversially, she continues to wear her hijab while naked with him and prays soon afterwards. Shamsie shows that beneath the veil a Muslim woman may well be far from the sexually repressed virgin/mother of stereotype.

'Obviously no touching, no kissing'

Sex and physical intimacy before marriage are typically considered, in the words of one of our interviewees, 'a very big no-no, Islamically speaking'. Ifrah was describing a conflict, as she saw it, between Islamic values and the Western idea that 'typical dating' involves 'two people going out, and then [getting] physically intimate as well at some point'. For her, sex is simply out of the question when young Muslims are dating: 'you are not going to hold hands, you are not going to do anything like that – at least, not until you are married'. With similar restraint, Waheed said: 'In our culture sex is forbidden before marriage. So obviously we don't get married until we are a bit older, so we don't really think about it until the time comes maybe.' This highlights the extent to which sex can be perceived as a taboo topic among young Muslims, something they would prefer not to think and talk about, at least not with our researcher.

Others were franker, acknowledging sexual desires that can be difficult not to act upon. Khadija felt that it is best to avoid premarital relationships altogether to obviate temptation:

> Obviously like relationships before marriage, you don't know what it would lead to. Obviously sex before marriage is forbidden in Islam, so obviously you don't know, you're in love with someone so deeply like you could commit the crime and like wouldn't realize it.

Khadija says 'obviously' a lot, evoking what she perceives to be common knowledge – that premarital sex is a 'crime' and that it is wrong to let passion get the better of you. Hassan similarly spoke of a clash between the Islamic ideal of abstention before marriage and what happens when young people date, observing: 'in an ideal world like you would go out but there wouldn't be any like touching, kissing, anything sexual in an ideal world. But again that doesn't happen'. Like Ifrah, he reflected on the difficulty of upholding 'Islamic values' in a society where being sexually active is a compelling social norm:

> They are just harder to follow if you are the only one who wants to follow those principles and other people don't. Do you know what I mean? That is difficult. And also like, you know it is kind of what is socially acceptable, what is the social norm in this day and age. So it is kind of, there are those challenges and it is easier to follow like British social norms as opposed to Islamic values. But just because we are following British social norms, it doesn't mean that those values, Islamic values, don't mean anything to us.

Here, Hassan speaks candidly of his struggle in navigating his British and Islamic identity and his anxiety about what is 'socially acceptable' for a young man of nineteen. These stories highlight how young British Muslims may feel both under pressure to be chaste and to be sexually active in different social contexts. In these accounts, religion and sex are in binary opposition, a theme that is also explored Hanif Kureishi's novel *The Black Album*, to which we now turn.

'The total effect of a Prince concert': Sex and secularity in The Black Album

Kureishi's second novel *The Black Album* (1996/1995), arguably his most didactic one, pivots on the eventful end of the 1980s in Britain that witnessed, among other things, reaction to the 1989 fatwa against Salman Rushdie's *The Satanic Verses* (1998/1988). The novel revolves around a tension between a spectrum of conflicting ideas – with secularism, hybridity and multiculturalism at one end and structural racism and extreme political Islam at the other. The air of uneasy transition that characterized the year 1989 unfolds via the Bildungsroman of a British Pakistani man, Shahid, who finds himself caught between clashing ideas of Islamic fundamentalism and Western liberalism, wavering between them and exploring both. While his brother Chili's 'relentless passion had always been for clothes, girls, cars, girls and the money that brought them' (41), Shahid is indecisive and impressionable. He is searching for some kind of validation of his identities, at once racial, sexual and literary (Shahid is an aspiring writer). While he feels drawn to charismatic fellow student Riaz and his anti-racist, community-oriented values, he is simultaneously attracted – in both the intellectual and sexual sense – to his Cultural Studies lecturer. This woman, Deedee Osgood, introduces him to the promise of free, uninhibited individualism.

The novel abounds in passages describing – often in quite graphic terms – Shahid's sexual acts with and fantasies about Deedee. When Shahid first meets Deedee, he is immediately beguiled by her sensual presence, which is represented in both visual and aural terms:

> He had, so far, successfully kept his eyes averted from her breasts and legs. But the whole eloquent movement – what amounted in that room to an erotic landslide of rustling and hissing – was so sensational and almost provided the total effect of a Prince concert that his mind took off into a scenario about how he might be able to tape-record the whisper of her legs, copy it, add a backbeat and play it through his headphones.
>
> (26)

The hyperbolically humorous image of an 'erotic landslide' conveys the extent of Shahid's sexual excitement. The comparison of Deedee's arousing susurrus to the music of Prince, whose album gives the novel its title, reinforces the idea that for Shahid, this woman holds out the promise of a pleasure not unlike the euphoria experienced at a pop concert.

While Shahid is awed by his friend Riaz's confident demeanour – his strict ideological and sexual boundaries – there is always within him an opposite and more powerful pull towards Deedee, who promises transgression of all such boundaries. In the initial meetings between them, Deedee is always described from Shahid's perspective in physical terms and with strong sensory resonances (see Chambers 2019: 41–68). For example, during the exciting honeymoon phase of their relationships, 'Shahid lingered a moment, thinking how brilliant she looked in her short skirt and wide-lapelled jacket, under which she wore a black bra' (55). Although Kureishi sets *The Black Album* up as a novel of ideas, the verve and glee with which he describes 'sex and secularity' (Kureishi 2011: 242) leaves little room for doubt as to which side of the argument he is on.

Shahid's affair with Deedee entails discussions about literature and music, as well as experiments with drug and sex. While physicality is the dominant feature of their connection, the bond also carries a cerebral aspect. Shahid's unbridled sexual experience with Deedee and drug-taking induces a trance-like state within his psyche: 'He could have slept but knew when he woke up life would be banal. Why did Deedee have to go? [...] Why hadn't he been able to ask his teacher to spend the night with him after such a high time in the swimming pool of dreams?' (65). Experiments with narcotics, sex and clubbing create an alternative nocturnal world for Shahid, starkly contrasting with his mundane daily life.

As Shahid fantasizes about Deedee, his sexual dependence on her becomes stronger. The following passage outlines his fantasies about submission and domination as he waits for her to arrive:

> [H]e [...] extract[ed] his dick and tr[ied] to stroke it in into shape. (Soon she would be there; he would lift her clothes up and lie next to her; in the morning they would go to college: lovers.) [...] [S]he was waking him! He stirred as she pulled him into her arms, warm as mother, where he dissolved.
>
> (65–6)

The extract opens with unashamed details of sexual acts and ends on a different, psychoanalytical or even incestuous note, when Kureishi uses maternal imagery to infer Shahid's complete surrender to Deedee.

Sexual pleasure serves to ignite Shahid's literary imagination. His experience with Deedee – physical, intellectual and a curious blend of both – imbues him with a creative energy: 'His typing fingers, sensing Deedee's body beneath them, danced on the keys too euphorically for the subject matter. He told himself that concentration was the cornerstone of creativity. He pulled himself together, but got an erection which just wouldn't go away' (76). Here we see a convergence of sexuality and literary creativity: the pen as phallus. Whereas the celibate religious leader Riaz is depicted as trying his hand at poetry but only producing clichéd and unimaginative verse, Shahid's literary powers expand and develop as he gains a wider range of sexual experience. This novel, with its unabashed delight in sexual scenes and imagery, offers a contrasting perspective to the more hesitant and shy accounts of sex from young Muslim interviewees.

'My mum left Mills and Boon books out'

How families talk – or fail to talk – about sex can either serve to reinforce or break taboos. Hanifa was amused by her mum's efforts to broach the subject with her as a pre-teen, describing the older woman's reservedly British approach of leaving popular romance novels around the house:

> My mum used to read Mills and Boon and it was the same in some of my aunties' households. They would have them lying around and so mum would be like 'Don't read that, it is rubbish'. And obviously I would read it ... And she says

that she left those Mills and Boon books out because she knew I would want to read them, because that is what her mum did. So I guess through that they have inadvertently given me a sex book.

These books were not particularly sexy – alluding euphemistically to sex rather than presenting it graphically – but they helped Hanifa make sense of her first crush. This story neatly encapsulates the awkwardness that parents may feel in talking to their children about sex, wanting to raise the subject but feeling unable to do so outright, and thus reinforcing norms of secrecy and discretion.

Safa, married in her early twenties, recalled how her family's silence on the subject of sex left her wholly unprepared as a new bride. She spoke of her anger and frustration with the older women in her family for not having offered advice or reassurance about first-time sex:

> My aunts are so close to me, but no one said that this is what you need to expect, and this is how it is. No one gave me that pep talk and just, well, what did you do? [...] and I was like: Mum, you knew all this. And my mum was like, 'That is all right, it took me a week to get used to things'. And I was like, that is not the answer to my question.

This story emphasizes the intergenerational transfer of the idea of sex as a taboo, with Safa's mum embarrassed and dodging questions with the defensive euphemism that she too had to 'get used to things' as a virgin bride. Hoping to avoid a repeat of her own sexual naivety, Safa believed it should be 'acceptable' to talk about sex, and plans to do so if she has children of her own: 'if I had a daughter, there is no way I would have let her go like that'.

Of course, it may be young people themselves who feel unprepared for frank conversations with their parents. Salim said he feels uncomfortable when he is watching TV with his family and sex or sexuality comes up as part of the storyline: 'watching anything like that with your parents, you don't want to'. In these awkward moments, he finds himself gauging his mum's reaction: 'I am trying to see – you know how she reacts to it and the fact that she never said anything negative at all, or anything I can remember, [...] perhaps I am underestimating her.' Unwilling or unable to discuss such issues openly, and having made assumptions that he will be met with socially conservative attitudes, Salim is trying to glean clues about his mother's views on and acceptance of modern sexual practices.

Aliya was far more upfront, arguing that there should be 'no shyness when it comes to seeking knowledge for the sake of God', including knowledge about sex. However, she observed that some of her peers do not share this view and get 'embarrassed' when parents bring it up. She offered the example of a Pakistani Muslim friend whose dad 'will openly talk to them about relationships and sexual relationships and stuff and boyfriends'. This advice comes much to his daughter's mortification: 'She was like "Whoa, my dad's talking to me about stuff like this and I'm like whoa, Dad, what are you doing?"' This story illustrates that premarital sexual relationships are not a taboo in every Muslim family, and that some Muslim parents are open to discussing these issues – whether or not their children want them to!

'Everyone thinks about sex'

While lack of premarital sex and frustrated desires are the subject of some conversations, others were more positive about not having sex, or not yet. In some instances, religious and cultural norms provide a welcome licence for not having sex that young Muslims are either unready for or not keen to have. Zohaib, a teenager we encountered in the 'Speaking to Stereotypes' interlude, readily acknowledged his virginity: 'I haven't had full sex but if I wanted to I could [...] I couldn't do it like with randomers'. Here, he expresses an aversion to casual sex, a lack of desire to have 'full sex' yet, rather than bemoaning any lack of opportunity. Bilal described his views on sex as somewhere in between his family's rule of 'no relationships at all' and the laidback attitudes of many of his peers who are in 'what I would call loose relationships'. While Bilal is 'completely fine' with people who prefer casual dating and sex, he reflected that for him personally, 'it has never been something that I am comfortable [with]'.

Others, while sharing the aspiration of sex within the confines of a loving relationship, resented having to hold back. Khadija, whom we heard from earlier in this chapter, avoids relationships to ensure she abstains from physical intimacy:

> If you have got a boyfriend and a girlfriend it is going to happen, and then – you know the sexual relationship, you are going to find each other attractive, it is not as if you are not going to even kiss or hold hands. And then when you do that, you hug them and stuff and then it turns into something else, and you are like 'Oh God, we were not supposed to do that! We won't next time.' But you can't help it if you do find them attractive.

This is a candid admission of sexual desire, evasive in its use of the second person as to whether Khadija has acted on these impulses. The young woman admitted to struggling with the Islamic ideal of chastity before marriage and a longing that she 'can't help', her choice of words suggesting an inevitability that young people will act on sexual impulses.

Hanifa described her long-standing curiosity about sex, from pre-teen school crushes to the now sharp interest of a sexually mature twenty-something. She spoke of her eagerness to get married soon in order to be sexually fulfilled:

> It is difficult not to have had any kind of intimacy with anyone for even kind of this long. Like it is hard. Everyone thinks about sex, everyone starts like starts getting interested in it. But I have been interested in it for ages, and to not have, to not have anyone is difficult.

She felt that, in the long run, having a sexual partner is essential 'for like my own mental health'. Elaborating on this desire, she said: 'I think that partners are a gift ... because obviously you could have sex with yourself, but I don't think it's going to be the same!' Hanifa laughed at this last observation, perhaps self-consciously at her frankness and inexperience, nonetheless offering a poignant commentary on the importance of intimacy in people's lives.

'Sex, lust, desire'

Hanifa spoke more directly about sex. In a creative writing exercise at a men's writing workshop in Glasgow, Adam listed the key ingredients for his short story as 'Sex, lust, desire. Young, naive, interested, excitable [...] and out on the "pull"'. Here, flirtation and lust are portrayed as a natural impulses for young people finding their way to adulthood. Azeem, who is gay, presented himself as more sexually experienced than his friends, describing himself as 'a bit more experimental with a few more' partners. He explained that in his first year of university, casual sex was important in affirming his identity and offered solace when he initially struggled to make friends: 'I was going and using these dating apps and websites and things, just to have somebody to talk to sometimes and just to have you know sex as well.' He now looks back on this period as a time of 'clearing my mind that I wanted to kind of engage with my sexuality in another way than just getting drunk and having sex'. Dissatisfaction eventually led him to go out and making friends on the gay scene who 'helped me learn to be more comfortable with it'. Azeem talks about sex without shame in a matter-of-fact way, describing how intimacy can be a validation and comfort, sometimes about fleeting moments of companionship rather than a romantic connection.

Others wrote about sexual desire – and sometimes its lack – within marriage. At a blogging workshop at Glasgow Women's Library, Zarina decided to research and write about anal sex, a subject that can 'raise a few eyebrows'. In her blog post, she explained that she chose the topic because 'I might eventually come across this issue at some point in my marriage', confessing that this 'fetish' is 'something which I find puzzling yet also a bit titillating'. While noting that Islam is not the only religion to treat anal sex as a taboo, Zarina is interested in what Islamic scholars have to say about it 'as someone who identifies as a Muslim first and foremost'. She notes that while some forbid the act, others argue that 'man and wife are permitted to derive all kinds of sexual pleasures from one another. Seems legit. [...] My advice, make sure you're following the right sheikh ;)'. In a later passage, she again turns to Islam to assert the importance of active consent:

> [A]nal is permissible as long as the wife 'consents', probably the most important word when we discuss any kind of sexual activity, what a profound meaning it has. I would say with the growing popularity of anal sex in the West (and let's be honest probably all over the world) many women would feel under pressure to oblige with their partners' requests. So can we really say they are truly and wholeheartedly consenting? Is there real excitement and anticipation for the actual act or is it just a selfless lover merely giving into their partner's desires? Does the pleasure overcome the pain? Are we looking forward to the Sunday morning tumble or are we dreading it?

In this blog, Zarina comes across as apprehensive at first, but her confidence grows as she speaks of sexual experimentation, knowing each other's kinks and respecting each other's boundaries within marriage, offering a bold defence of sexual agency.

A less positive view of sex within marriage emerges in Taibah's untitled play, also written at a workshop at Glasgow Women's Library. The play focuses on Harris and Aliza, whom we first met as young lovers in the dating chapter. The play's early scenes show Harris's attempts to woo an initially sceptical Aliza. It then jumps to a scene three years later, in which the unhappy husband and wife argue about Harris's partying and Aliza's newfound piety following a miscarriage:

> Harris: Pfft. I have needs, Aliza. Ever since you took on that hijab and praying all Godly hours of the day. You –
> Aliza: What on earth are you talking about? What needs?
> Harris: Sex, Aliza. I'm talking about sex. When was the last time? Do you even remember?
> Aliza: What on earth. Ramadan just went by.
> Harris: People do have sex during Ramadan. It's allowed you know. When you're not fasting.
> *Beat*
> Aliza: Hold on a second. What's sex got to do with you coming home at 12 at night?!
> Harris: It's got everything to do with me coming home late at night. God damn it. Why should I come home early? To what? You the Hijabi Nun. I don't even want to look at you any more.

By juxtaposing Harris and Aliza's early courtship with this tense exchange, Taibah demonstrates that the initial spark of sexual attraction can fizzle out after marriage, eroded by life's banalities and, in this case, shared trauma. In a closing soliloquy, Aliza confesses that she used to feel uncomfortable around Harris and his friends: 'He loved that he could flaunt me around with him like his trophy wife. He always had that "cat got the cream" look on his face […]. I never liked the ogling. I never liked the smirks and the eyeing-up.' She takes solace in her hijab as 'a piece of cloth that draws a boundary', angry at his rejection of her without makeup and fashionable clothes. Ultimately, she retreats from him sexually as she senses his lack of desire for her.

'Ready for the big night'

For those who refrain from premarital sex, the wedding night and early days of marriage may be unnerving, particularly when both partners lack experience. In a blog post entitled 'How To Be a Man', Nazia imagines the 'big night' from the perspective of an anxious groom:

> He has a long day peppered with many a guy conversation asking if he's 'ready for the big night'. Penis enlargement apparatus, pills to help you get it up or keep it up are all common gifts exchanged between friends in the runup to the wedding. Many a well-meaning tip is passed on; in a world of lacklustre Muslim

sex education and violent mainstream porn the first-time groom feels nervous, exhausted and even afraid of this new found 'manly' act he is supposed to perform. He's not sure how to kiss her, so he doesn't. He's not sure how to touch her first, so he doesn't. He's not sure how to please her, so he doesn't. He's not sure how to last, so he doesn't. Hardly the first time he dreamt of.

This story highlights how a dearth of opportunities to discuss sex may be detrimental to a quality sex life. Also stressed is the gap between high expectations and the awkward reality of first-time sex. Nazia also explores what sexual anxiety might feel like from a male perspective, with all the anxieties around having to make the first move.

Safa explained how, on her wedding night, she was utterly daunted at the prospect of being intimate with her new husband because she had no idea what to expect:

> I don't understand how you can like know someone for like, like you have just had your *niqah* [wedding ceremony] and you can be intimate with them … I found it really difficult, because obviously when you are faced with the situation you don't know what to do. I actually didn't I was oh God, I was like I can't believe … Because I have not even been in a relationship, I have not even spoken to a guy like in a different way or anything like that and stuff. So it was quite difficult for me. I found it really hard, and very off-putting. And I said it to my husband, I was like, 'Oh no, I just want to go home.'

This account is touching in its naivety and honesty, illustrating that some young Muslims may not feel ready for sex at the point of marriage, nor necessarily have a positive first experience. In the 'Married' chapter, Safa described her relationship with her husband – a distant cousin with whom she had an arranged marriage – on good terms, whilst acknowledging that they were both 'shy' at first. Here, she draws attention to the abrupt transition from not dating before marriage or spending time alone with men, to living and sleeping with one.

For young Muslim women who wear modest dress, the prospect of undressing for the wedding night can be a source of anxiety. Esha spoke of a younger cousin who, ahead of her upcoming marriage, is 'really scared' about this:

> She is really scared, she is really self-conscious about her body and she is just not a very cuddly, sexual kind of a person. Um, so she is, just feels like it is going to be really awkward. And I was saying to her, it is different you know when you have always been covered up and it is your first partner and you are married to them and you know that there [are] expectations and you know young girls, and I don't know maybe old girls as well, have this thing, okay he is going to want to see me naked and how am I going to go about that.

Some of this anxiety relates specifically to religion and culture – the prospect of removing her hijab and clothes in front of a man for the first time. There are also, however, elements of body-consciousness and worries about intimacy as a person who does not enjoy being tactile or 'cuddly'. Esha, who was a virgin herself when she married, has been trying to offer her cousin reassurance, drawing on her own experience of exploring sex with her husband:

> I was just explaining to her to that you don't really just walk in naked. You just take things slowly and you do what you are comfortable with. […] I am open sharing things like – we talk about everything. So if there is anything we are uncomfortable with or feeling really shy to do let's keep the light off or, you know things like that … You sort of work out together what to do.

In contrast to Safa's story of feeling clueless about what to expect, Esha's account underscores the importance of peer support among young Muslims in preparing for first-time sex, and of communication between husband and wife. Like Safa, she acknowledges that sex can be 'awkward' and that newly married couples can feel 'uncomfortable' and 'shy', but suggests that it is best to talk through these feelings.

From these stories of shy and hesitant newlyweds, we turn to a contrasting example from published literature where piety and religiosity meet with sexual boldness.

'A world other than that of bodies and senses': Sex and religion in Home Fire

Winner of the Women's Prize for Fiction in 2018, Kamila Shamsie's acclaimed novel *Home Fire* (2017) takes its inspiration from Sophocles's *Antigone* to narrate a tragedy borne out of our ruthlessly violent post-9/11, post-Arab Uprisings era. The novel primarily grapples with the issues of radicalization and citizenship in the context of contemporary Britain. However, it also presents a complex depiction of sexuality and religion. The novel revolves around the calamitous fate of the British Pakistani Pasha family after the only son, Parvaiz, follows in the footsteps of his long-absent father to become a jihadist. Parvaiz's twin sister Aneeka is determined to bring her brother home when Parvaiz becomes disillusioned with ISIS's violent bigotry and longs to return to England. A chance meeting between their older sibling Isma and the son of Britain's first Muslim Home Secretary, Eamonn (an anglicized/celticized version of the name Ayman), leads the latter to visit the family's house near Wembley. There Eamonn and Aneeka meet for the first time and quickly embark on a sexual relationship.

Shamsie's outspoken Antigone figure is the nineteen-year-old law student Aneeka, who is intelligent, headstrong and religious. Later in the novel, while declaring his love for Aneeka, Eamonn describes her to his father as follows: 'She prays. Not five times a day, but every morning, first thing. Doesn't drink or eat pork. She fasts during Ramzan. Wears a hijab' (106). The question that his father, the pro-assimilation politician Karamat Lone, immediately asks is whether Aneeka is comfortable with physical intimacy before marriage, which Eamonn answers affirmatively. This implies that Shamsie's heroine does not conform to conventional ideas of the prudish chastity of hijab-wearing, practising Muslim women.

Indeed, the way Aneeka's relationship with Eamonn starts and continues, with their sexual compatibility often highlighted in the novel, breaks many stereotypes. (This is true even if there are questions over Aneeka's real motivations, since initially at least she plans to enthral Eamonn so that he will persuade his father to let Parvaiz back into Britain.) When Aneeka comes to Eamonn's flat for the first time, having met him only hours before, Eamonn doesn't know what to make of her: '[I]t was hard to know what to want of a silent beautiful woman in a hijab sipping coffee in your flat' (68). Readers share Eamonn's puzzlement, for pious behaviour and religious fervour are not usually considered compatible with sexual boldness.

The first sexual encounter between Aneeka and Eamonn is portrayed in euphorically nervous romantic terms, and showcases Aneeka's initiative and agency in the sexual act: 'Taking his other hand, she placed it on her breast but over her shirt. That was still confusing as a signal until he realised, no, not her breast, she had placed his hand on her heart, which was beating frantically' (69). This quickly progresses to an exciting and satisfying sexual experience, and one which even holds out the promise of love. To understand the dynamics of their sexual relationship let us turn to another passage that describes their act of lovemaking:

> To start with she'd been hesitant, tentative. During their first kiss, she'd broken away, and had started to put her hijab back on, before his entreaties convinced her to stay. [...] [A]nd they set about discovering each other in that slow-quick way of new lovers – testing, exploring, building on what each was learning about the other.
>
> (69–70)

This passage depicts the usual hesitations around getting intimate with someone new, while gradually their mutual readiness and compatibility take over the initial disquiet. The verbs used from Eamonn's focalization to describe the lovers' exertions – 'testing, exploring, building' – are quasi-scientific, chiming with geographical discoveries and feats of engineering, and suggesting his Westernized worldview at this early stage in the novel.

Interestingly, readers witness Aneeka's curiously provocative sexual gesture in which she continues to wear her hijab while making love to Eamonn: 'she continued to undress until there was nothing left but the white scarf covering her head, one end of the soft fabric falling just below her breast, the other thrown over her shoulder'. She asks Eamonn whether she should leave on the veil, framing this as a question 'not because she doubted his desire' (71) but because she wants his wholehearted endorsement. Shamsie peels away layers of received ideas to show that Muslim women, including hijabis, have a range of attitudes towards sex and are not automatically abstemious. Aneeka's sexuality, not by chance, seems to be in harmony with her deeply devotional self. The following passage describes Aneeka from Eamonn's perspective when he sees her absorbed in her morning prayer:

> [H]e couldn't help watching this woman, this stranger, prostrating herself to God in the room where she'd been down on her knees for a very different purpose just hours earlier. It was, finally, the depth of her immersion in a world other than that of bodies and senses that made him go back to the bed, wondering if she'd return.
>
> (70)

This juxtaposition of Aneeka's sexuality and faith complicates the dichotomy of spiritual and carnal (Chambers 2019: 169–211).

The couple's physical intimacy, for Eamonn soon turns into love. This previously suave and unmovable young man finds himself 'almost incapable of thinking about anything but her. And not just the sex, though he thought about that often enough. The other things also' (74). While sexual experience is a constitutive element in their love, it is not the sole criterion. This is evident in Aneeka's reaction when Eamonn 'proposes proposing' to her:

> For a moment he thought he'd made a terrible mistake, Aneeka looking at him as though he'd said the craziest thing in the world. And then her mouth was on his, his hands on her shower-warm skin, everything he wanted in the world right here, right now, this woman, this life, this completeness.
>
> (91)

The repetitive and affirmative tone of the words calls forth passionate love while their bodily expression of affection carries an evocation of the sincerity and warmth of young lovers.

Conclusion

The taboo of sex was nowhere more evident within this project than in initial attempts to recruit young Muslim interview and workshop participants using the project's original title, 'Storying Sexual Relationships'. Sex was soon dropped from the strapline, proving too loaded a term and off-putting to the young people we wanted to engage. Yet, as this chapter has shown, when young Muslims are invited to speak and write about their relationship histories, the stories they tell make it clear that sex is an integral part of their lives. In many of the stories within this chapter, sexual experiences are inflected by religion and culture. Sometimes this is constraining – when young Muslims want to talk about sex but feel as though they can't, or want to have sex but feel obliged to wait until they are married.

At other times, religion and culture can be fonts of sexual agency and fulfilment, in asserting choices about when (not) to have sex, about active consent, and in exploring sex with your spouse. Young British Muslims live in a sexualized society, one in which a religious group that, as a rule, abstains from sex before marriage may be unfairly pigeonholed as strange or passionless. This chapter has demonstrated both that premarital chastity is far from a universal norm among young Muslims, and also that sexual curiosity and desire finds expression in all manner of ways.

Table 7.1 Interviews quoted in Chapter 7, 'Sex'

Name	Gender	Age	Relationship Status	Location
Aliya	Female	24	Married	Newcastle
Ifrah	Female	21	Single	Yorkshire
Waheed	Male	21	Single	Glasgow
Khadija	Female	19	Single	Newcastle
Hassan	Male	29	Single	Yorkshire
Hawa	Female	25	Married	Yorkshire
Hanifa	Female	22	Single	Glasgow
Salim	Male	24	Single	Newcastle
Safa	Female	22	Married	Yorkshire
Zohaib	Male	19	Single	Newcastle
Bilal	Male	22	Married	Yorkshire
Azeem	Male	26	Single	Newcastle
Esha	Female	27	Married	Yorkshire

Table 7.2 Workshop participants and convenors quoted in Chapter 7, 'Sex'

Name	Gender	Age	Workshop Series	Role in Workshop	Title
Nazia	Female	Not stated	6. Blogging, Glasgow	Participant	'The First Time'
Adam	Male	Not stated	8. Fiction, Glasgow	Participant	Writing exercise
Zarina	Female	Not stated	6. Blogging, Glasgow	Participant	'Anal Sex'
Taibah	Female	36	4. Playwriting, Glasgow	Participant	'Untitled'

Chapter 8

Dreaming

I still would love the happy ending, I would love to meet somebody, somebody that'll be there for me and look after me. Because I see my brother, he's married now and he's got a wonderful relationship with his wife. And I would like to have that.

(Mumtaz, twenty-three, interview)

The hardest part about dating while desi is rejecting the idea of a surprise love, of a lifelong commitment blossoming with someone you've spent two hours with. It's the stupid Bollywood narrative we love to indulge in that becomes hurtful when compared to our real lives.

(Maria Qamar, *Trust No Aunty* (2017: 75))

Many young people dream about the future, and young Muslims are no exception. Their dreams encompass passing daydreams to cherished hopes of finding 'the one'. The stories they tell of sexual attraction, love and marriage speak of future possibilities. The two quotes that open this chapter juxtapose dreams borne out of Bollywood fantasies and real-life experiences, in which dreams don't always turn out as planned. Mumtaz, a divorcee, still believes in happy endings, taking inspiration from her brother's 'wonderful' marriage to keep searching for a soulmate. In her humorous semi-autobiographical graphic novel *Trust No Aunty* (2017), Maria Qamar rejects the romantic tropes of film and fiction to forge her own path. Our book is primarily concerned with Muslim relationship stories, but of course not everyone dreams of romance or rescue by a Prince Charming. Some of the stories in this chapter narrate dreams of escape (like those of the teenage protagonist in Almas Khan's *Poppadom Preach* (2011)) and dreams of becoming, coming out or finding a voice. This chapter recounts dreams that are variously curious, joyful, bittersweet and sad, to reflect on how young Muslims are rewriting the script of their lives.

Sensuous dreams and sexual fantasies

In short stories written in creative writing workshops, young Muslim men and women used fictional characters to explore sexual fantasies, describing moments of attraction in sensuous detail. In a short story entitled '"Qabool": The Happily Never After', Haris, writing in a female voice, portrays the glamour and eroticism of the celebrity couples that his unnamed protagonist admires:

> It used to be so lovely watching the beautifully dressed, meticulously powdered women on the TV channel, Star Plus, play joyfully with their loving husband on their neat and tidy king-sized bed. I used to get a thrill when the six foot two, broad-shouldered man would rescue the innocent, attention-seeking woman in the Hollywood movies. Don't get me started on the excitement I used to bottle in when the athletic, fair-skinned Indian couples used to dance incredibly under the glowing rain in a precisely executed routine.

As the title suggests, Haris is critical of this romantic ideal. His story is a morality tale about the dangers of temptation, detailing a young woman's regret at being swept off her feet and into a so-called love marriage. Employing gendered stereotypes of muscular alpha males and frivolous damsels in distress, this passage hints at tantalizing dreams of flirtation and foreplay.

In the same creative writing workshop in Rochdale, Farid wrote a story called 'Dreams'. This story has a more everyday setting: the library where its central character, Simon, works. Simon has a crush on one of the regular visitors to the library, Sarah, and is noticeably excited to catch sight of her in one of the aisles: 'She slowly skims the books, running her finger across the spines until she sees the one she wants. She lifts up the book from the shelf, puts it on top of the previous two books she's picked out, and goes to the checkout counter.' In this passage, Simon's thoughts linger on the haptic sensation of Sarah running her fingers along the spines of the books as she makes her choice, hinting at sexual possibilities underneath a simple story of 'boy meets girl'. This story captures both a momentary fantasy and a young man's cherished hope of working up the courage to ask the object of his desire out.

Meena's short story 'Rearranged' itemizes the dating exploits of Sapna, whose very name means 'dream'! She is an ageing woman accorded a new lease of life in widowhood. In this story, dating is part of Sapna's wider personal awakening and desire for new experiences:

> Along with her increasingly experimental cooking and vocabulary, there had been many other changes to Sapna's life in the three years following her husband's death. She frequented trendy cafes in Glasgow's West End. Ordered courgette cake and thimblefuls of macchiato from tattooed men in leather waistcoats and sculpted moustaches. She went to New Look and bought jeans. Jeans! […] She'd only started this thing out of curiosity. She wasn't seriously thinking of remarrying at her age. It had all just been to see … was there anyone out there like her?

> (Chambers et al. 2020: 101, 104)

Meena makes allusions to Sapna's sexual desire by dressing her in tight-fitting clothes and describing the new, younger, on-trend men whom she likes to hang out around, men who are nothing like her late husband. Meena's insistence that her protagonist is only curious contrasts with the quiet plea 'was there anyone out there like her?' This suggests that beneath Sapna's delight at flirting with possibilities, she is dreaming of something more.

The road not taken

In 'Rearranged', Sapna's password for her online dating profile is 'theroadnottaken', an apparent reference to her regret about 'years of bland indifference' amid a loveless marriage (101–102). In widowhood, Sapna feels that she has a second chance to live the life that she dreamed of. In other stories, dreams of what could have been are at once pleasant and painful, reflecting on moments that have passed. At a creative writing workshop in Bradford, Bilal responded to the prompt 'A time you loved someone'. He wrote a first-person narrative from the perspective of an unnamed narrator (whose gender is not revealed), who rues failing to pluck up the courage to share their feelings with a former crush: 'It was never anything more than those looks – moments and conversations when all I really wanted to say and scream was how much I loved you'. Speaking of unrequited love or unspoken possibility, this ambivalent passage depicts the frustration of a dream unfulfilled.

Sofia's play 'Life As We Know It' follows forty-something protagonist Maryam as she gently resists her concerned family's attempts to marry her off before it's too late. In the following extract, Maryam has a flashback as she awaits a visit from a prospective *rishta*:

> It's June 1999. The warm heat of the afternoon sun beats down on Maryam and although exam season is in full swing, most students are sitting out with their books on the grass area in front of the library rather than sweltering inside. She runs up the stairs to the fourth floor and finds him sitting in their usual spot in the now deserted building.
>
> Maryam: How long had he been there waiting? Not one hour, not two, no not even three. Five hours. Like I said, we didn't walk about with smartphones in our pockets in those days. We just waited. And if someone really liked you, then I guess they came in at 8 a.m. and sat and waited for five hours until you turned up if they wanted to spend time with you.

This brief flashback sequence is juxtaposed with Maryam's reluctant participation in the introduction process. Perhaps she is thinking back to her first love, reminiscing about a relationship that long since ran its course, or one that was cut short abruptly. The play contrasts Maryam's daydream of a time when she loved and was loved by someone, to her present circumstances: single, and grudgingly agreeing to a formal introduction to a stranger.

Real-life stories, too, look back at what could have been. Salim, now in his midtwenties, reflected on a time when he dreamt of his friendship with the 'perfect' girl becoming something more:

> I was close to this girl, we both started sixth form at the same time and like in my head she was the perfect girl for me, like everything just worked out really well. I'm still friends with her now to be honest. Like it didn't work out, nothing really happened, it was just like we kind of – well I know I liked her a lot but it just wasn't working out like the way – like I feel like as I got to know her more, she became a better friend.

Here there is a faint sense of regret: it is clear that Salim still harbours affection and admiration for his friend. Yet, in hindsight, he recognizes that the moment has passed and that her perceived perfections were a figment of his imagination, as he reconciles his dreams of romance with the intimacy of friendship.

'Somebody you can get along with': Dreams of marriage

Looking to the future often involves conjecture about whom one might meet and, for those who envisage following a well-trodden path, dreams of one's future spouse. Haroon, during a creative writing workshop at his college, invented two characters whose relationship develops out of friendship. Billi is 'brown' and 'doesn't know English', while Aida 'loves arguing' and is 'very loud'. The story, roughly drafted, is evidently written from Billi's perspective: 'It's on a Monday when it was Aida and Billi's wedding. It was Billi that ask for her to Marry and she Said YES' [...] They loved each other to bits as they've been together for so long. That's why Billi wanted to marry her'. This scenario confounds some British Asian cultural norms by envisaging a match in which the wife is more powerful than the groom, with Billi admiring Aida's outspoken confidence.

Conversely, some young Muslim women shared dreams of marriage on equal terms. Muneera, contrasting her hopes for the future with a friend's recent divorce from a man who went to prison for sexual harassment, said her ideal husband would be 'someone who's not controlling I guess':

> When I hear stories like that, it just makes me ... really scared about you know, the future, obviously. I know that's only one person and I know like you can't stereotype like that, like if one person's like that it doesn't mean everyone's like that. But the qualities I would want is just kind of, you know, respectful, chivalrous, understanding, caring, respectful towards women especially.

From this we can infer that dreams about the future may be informed by fear as well as hope. Muneera draws on a friend's story to express her worry about unwittingly entering into a controlling or abusive marriage. She repeats her wish for a 'respectful' husband, prizing this quality above other criteria in her dreams of a decent man.

Janan, a little older, reflected on how her dreams about her ideal husband have changed over time, from the 'cliché' happy endings of Bollywood and Disney to the simple hope of meeting someone 'down to earth':

> I think you know, you don't really need to tick all the boxes, I just want somebody who's down to earth and I can have a good laugh with. But yeah, it's kind of cliché but you know, at high school we did watch Bollywood and we did watch all the Disneys and you know, you watch fairy tales and it's all perfect and you think, 'Oh yeah, I want that.' But yeah, no, I don't at all. I just want somebody to well be decent, to be honest with you, and I think that comes from also experiences of just different guys I've been introduced to and talked to and met as well, and I've just thought, 'Oh God,' you know. Like you have no respect for women, you don't know how to talk. Yeah, [I] just want somebody down to earth and I'd be happy.

Here, Janan contrasts her ideals in her thirties with the naivety of the 'perfect' fairy tales she dreamed of when she was younger, also reflecting on past disappointments when meeting prospective suitors. Aqeelah, recently married, shared Janan's disillusionment with the 'happily ever after' romances portrayed in Bollywood and Disney, which she described as 'kind of cliché boy meets girl, somebody has an issue with it on either side ... but all ends well'. She felt that this leaves people wanting the 'Prince Charming perfect guy' or 'perfect princess', rather than thinking seriously about what qualities they are looking for in a life partner.

On a similar theme, in '"Qabool": The Happily Never After', Haris warns about the dangers of love marriage through the eyes of a naive young protagonist who soon regrets her decision: 'How wrong I was about relationships ... I thought it would be sweet and romantic like the times we used to speak on the phone till three in the morning. I couldn't imagine it being an atom's weight of negativity'. In Haris's unfinished draft of this story, we never learn the reasons why marriage soured, but the writing hints at broken promises and the difficulty of 'two completely different specimens with different lifestyles coming together ... sharing the same bed, the same toilet, the same living space under one testing roof'. This story contrasts fantasy with reality, albeit a little crudely, to suggest that romantic fantasies can be deceptive and make the dreamer a poor judge of character when entering into marriage.

As we saw in Haroon's story, young Muslim men can also dream of happy marriages that defy negative stereotypes of domineering husbands and subjugated wives. Arshad, whom we met in the 'Married' chapter discussing the breakdown of his first – arranged – marriage, reflected on how that experience shaped his hopes for his second marriage, in which he has had much more dialogue with his wife about their shared dreams for the future:

> I was actually devastated when my first marriage ended. I tried everything to bring her back but you know, she didn't want to ... Now I think going forward, I think a woman has to – you've got to know the lady, in this day and age now

you've got to know the lady, what she wants. You've got to meet her and talk to her and realize what she wants in life and what her goals are in life and what your goals are in life.

When asked what's important to him in his life now, he replied 'having a good relationship with my wife, supporting her'. In dreaming of a successful marriage second time around, he held himself to account as a husband who wants to see his wife flourish.

'Everybody wanted this to work out'

Sometimes, dreaming about the future means reconciling your own desires with those of others, and sometimes those desires prove incompatible. Divorcee Mumtaz had looked forward to her arranged marriage and hoped for the best. She had believed that her (now ex-) husband had a similar outlook, and at the start things seemed promising. She recalled assuming 'he's got my way of thinking and love would grow. But the love never grew because we were two different people wanting two different things out of life.' For Mumtaz, facing up to the fact that she could not grow to love her husband was a difficult realization. She blamed herself for their divorce, and felt guilty about the hurt that she perceived she had caused to everyone involved in the match:

> Everybody had so wanted this to work out so much, I was under so much pressure. It wasn't just from my mum, it was my brothers liked the boy and they were quite happy for it all to go ahead. And in a way I feel I've ruined it all now ... And I feel sorry for my husband, my ex-husband, as well because like he had that expectation as well; and obviously going back to what he saw with his own parents and what he wanted, I couldn't give him that.

When Mumtaz foreclosed one possible future for dreams of a better marriage, she did so in spite of the obligation she felt to her then-husband and both of their families. Her story ends on a cautiously optimistic note, as we saw at the opening of this chapter, but it also illustrates how the dream of a successful marriage can be shaped by obligations to please one's family.

When young Muslims dream about the future, they tend to envisage relationships in which couples are part of families and communities. Salim, looking ahead to his future marriage prospects, explained how his desire for more independence is at odds with his parents' hope that he will continue to live in the family home:

> My mum and dad really want it, they really want us to all live in one house and like, it is their dream I guess ... If you'd asked me like a few years ago, like I would have liked that idea too but I feel like it's at that point now where like you can't have that many people in one house. Like especially when like you've got such strong personalities. Like everyone wants to do their own thing [...] and like I feel like you've got to kind of let that happen now.

Here, Salim reflects on how his dreams about the future have shifted over time, and also how he has to contend with the dreams of others. If he chooses to live apart from his parents after marriage, he must do so in the knowledge that it will break with tradition and forestall the future they imagined of a happy extended family household.

Dreaming and becoming

While some dream of romance, others seek happy endings that are about personal self-fulfilment. Saamiya, alert to her parents' wish for her to get married, dreamed of coming out to them about her sexuality but felt this would be impossible. She recalled how, in her loneliness and frustration, she used to think that marriage might offer a solution:

> Part of me was thinking: 'Oh I would just like to get married,' because I was feeling lonely or whatever … I was like, 'Why am I feeling lonely?' It is because I have got nothing to fill my time. Why do I not have anything to fill my time? Like I am not, I just go to work and I go home and I do nothing. Why is that? Like who am I? And I had forgotten who I was in that. So then I started doing other things, like I started reading again.

For a teenager, Saamiya offers a mature perspective on romantic dreams, recognizing that such fantasies are not always an expression of one's innermost desires. Sometimes, they serve to alleviate boredom or speak to something that is missing from one's life. While Saamiya did dream of the possibility of a loving same-sex relationship, her more immediate wish was to know her own mind and make time for hobbies that are important to her.

These themes – knowing yourself and pursuing your passions – emerged strongly through creative writing, speaking to the power of this medium for helping young Muslims to find a voice. In a play called 'Cake and Eat It', Meena explores tensions surfacing in a marriage in which the central characters ultimately want different things. In the following scene, Diyah is trying to persuade her husband Adaam to travel with her to the United States so she can attend a creative writing course:

> Diyah: Come on, you know it's what I've always dreamed of. It's a brilliant opportunity, we'll travel, we'll have so much fun.
> Adaam: No. We should go to Dubai. Food is halal, we'll hire a fast car, drive around.
> Diyah: The course isn't in Dubai. Oh forget it …
> *Pause.*
> Adaam: Make us some tea, would you?
> Diyah: Yeah, *that's* what I'll do. I've just been at work all day. At lunch I had to go to the bank because you forgot then I had to rush home, put a load of washing in, make dinner, clear up but of course, I'll be the one to get up and make you the tea!

The couple's contradictory natures are illustrated by Diyah's long-nurtured ambition of writing and Adaam's craving for fast cars and good food. After a pregnant pause, his request that she make tea prompts Diyah to vent her frustration at the daily drudgery of their domestic arrangements. This story is both about a dream that hasn't lived up to expectations and about the escapist dreams that follow, as Diyah envisages an independent future.

As this play excerpt suggests, many young people dream not only of Mr or Ms Right but also of their own fulfilment, for example through becoming a writer, a filmmaker or a happy and successful person in their own right. It would do a disservice to the complex and varied writing coming out of professional publishing houses and our own creative writing workshops alike to reduce Muslim authors' accounts of young people's dreams simply to their love lives. In this regard, it is worth looking at an exemplary short story from the anthology that emerged out of the writing workshops we organized in Bradford, Leeds and Glasgow. As noted in Chapter 6, 'Married', the keener among the new and emerging authors who participated in these workshops eventually published their stories. Their writing was showcased alongside more well-known, already-published authors in an anthology of Muslim women's writing about love and desire entitled *A Match Made in Heaven* (Chambers et al. 2020). One striking theme that crops up again and again in the stories presented in this book is the multidimensional nature of Muslims' dreams for the future.

In one of the stories, entitled 'Moments in Time' and written by Sunah Ahmed, a participant at the Glasgow workshops dealing with fiction, readers spend the twenty-four hours of her birthday with the protagonist, Leena. This young woman character feels unfulfilled in her marriage to Ali, who has apparently forgotten her special day. Throughout the day, Leena recalls and reflects on time she spent at university in a relationship with a fellow student named Isa. This relationship had come to an end when Isa followed his dream of becoming an author by heading to the United States to do a creative writing course. Leena had hoped their connection could continue at long-distance, but Isa had tunnel vision about his quest for a literary life and refused. Ultimately and with bitter regret, Leena had opted for an arranged marriage with Ali. This husband of three years is a simple but loving man, whose hard labour at a takeaway leaves him smelling of 'mustard oil and sweat' (134), much to Leena's disgust. One of the things about Ali that Leena disparages is his lack of interest in the arts. Like her ex-boyfriend, Leena is attracted to the artistic world. In her case, while she enjoys novels it is painting that she loves and aspires to. Meanwhile, Ali thinks practically that 'books wouldn't pay the bills' and can barely 'suppress his yawns' when confronted by a gallery (139). In the 'moments in time' traced in the story, much of Leena's continued yearning for Isa stems from the glamorous creative and intellectual world he now occupies. Isa has become a successful novelist, and the story culminates in the revelation that Ali, far from forgetting Leena's birthday, has marked the occasion by getting a signed copy of Isa's novel for her. Ali has met Isa at a signing in the local bookshop in order to ask the novelist for his autograph, since he knows his wife to be a fan of Isa's work (though not the reason why). The discovery that Isa is back in his home city tempts Leena to sign up for a writing workshop he is running in Glasgow. However, ultimately she seems to realize that her dreams of Isa are tied up with the creative life he is living and which she covets. Ali's kind solidity, and the support he gives to Leena's imaginative pursuits even though he does not share them, leads the young woman to switch off her laptop before completing the online form for Isa's workshop. She then heads to bed with Ali, whom she calls 'husband' for the first time without resentment. Readers may hope from this that she will be able to become a fine artist, as her dreams of expressing herself on canvas are more valued by Ali than she had hitherto understood. From young Muslims' accounts of dreaming and becoming, we now turn to a novel whose protagonist dreams, as Saamiya once did, of marriage as an escape route.

'Princess Dilly's story should have a happy ending': Dreams of escape in Poppadom Preach

Almas Khan's 2011 novel *Poppadom Preach* depicts an oppressive environment within a Pakistani Muslim family living in Britain. Critic Esra Mirze Santesso (2013: 162) observes that Khan's chosen genre of young adult fiction by British Muslim writers often uses a formulaic setting that does not go beyond well-worn plots – the protagonist typically has an abusive father, an insensitive mother and is herself a rebellious teenager. Santesso is not, however, entirely dismissive about the literary worth of *Poppadom Preach*, and maintains that the novel to some extent departs from the stereotypical 'disorientation narrative' (163) by presenting a protagonist who is confident in her British identity (164). The story is told through the focalization of teenage protagonist, Dilly. We witness her overbearing mother's coercive behaviour, and a terrifying father who becomes violent at the slightest provocation – even the most trivial act of disobedience from his daughters. The novel revolves around how Dilly navigates her chaotic and confining Shah family while harbouring a dream to break free. The defiance and assertiveness Dilly embodies is evident from the novel's outset, as she declares: 'I'd given up waiting to be rescued by a dashing young prince and had decided to figure it out for myself' (Khan 2011: vii). The dream here is not of a Prince Charming appearing as a saviour, but to be self-sufficient enough not to depend on him.

For Dilly, a dream relationship is one that would that would free her from the 'shackles' (vii) of rigid familial norms and customs and give her space of her own. She worries about whether her long-term exposure to such a repressive environment will result in her imbibing some of her parents' unattractive traits, especially the domineering nature of her mother. She hopes that her future husband will liberate her by having an entirely opposite personality to the ones she has grown up with. She speculates: 'It seemed to me that my only hope would be to find a husband who wasn't too strict, one who wanted his children to be free. In other words, nothing like my own father' (299). The desire for a relationship, as expressed in these lines, is formulated as a response to the current crisis facing the teenage protagonist. Dilly's relationship yearnings relate to her immediate context – her oppressive parents, whose hold she wishes to escape by any means. She hopes her future husband will be self-reliant: 'Any man who took me on would have to be independent enough to want to set up his own home; moving into my parents' house would be a disaster' (374). In a way, what she is looking for is a ready-made household, but one that differs in every respect from her current unhappy home.

At the end of the novel, when Dilly is about to go to Pakistan to attend her sister's marriage, her mother apprehends that Dilly's father might attempt to marry her off to a nephew. She forewarns Dilly and sternly asks her to avoid marriage by all means. Initially surprised by her mother's concern, a rare occurrence in the span of her teenage life, Dilly soon realizes that her mother's sole fear is an imminent loss of control over her daughter. As a baffled Dilly asks her mother for an explanation, the latter says, 'You're my […] slave, you have to stay single for me. I don't want you working for anyone else' (373). When Dilly understands her mother's selfish motive, escape through marriage becomes an even more treasured dream:

> Finding myself a husband was at the bottom of my 'to do' list.
>
> But later that night, as the coach cruised down the motorway towards Manchester, I stared dreamily out of the window and hid my smile behind my veil. I'd made up my mind: I was going to get married. […]
>
> I'd persuade my new husband to let me finish my education, and find myself a job. Then I'd dump him. […]
>
> Surely it was time for me to break free from the shackles of tradition? It was only right that Princess Dilly's story should have a happy ending.
>
> (374)

Here, Dilly harbours no romantic hopes, but rather dreams of marriage as a stepping-stone towards freedom. That said, the ending of the novel hints towards the complicated marriage to unfold in a possible sequel, as it ends with the following lines: 'While I was preparing to divorce someone I hadn't even met yet, he was preparing to make sure we stayed married for the ten years it would take him to get his British passport. But that, as they say, is another story' (374). This conclusion suggests that breaking free from home by marrying in Pakistan will likely pose further obstacles to Dilly's dream of independence.

'I didn't want to be saved': Dreams of down-to-earth romance in Trust No Aunty

The graphic narrative *Trust No Aunty* (2017) by Maria Qamar has a humorous style and is presented as a 'survival guide' (back cover blurb), with chapters on career, love, relationships and lifestyle. Her protagonist Maria's immediate challenge is to 'survive' the complexities of cultural hybridity, growing up as she does in a South

8. Dreaming

Asian household in North America. In terms of its genre, it should be noted that the graphic narrative is an umbrella term which includes nonfiction. *Trust No Aunty* is thus memoir-like, drawing on Qamar's own experience of being raised as a 'desi' in Canada, where she moved nine years after her birth in Pakistan. This particular location of Canada (or more broadly North America) is mentioned once or twice in the book. Qamar also takes a syncretic approach, which is understandable given that she explains: 'I was born in a home which was half Gujarati and half Bihari, by way of Bangladesh but located in Pakistan' (2). She accordingly sprinkles her book with references to India as well as Pakistan, and Hindu or Sikh names as well as Muslim. What is significant about the cross-cultural, diasporic context is that it is equally relevant to the British South Asian diaspora. It is impossible and nor is it necessary firmly to determine the locations housing both the fictitious characters and the real-life personalities (Qamar sometimes mentions her parents) of this survival guide.

In this graphic novel Maria Qamar uses bold pop art panels to accompany her tongue-in-cheek commentary on the ageing South Asian woman affectionately and scornfully addressed as 'Aunty'. Such women are obsessed with other people's affairs and always keen to interfere. Qamar is both caustic and empathetic about the aunties, ready as they always are to shower young girls with advice. They are especially interfering when it comes to relationships.

Trust No Aunty explores a young woman's dreams, and the obstacles she faces in following them. Though some of these obstacles are rooted in tradition, others are more contemporary. Like many young people with South Asian heritage, Qamar's teenage self is drawn to the Bollywood dream factory. But Qamar does not care to revel in Bollywood dreams. She takes issue with the Mumbai film industry, interrogating its production line of fantasies and stereotypes, as well as its hackneyed portrayals of South Asian people and their lives. Qamar recalls being influenced as a teenager by such superficial portrayals, which are glaringly outlandish and exaggerated while glorifying traditional customs. She discusses the disillusionment such portrayals eventually resulted in for her, as we saw in the quotation that opens this chapter, where Qamar complains that the 'stupid Bollywood narrative' of love at first sight is hurtful and unrealistic (75). With palpable irritation, she observes a stark contrast between the Bollywood 'dream' and her personal experience.

Her desire for a romantic, film-like relationship, Qamar explains, gradually matured into a greater understanding of herself:

> I began to have a good time not picturing myself as the damsel in distress because deep down, I didn't want to be saved. [...] I've let go of my dreams of finding Mr. Right at the traffic light, and embraced my freedom to choose what is really right for me.
>
> (74–5)

Qamar goes on to lambast widespread and tired portrayals of relationships, preferring to reflect on the real challenges that young couples might face: 'there are no Bollywood films about your potential partner earning less money than you, or the tension that might come from asking your husband to sacrifice his career to become a stay-at-home dad'. Debunking the Bollywood ending, she goes on: 'The love of your life won't be the lunatic that proposes to you the fastest.' Instead, she concludes, 'It'll be your best friend who understands the incredible obstacles you will face together as partners, lovers, and maybe parents' (75). In addition to criticizing a lack of imagination in Bollywood films, these lines also suggest a dream of a relationship that is more equal, with both partners pulling together and sharing household chores. The passage concludes with markedly dreamy undertones, as Qamar expresses her desire for a love story that is both dreamlike and down-to-earth: 'I know that one day I will create my own romantic comedy with someone who cherishes me enough to commit a cheesy gesture, but also supports me in tangible ways that go beyond flowers and candy' (75). Just as in rom coms, she hopes that her own romance will involve the occasional saccharine declaration of love. More important for Qamar, though, are tangible shows of support from a partner in everyday life.

Later in the book, Qamar discusses social acceptance of love relationships and marriage. She writes that people are often under the spell of cultural conformity to such an extent that their apprehensions about others' gossip loom larger than the reality. Even while dealing with this difficult subject, Qamar remains upbeat. Reflecting on relationships and sexual taboos, she highlights the subversive spaces inherent in South Asian traditions:

> All in all, we've got to stop worrying so much about what others think of our families and focus on talking more with one another. [...] [W]e come from a beautiful liberal, colorful culture; hell, we're the ones who created the Kama Sutra. We've been rooted in thinking outside the box for as long as we've been around. It's only fair that we continue breaking barriers and end stigmatizing lifestyles that are different.
>
> (168)

This quotation, with its assertive tone, intimates a dream of an inclusive community that thinks creatively and can accommodate non-normative relationships. Qamar expresses her desire for more communication and the creation of a hospitable space in which one's 'dream relationship' might thrive.

Here, the dream has matured. What started out as the search for an ideal man, moulded and glamorized in the one-dimensional space of a Bollywood film, has evolved in the form of a dream for something more. Such a dream incorporates, but is not limited to, union with a significant other. This brings the story back to its 'desi' origins and the author's emphasis on navigating cultural hybridity. Qamar advises young women to make the final decision about their own marriage, even if preliminary recommendations come from their mother or elders. In a section entitled 'What to Look for in an Arranged Husband/Partner', she illustrates a checklist of qualities, which is at once hilarious and serious. Echoing hopes and fears expressed by our research participants, the very first quality in Qamar's checklist is 'Respects women', which is followed by the parenthesis 'and not in a because-this-could-be-my-sister-or-mother kinda way'. The checklist also specifies that potential husbands '[c]an cook biriyani' and '[s]upport […] your decision to become famous as hell' (90). These are dreams for – more than a man – respect, equality and fulfilment.

Conclusion

Dreams are about playing with possibilities, sometimes – but not always – with serious intention. In dreaming about the future, young Muslims are exploring the prospects for whom they might meet, fall in love with and marry, and for how they might live their lives. Some dreams follow a conventional path to marriage, treading well-worn clichés of boy meets girl. And yet, even in these stories, young Muslims caution against the seductive power of fairy-tale endings and 'perfect' love interests, acknowledging that real relationships require work.

Dreaming is often about wish fulfilment, which means that some of the stories told in this chapter have a strong current of individualism running through them – because dreams are allowed to be selfish. It is also possible to dream with and for others: to share dreams with your spouse for your future life together, to dream of your family's acceptance of your lifestyle, to dream that you and your ex will find new loves. Dreaming gives young Muslims permission to ask and explore what they really want, and not just in a romantic partner. By making space for creative writing – an ideal conduit for dreaming – this project has provided opportunities for young Muslims to find their voice through creative endeavour, helping them to realize ambitions of publishing and to believe that what they have to say has value.

Table 8.1 Interviews quoted in Chapter 8, 'Dreaming'

Name	Gender	Age	Relationship Status	Location
Mumtaz	Female	23	Divorced	Glasgow
Salim	Male	24	Single	Newcastle
Muneera	Female	22	Single	Newcastle
Janan	Female	30	Single	Glasgow
Aisha	Female	27	Single	Yorkshire
Hasnaa	Female	16	Single	Newcastle
Saamiya	Female	18	Single	Glasgow
Arshad	Male	29	Married	Glasgow

Table 8.2 Workshop participants and convenors quoted in Chapter 8, 'Dreaming'

Name	Gender	Age	Workshop Series	Role in Workshop	Title
Haris	Male	25	7. Fiction, Rochdale	Participant	'"Qabool" – The Happily Never After'
Farid	Male	26	7. Fiction, Rochdale	Participant	'Dreams'
Meena	Female	35	4. Playwriting, Glasgow	Participant	'Cake and Eat It'
Bilal	Male	22	2. Creative writing, Bradford	Participant	'A Time You Loved someone'
Sofia	Female	37	4. Playwriting, Glasgow	Participant	'Life As We Know It'
Haroon	Male	Not stated	3. Creative writing, Sheffield	Participant	Writing exercise
Farah	Female	25	5. Fiction, Glasgow	Participant	Poems

CONCLUSION

[F]riends came bearing stories, one after another, and they seemed to provide, if not answers, at least milestones and signposts.
(Rebecca Solnit, *A Field Guide to Getting Lost* (2017/5: 15))

[L]iterature creates the world and cosmopolitan bonds in at least two ways. Through the powers of figuration, it enables us to imagine a world. But more important, through the pleasure it arouses in us and our desire to share this pleasure through universal communication, literature and its criticism enhance our sense of (being a part of) humanity.
(Pheng Cheah, *What Is a World?* (2016: 44))

The stories in this book, in the words and voices of young British Muslims, have been engaging and in some cases surprising. They may wrong-foot some non-Muslim readers where they contradict things they thought they knew about Muslims: stereotypes and misconceptions. They may also startle certain Muslim readers, particularly where they say things that may have been seen as unsayable, and explore possibilities that may have been seen as impermissible or haram. Engaging and surprising are not ends in themselves; these qualities empower a story, enabling it to travel and to matter. The stories told in this book – from those that focus upon the ordinary and non-sensational to those that confront big issues – lay down much-needed maps, not only for individuals on the brink of sexual experiences and relationships but also for societies hampered by divisions and misunderstandings.

Young British Muslims are breaking silences in many different ways: in conversations with friends and peers; in online spaces and platforms such as blogs and YouTube videos; in diary entries and creative writing; and in the printed word. There are differences between stories presented as fact, and their overtly fictional counterparts (Phillips and Kara 2021). Fiction presents opportunities for 'empathy and self-reflection through relatable characters' (Leavy 2015: 56). Furthermore, stories and novels explore experiences through 'fantasy, fabulation, distortion and invention' (Mort 2013: 219). Nonfiction brings other qualities and possibilities. Different fiction and nonfiction media also allow for a wealth of forms of exploration and expression. Interviews tell truths that scripts do not; scripts tell stories that poems do not; and so on.

Despite these differences, some common threads run through the different settings and media in which young Muslims are speaking and writing about sexual relationships. These revolve around ways of breaking silences about sex and sexual relationships. In the first interlude – 'Coming to Terms' – we identified three ways in which young Muslims are aerating these risqué subjects: starting with clichés, chatting with friends, and thinking aloud (through the spoken or written word). Cutting across each of these, in the course of this book we have observed a number of ways of using words to speak about sexual relationships. We use the verbs 'to speak' and 'to utter' broadly and inclusively: to encompass the written as well as the spoken word. In the next section, we draw together some of these tactics, before going on to ask what they make it possible to say (about relationships) and do (by making relationship choices).

Tactics

Young Muslims are breaking silences about sex and sexual relationships by: (i) speaking indirectly, hypothetically and conditionally, (ii) working with the devices of the storyteller and the writer of fiction and (iii) communicating directly and in some cases defiantly. These tactics revolve around storying, which has been a central conceptual strand of this book. As such, this is an appropriate point to review the ways in which we have contributed theoretically as well as substantively to understandings of storying, and to suggest what our distinctive contributions have been. In the Introduction, we drew together the literature on this subject, finding that storying is an inclusive term, encompassing diverse practices which range from everyday speech to oral storytelling, and from literary work to research methods. In each of these settings, we found, stories and storying serve many purposes, from entertainment to exploration of sensitive subjects which people find hard or impossible to address more directly. Over the course of this book, through our interdisciplinary attention to stories told and written by young Muslims, we have advanced these understandings of stories and storying in relation to both content and broader theoretical frameworks. Too often, social sciences approaches to storying exist in a separate silo to those from the arts and humanities, and vice versa. In this project we have brought the two into fruitful dialogue. Literary studies' methodological tool of close textual analysis has been illuminating, not just in exploring published texts but also in reading interviews. Equally, social scientific attention to lived relationship practices has helped us to situate and comprehend stories that are told and written, and to better understand their impact and significance. In this way, our interdisciplinarity has brought with it insights into stories and storying, and to what it means to speak and to represent oneself and one's relationality. Speaking, particularly for young Muslims, is foundational, but not free. As Khurram Hussein argues in *The Muslim Speaks* (forthcoming), the words you say and write enable you to be heard, recognized, acknowledged and affirmed as a social and political being. Speaking the world into existence, you may find your place in it and come to belong. So it matters if

Muslims are constrained in what they can say, how they can speak; and it matters when Muslims find ways to break silences and explore and expand possibilities. We develop these broader theoretical points in the remainder of this Conclusion, beginning with the three tactics introduced above.

First, where speaking and writing is difficult and complicated, as it often is for young Muslims tackling the subject of sexual relationships, there are advantages in speaking indirectly and dropping hints and euphemisms. By making hypothetical utterances about what they and others might have done or do, they allude to their sexual relationships, past, present and future, without giving away too much or taking foolish risks. Recall that Ifrah, who had studied away from home, spoke hypothetically about how student life might have changed her. She reflected that she had become more open to things she would have previously considered off-limits, such as meeting 'guys', though she steered clear of specifying whether such meetings had actually taken place. Haris, who acknowledged that it was easier for men than women to admit to having premarital sex, went on to admit that he had done so. He resorted to speculative language, though, when explaining why he would advise others to save themselves for marriage. As he put it, failure to do so could mean that the sex within marriage might not seem as good, undermining the marriage itself. Similarly, in the 'Dating' chapter we saw how Hiba used postulations and conditional (subjunctive) verbs to speak about her brother, her knowledge of her brother and ultimately herself. Their 'parents wouldn't have approved' if her brother had a girlfriend; 'if he did anything like that it would have been in secret'.

Hypothetical and conditional language opens up space for uncertainty and ambiguity. Here it is possible to start exploring possibilities in the absence of premature certainty about anything to do with sexual relationships. It can be liberating, as we have seen, to find a way of admitting and expressing uncertainty. Think back to the fragmented speech, loosely stitched together with words such as 'like', 'okay' and 'so', in which Hassan circled around his subject, admitting that he still wasn't sure where he stood on certain issues. In his splintered speech, Hassan began to articulate something, even as a throat-clearing exercise.

A second set of tactics which runs through this book and through the ways in which young Muslims are breaking their silence works through storytelling and fiction. This finds many homes: from the pages of published works, of course, to the rumours and hearsay that pepper everyday conversations and to the scenarios that young Muslims concoct as they explore and represent their own lives. The latter include conversations, rehearsed aloud or played out in their minds, in which young people come out to parents or proposition would-be lovers; and, of course, sexual fantasies. Some of these sexual relationship fictions take written form; this includes the plays and short stories written in the Storying Relationships workshops. When Hiba spoke about a hypothetical brother and his girlfriend, she echoed the ways in which storytellers and writers of fiction conjure up characters, exploring relationship possibilities without directly implicating themselves or their readers. These authors are able to slip between the cracks of ringing true on the one hand, and on the other being factually accurate. Roopa Farooki can write about 'the salty-sweetness' of her characters' 'lovemaking', inviting readers to imagine 'the sticky heat of their bodies' (Farooki 2007: 44–5), without revealing the details of her own relationship. And so it is with all the fiction we have encountered in this book. Readers may wonder how writers knew about particular experiences and speculate as to how much of the author's personality or life is revealed through his or her characters and stories. However, they are usually left guessing. The advantages of fiction include displacement, where authors write about he, she, they or you without needing to reveal the real me or I except through the artifice of the first-person narrator. Moreover, fiction (in common with some other forms of creative writing and storytelling) allows for more than one point of view, and it frees up the author to explore these perspectives without endorsing any of them. This point overlaps with another, which we introduced in the first interlude. By speaking and writing in clichés and framing stories within genres, it is possible to obscure the individuality and specificity of the individual voice. Rather than a failure of 'freshness, energy and reverberation of voice' – Martin Amis's withering assessment (2001: 19–20) – cliché can function to protect speakers and authors. These vulnerable speaking or writing subjects may appear to be reciting a script rather than speaking directly from their own experiences, while at the same time providing audiences with something they can immediately recognize and follow.

Though storytelling takes many different forms, it relies upon a number of devices, which include the use of specific and vivid details that can bring stories and characters to life, placing them in particular times and places. Details lend authenticity, add sensuous appeal and emotional impact and draw audiences in. In Noura's short story, 'Her Trials', it is not insignificant that the female protagonist is wearing 'winged eyeliner' and is armed with her 'favourite black handbag, with its own small sprinkling of metal studs'. These details complete the 'kick-ass look' she needs to face her cheating husband (Chambers et al. 2020: 33). It matters, too, that Amna in Rehana Alam's novel *The Tea Trolley* (2017) is wearing 'a cream colored shalwar qameez and a chiffon dupatta' (24). These sartorial touches draw the reader into this scene, while making some serious points: showing the reader how this prospective bride has taken care over her appearance, and how much rides on the brief impressions afforded by a typical *rishta* meeting. Here, the contrivances of creative writing and storytelling tessellate with real life, where they subsequently make an impact. The potential impact of a filigreed detail, though more closely associated with the 'show don't tell' traditions of creative writing than the 'tell then evidence' traditions of formal academic scholarship, is recognized by writers, storytellers, critics and communicators of all stripes.

Third, in contrast with those who speak indirectly, whether through noncommittal, conditional language or through the veil of fiction, some young Muslims are speaking directly and defiantly, breaking taboos about what can (and cannot) be said about sex and relationships. Some of the conversations in the workshops we ran became animated and sexually frank. Participants drew upon these permissive exchanges in their writing in works ranging from a blog about anal sex to a short story in which a suitor suggests the use of clingfilm as a prophylactic. Published writers, encountered in the course of this book, also speak directly about sex and sexual relationships. Memorable scenes include the moment from Mohsin Hamid's *Exit West* (2017: 33), in which a conservatively-dressed woman goes home with a buff musician. The sex isn't great – she merely 'shuffle[s] off the weight of her virginity' – but there is truth in this too: sex *can* be disappointing, especially if it's not the kind of sex a person really wants. This couple quickly go their separate ways, and the woman forms a much more serious relationship with another male partner. They too eventually split up, and both go on to explore other possibilities later on; for the female character, this takes the form of a same-sex relationship. In this respect, *Exit West* takes its place among other books, including novels such as Amjeed Kabil's *Straightening Ali* (2007) and Hanif Kureishi's *The Buddha of Suburbia* (1990), in which young Muslims explore same-sex desire. Moreover, young Muslims are among those who read these stories, and go on to think and talk about them, breaking silences as they go. Young Muslims are breaking other silences which hang over the subject of sex and sexual relationships: not experiencing sexual desire; feeling lonely; preferring to remain single; experiencing sexual abuse; enjoying masturbation; experimenting with unconventional sex; and so on. Though comical, Mateen's shriek – when he tries to speak to the boy he desires in Yusuf's short story, 'What If?' – exposes his loneliness and isolation, the distance that stands between him and romantic fulfilment.

Through these gambits, young Muslims are now speaking and writing about sexual relationships, both as they are and as they might be. But what are they saying? We have ended each of the eight substantive chapters with conclusions about the things young Muslims are saying of the dimensions and stages of sexual relationships: Single, Meeting, Dating, Love, Pressure, Married, Sex and Dreaming. Here, as we continue to draw together the themes of this book, we will begin by briefly recapping the findings of each of these chapters before highlighting cross-cutting themes, once again taking our points of departure from the interludes – in this case, from 'Speaking to Stereotypes' and '(Not So) Different'. Doing so, we answer the fundamental question: what have we learned about young British Muslims' sexual relationships?

Relationships

When young Muslims speak and write about sexual relationships, they might hold up a mirror to the lives they are already living. Sometimes they are speaking less directly, perhaps to imagine how things could be better, to warn about how they could be worse or to explore and to open up possibilities surrounding sex and relationships. This means that the stories which we have explored in this book do not present the most literal or factual pictures of young Muslims' sexual relationships. Accordingly, for detailed, factual information about who has sex with and/or marries whom, where and when, and for understandings of the social contexts and diasporic geographies in which these relationships are agreed and formalized, we defer to social scientists who have conducted more conventional ethnographies, interviews and statistical surveys. Our goal has been to complement rather than replicate such work, providing new insights into young British Muslims' sexual relationships, and into their thoughts and feelings, hopes and fears, plans and expectations when it comes to these relationships. With this definitional remit and scope in mind, the following paragraphs reprise the findings of each chapter, which we then pull together.

The order in which we have placed these chapters roughly parallels that in which many Muslims experience (or expect to experience) and story their relationships, though this temporal sequence does not hold true for all, and not everyone goes through all these stages. This typical but not universal order begins with being single, an experience followed by meetings, with marriage and sex further down the line – usually in that order. Of course, some remain single; others find themselves single again, after separation or bereavement; and not all married couples are sexually active. We have put the chapter on dating before that on marriage, though not all young Muslims date at all, and some only do so after they marry, as they begin to get to know their spouse. Likewise, we have put love before marriage, though many Muslims speak of falling in love (or hoping to do so) after marriage, given the limited contact some experience before making this commitment. Other chapters – on pressure and dreaming – could appear anywhere in the sequence; they are experienced differently by different people, and for many they never go away.

Stories about single life, which we explored in the first substantive chapter, convey mixed emotions. These range from the freedom, friendship and possibility known by some people, some of the time, to experiences of anxiety, uncertainty and loneliness. Stories about single life speak variously of yearning, waiting and searching, both for a spouse and for a path in life. They also affirm the existence of the single adult Muslim, contradicting the widespread depiction of Muslims as people who segue abruptly from innocent childhood to married adulthood. Muslims tell different stories about single life and have different experiences of it, but for many this is an important stage in life, a time of relative freedom and exploration, the significance of which may endure in later life.

Introductions and meetings typically punctuate the tales young Muslims tell about their lives before marriage – and, furthermore, the stories that older Muslims relate about when they were young and single. These are heady and sometimes funny tales, shot through with strong and mixed feelings of excitement, anticipation, hope, desire, embarrassment, nerves, self-consciousness, desire and humour. All this is complicated and animated by intergenerational dynamics, stemming from the stakes that family members have in a potential relationship, and their interests in either encouraging or blocking it. Some of the characters in these stories appear compliant, content to rely upon introductions arranged by their families, or resigned to these customs. Others proactively seek out their own partners or actively acquaint themselves with those they have been introduced to, or have already become engaged to or married. These stories unfold the time spent together by prospective spouses, avoiding physical contact until they are married, and involving a chaperone if they meet in person. As such, they narrate an idea that has been gaining in currency and which we discuss in this book: halal dating. Meanwhile, other stories tell of unmarried Muslims who are less restrained, and may be dating for pleasure rather than to line up a husband or wife. These stories, dealing as they do with experience and desire, break silences and challenge stereotypes.

In the stories that young Muslims tell about sexual relationships, love is important. That said, it may well not be universal, explicit or necessarily in the places where non-Muslim audiences might expect to find it. In some cases, love stays beneath the surface, as a feeling or experience that young people struggle to acknowledge in words. In others, it appears in clichés and platitudes. Yet, where the present chapter has scratched the surface, Muslim love stories emerge that are at once culturally distinctive – with love *after* marriage, and lovers guided by Islam – and have widespread appeal. In interviews, workshopped stories and published literature, there are manifold expressions of hopes and dreams: to fall in love at some stage, and to stay in love with one person.

Another way in which Muslims' relationship stories stand out from the mainstream – without being unique, since they have things in common with other arranged marriage cultures – is in the pressure they portray. These stories speak of young people under immense pressure to get married to a person of the opposite sex, doing so at a particular time in their life, and with a spouse approved by the family. This pressure is uneven: loaded especially heavily upon female characters, who are bound more tightly and explicitly by patriarchal notions of *izzat*. Though to a lesser extent, male characters also carry the burden of familial expectations, which range from providing for their family to delivering supposedly unrehearsed but virile performances in the bridal suite on their wedding night. While some of the stronger, more dramatic stories speak of the intense pressure that is felt by some, our interviews and creative workshops also gathered quieter and more mundane accounts, which present more gradated pictures of the pressures experienced (or not) by young Muslims. These stories also illuminated some of the ways in which these young people are successfully negotiating and resisting such pressures.

Marriage is central to the stories young Muslims tell about sex and relationships. Though, as we have seen, many young Muslims enjoy and value the time they spend as single adults, and though some take the opportunities it provides for dating or alternatively for enjoying friendships, marriage is pivotal in this book. While most chapters addressed the ins, outs and implications of getting married, the 'Married' chapter focused more specifically on *being* married. We explored resonant stories – about bickering with a spouse, and deepening affections – as well as more distinctively Muslim marriage experiences, such as marrying into an extended family household and dealing with disappointment when marriage does not lead to love or a fulfilling sex life. The stories we have explored in this chapter, varied as they are, show that marriage means different things to different Muslims. For some it means more than a happy ever after. Marriage may involve an ongoing search, questioning what the union is and can be, why it doesn't always work and how young Muslims can shape it in their own interests and images.

When sexual relationships are framed largely (if not exclusively) in terms of marriage, sex may recede in importance. Still, this book presents varied, sometimes entertaining, often taboo-busting pictures of sex: good and bad sex, enthusiastic and dutiful sex, licit and illicit sex. Though the s-word proved initially off-putting to some of the young people we invited to participate in interviews and creative workshops – prompting us to drop the 'Sexual' from our original project title, 'Storying Sexual Relationships' – once they got over their shyness many eventually warmed to the subject. The stories they came to tell make it clear that sex is – or will be, they hope or expect – an integral part of their lives. And sex does not necessarily wait for marriage. Premarital chastity is far from a universal norm among young Muslims, and many of the unmarried Muslims who are not having sex are dreaming, thinking, talking, reading and writing about it. Dreaming about sex and sexual relationships, and articulating these dreams in the stories they share, young Muslims are toying with possibilities, mapping out divergent pathways for their own lives. These are of course not the only things on their minds. Many, particularly those who find ways to prolong their single years, dream about much more than meeting the right boy or girl and proceeding to a fairy-tale ending. Dreams take other forms too, and involve other kinds of relationships. 'I chose a string of boyfriends over one solid partner', said Noura defiantly. 'But only because I believe I can find my partner after I have found my power.'

Across these chapters and findings, a number of cross-cutting themes emerge, which pick up on themes we introduced in the second and third interludes: on the ways in which young Muslims are speaking to stereotypes and the extent to which the relationships they story are indeed distinctive: (not so) different. First, many of the stories we have entertained in this book contradict the stereotype that Muslims do things differently when it comes to sex and relationships. Muslims are portrayed as powerless and unhappy in love, driven by family, tradition and religion rather than passion, pleasure or personal desire, and self-destructively conformist (Chambers et al. 2018). This stereotype is important because it casts the Muslim as an alien and problematic figure, underpinning Islamophobia and interrelated forms of racism, and defining a divide between Muslims and all others. And yet, many of the stories in this book will resonate among non-Muslim audiences. If not universal – but what really is? – neither are they unique. Some of the things young British Muslims say and write about sexual relationships are quite ordinary, and neither unique or distinctive. Muslims are not alone in feeling tongue-tied, like the fictional Mateen in Yusuf's short story, when they finally meet the person they want. Nor are they unique in feeling anxious about the risks of a new relationship: developing feelings that may not be reciprocated; surrendering their independence; making themselves vulnerable. Young Muslims are not alone in experiencing physical desire, which draws them to another person without any certainty about what will happen next. There is a plangent simplicity in Mobeen's short story, penned in a workshop in Rochdale, in which a boy is attracted to a girl in his class simply because he 'liked the look of her, thought she was pretty'. Some other tropes and discoveries running through the book are equally ordinary: stories showing that love can be flawed, imperfect and sometimes painful, as well as a source of great joy and comfort (see the findings of the 'Love' chapter); pictures of established couples who bicker more and have sex less but, in some cases, grow in their love. Attention to ordinary things – those small details of life which chime with readers' experiences – can serve to humanize those who have been cast as curiosities and exoticized, showing that they are not so different after all (Garland-Thomson 2009).

But, as we argued in the third interlude '(Not So) Different', while many differences between Muslims and others are exaggerated and simplified by the mainstream press, other differences remain. The following paragraphs provide two examples of distinctive (but not always unique) ways in which Muslims speak and write about sexual relationships, building upon the stories that we elicited and explored in this book.

First, for many young Muslims, sexual relationships are fundamentally religious, framed by Islam. Muslims are not alone in bringing their faith and religious principles to sexual relationships, though of course they are unique for bringing *Islam* into their lives in this way. Many of the stories in this book tacitly echo the hadith that teaches that '[w]hen a servant marries he fulfils half the religion; so let him be conscious of God regarding the other half' (Eaton 2008: 84). As we saw, 'Shelina's' romantic quest in *Love in a Headscarf* begins with her understanding that marriage is 'half your faith' (Janmohamed 2009: 56) and that men and women are 'From a Single Soul, Created in Pairs' (Janmohamed 2009: 178). Given the importance given to marriage in Islam, for many Muslims sexual relationships are virtually synonymous with marriage. The predominance of marriage, coupled with barriers to speaking and writing openly about sexual relationships outside wedlock, have not silenced other voices. Indeed, this book has brought to light the sexual life that is experienced and/or imagined outside marriage, but still within a religious framework of some kind. This ranges from halal dating to premarital and extramarital sexual relationships, in which those involved are conscious of the religious boundaries they may be crossing, even as they traverse them. There is an undercurrent of tentative self-examination in Mobeen's story about a boy attracted to a girl simply because he 'liked the look of her'. Rather than narrating events, this story implicitly and simply reflects on whether it is right for a Muslim to be driven in this way, to allow his eye (and his libido) to lead. Even in an at-times overtly erotic story we examine in this book – *Exit West* – one of the protagonists finds it impossible to forget his religious principles. Nadia is taken aback when Saeed demurs to sex before marriage. They find pleasure in sex short of penetration, though.

A second example of the ways in which Muslims' sexual relationship stories are idiosyncratic, standing outside the mainstream, resides in the large cast of characters involved in these stories. Illustrating, perhaps caricaturing this point, set-piece *rishta* scenes involve members of two families, gathered while the prospective couple steal glances at each other across the crowded room. We have encountered these scenes in many forms, from novels like Rehana Alam's *The Tea Trolley* (2017) to tales related directly by young people. Before such formal gatherings take place, a lot goes on behind the scenes, with many people involved. Aunties, who are often portrayed as comic and controlling, are central to these proceedings. Recall the 'creepy' aunties, demanding to know the vital statistics of young women in the family and instructing them to 'walk up and down the room'

(Aqeelah's story was discussed in the 'Meeting' chapter). Interfering auntie figures – in this case neighbours – are also satirized in Heena's untitled play, where two older women are gossiping about a young woman they see in the distance and mistake for a neighbour's daughter. 'You know, these girls bring so much shame to their parents', judges Samira, before realizing this is her own daughter, holding hands with a boy on the street. Heena's story explores how families, friends, neighbours and communities play their parts in preventing, policing and discouraging some relationships, while condoning, sanctioning and pressing young people into others. The liberal use of the word 'auntie' underlines the sheer number of people who get involved in these communitarian rather than individualistic relationships.

The singularity of Muslims' relationships and relationship stories demands qualification, for two reasons. First, Muslims are distinctive but not unique in Western countries, since the stories they tell overlap with those of other ethnic and religious minorities. This is exemplified in the long cast of characters, which we have observed as characterizing their relationship stories. This reflects the extent to which their close and distant kin as well as community members get involved in marriages and other relationships. These (usually older) people lean in for a range of reasons, which they tend to present as religious but are in reality entangled with cultural and economic traditions and interests. In this respect, Muslims' marriage traditions overlap with those of others who share South Asian heritage. Families may have religious reasons for policing the virginity of unmarried women, but they also see the latter as fundamental to the purity of their bloodline, social standing and, in turn, their livelihood (Abboud, Jemmott and Sommers 2015; Amer, Howarth and Sen 2015; Buitelaar 2002; El Feki 2013; Khan 2012). Though common among British Muslims, particularly those with South Asian heritage (Shaw 2000, 2001; Mohammad 2015; Qureshi, Charsley and Shaw 2014), these business-like marriages are not exclusive to Muslims, nor are they intrinsically Islamic; other (British) South Asians practise them too (Afshar, Aitken and Franks 2006; Dale and Ahmed 2008).

Muslims overlap with others in another way, which has increasingly but incorrectly become identified with Muslims above all other minorities: the portrayal of Muslims as homophobic, and of gay and lesbian Muslims as uniquely embattled. In the third interlude, we acknowledged the heteronormativity and homonegativity of many Muslims, and saw that it can be harder for Muslims than members of the wider society to opt out of heterosexual marriage and into same-sex relationships. We acknowledged that heterosexuality is still effectively compulsory for many Muslims, given that 'marriage is obligatory for all Muslims' (Siraj 2009: 43; see also Yip 2004b). Without downplaying any of these important points, we added, however, that Muslims express a range of attitudes towards homosexuality, and have different experiences of being gay or lesbian. Not all Muslims take a hard line on this subject (Shannahan 2009). Some attempt to follow 'Islam's explicit condemnation of homosexuality' (Siraj 2009: 41) and harbour negative attitudes towards homosexuality, but others do not. Moreover, the range of attitudes that Muslims take on this subject broadly resembles that of the other Abrahamic faiths (Yip 2004a) or those they often call People of the Book. Here, as in other respects, the otherness of Muslims has been overstated. Joseph Massad (2015) finds a logic in this, arguing that Europeans, presenting themselves as liberal, have constructed Muslims and Islam as illiberal. There are elements of truth in their claims about the heteronormativity and homonegativity of Muslims, but these claims skim over important facts and exceptions, and they are fundamentally circular. In this book, we have heard stories about gay-friendly imams and happily gay and lesbian Muslims, placed alongside those of heteronormative mothers and young gay and lesbian Muslims who feel isolated and constrained. This nuanced picture contests easy but simplistic claims about either the homophobia or the homophilia of Muslims and Islam. This supports the broader conclusion that it would be wrong to portray Muslims as just like everyone else, or as unlike everyone else; their sexual relationships are ordinary in some ways, unique in others, and somewhere between these extremes in still others.

Choices

Through stories, young Muslims are not simply reflecting their lives or finding meaning in things they are already doing; they are making choices about how to live their lives, and explaining those choices to themselves and then to others. As we discussed in the Introduction, Ken Plummer (1995: 1) elucidates, 'Whatever else a story is, it is not simply the lived life. It speaks all around the life: it provides routes into a life, lays down maps to follow, suggests links between a life and a culture.' For most of the young people we have met over the course of this book, the storying of relationships takes place primarily within their own heads, also in creative writing that is never shared and conversations that are imagined and rehearsed long before they are spoken aloud – if they ever are. Once they have come to their own conclusions and rehearsed their reasoning privately, they have the words to communicate better with their families and communities. In doing so, they are necessarily confronting and exploring questions about what it means to be Muslim. Many are making choices and finding fulfilment through rather than in opposition to faith and family. Choice refers to the 'capability of actors to make decisions' based on their own interests, experiences and desires (Burns 2015: 198). To make a choice is to affirm the 'capacity for action', which is how Saba Mahmood (2001: 203) understands agency. This is generally seen as 'inherently positive' (Evans 2013: 47) because it denotes 'the ability for individuals to have some kind of transforming effect or impact' in their own lives and 'on the world' around them (McNay 2018: 39). This kind of optimism can also be found in Philip Lewis and Sadek Hamid's *British Muslims: New Directions in Islamic Thought, Creativity and Activism* (2018). These religious studies experts identify positive reformist practices as coming out of tripartite contributions by women, the English language and culture (or what in their final chapter they call 'Muslim Cool'). The present volume takes forward the focus on women (and men) and how they are working creatively and boldly with the English language and cultural production.

Ayaan Hirsi Ali (2006: 24) has asserted that the Muslim who wishes 'to liberate him- or herself [...] must first come to think differently about sexuality'. But, whereas Hirsi Ali speaks of young people liberating themselves *from* Islam, we have encountered some young men and women who are liberating themselves *through* their religion. These findings slot in with those of researchers such as Pnina Werbner, Haleh Afshar and Andrew Yip, who have shown how young British Muslims, while making their own life choices, are skilfully negotiating rather than turning their backs on faith and family. Sexual liberty does not automatically involve conflict with Islam or vice versa. Importantly, storying sexual relationships involves artful, delicate and attentive communication, with respect being shown for parents and elders within the community, and for religious principles. This tends to leave relationships with families and communities intact, and even stronger through the dialogue.

Where young Muslims story the choices they are making, they address the stereotypical portrayal of young Muslims as passive figures, who have little control over their relationships, simply following the dictates of family, tradition and religion (Chambers et al. 2018). We have argued that young Muslims can be burdened by the need to speak to such stereotypes, and thus to speak defensively, with a non-Muslim audience in mind. And yet, these stories are also vehicles for finding and making choices. These include decisions about when, whether and how to marry, as well as choices about other possibilities, ranging from staying single and chaste to experimenting with a range of sexual partners and roles (Daneshpour and Fathi 2016; Ouis 2007).

Young Muslims have agency in their sexual relationships because, however much pressure they are put under by family, community, culture and religion, they are not generally forced into anything. There are well-documented and important exceptions to this, of course, particularly in the form of forced marriages, and corrective and punitive expatriations, in which transgressive young people are sent off to relatives 'back home', often in Pakistan. But most young British Muslims most of the time are pressured rather than forced into particular relationships, and out of others. This, as we have seen in this book, involves pressure exerted through families, in which parents, aunties and siblings set and enforce variously explicit and implicit rules. In some cases, these rules are presented as advice or guidance. In others, they materialize as instructions to get married. (Tahir said his older brothers 'get it every single day. Get married!') Pressure is also exerted through cultural and religious norms and codes which revolve around marriage: the fundamental principle that every adult who can get married to a member of the opposite sex should do so; further, that they should consummate this marriage and enjoy sex within it – but only within it. This principle, as we learned, has three key dimensions: heteronormativity, homonegativity and premarital virginity.

Pressures should not be underestimated. Pressure – usually to marry a 'suitable' person of the opposite sex, and to refrain from same-sex and other forms of pre- and extramarital relationships – is often intense, suffocating and hard to bear, particularly for those who find it difficult or impossible to conform. And yet, this pressure does not usually amount to coercion. Young people – some more than others – find room for manoeuvre: 'wiggle room' (Ahmed 2014). This may mean overt resistance: openly refusing to follow the wishes or rules set by family members or to conform to community norms. Or, conscious of the costs of outright rebellion, young people sometimes opt for more subtle forms of resistance: doing things they want to do (such as dating), not doing other things that other people want them to do (such as marrying and starting a family at a young age) while appearing to conform. One might call these 'weapons of the weak' (a term coined by Scott 2008: 1) or, more accurately, the pragmatic and diplomatic actions and negotiations of young people who know the value of keeping in with family and kinship groups since economic livelihood remains bound up with marriage (Dale and Ahmed 2008; Hélie and Hoodfar 2012). Tahir, whose parents have been pressuring him to marry since he was a teenager, has been able to buy time for himself without forcing any conflict. He simply stays in the shadows while his parents concentrate their energies on his still-unmarried older brothers. There are limits to all this, of course; these young people are negotiating the details of their marriages, not questioning the fact of marriage, or their heterosexuality.

While young Muslims are finding and making their own choices, whether by breaking rules and refusing to do what they are told or by resisting pressures and expectations, others are exercising agency by negotiating wider sets of norms in which religion intersects with ethnicity and heritage. Some are resisting their parents' assumption that they will take spouses from Pakistan, and otherwise follow Pakistani-identified marriage customs (Charsley 2005a, 2005b; Charsley and Bolognani 2017). Others, by embracing Islam, are rejecting cultural traditions and norms, challenging parents while staying within the bounds of familial acceptance and religious respectability. As Pnina Werbner explains, identification with Islam 'empowers these young men and women with the right to choose their own marriage partners, even against the will of their parents'. It also offers licence to 'accuse their parents of being ignorant, locked into false or mistaken parochial "customs" and "traditions" of the old country' (Werbner 2007: 171). Meanwhile, these young Muslims are retaining strands of cultural heritage, deciding which traditions they want to retain and renew and which to jettison, in each case with implications for their relationships, above all their marriages. They are mobilizing their religion and heritage without being driven by either of these (Phillips et al. 2020).

But, while young British Muslims are breaking silences about sex and relationships and are thus identifying, making and explaining a greater range of life choices, some of these possibilities are more realizable for some than others. Agency is unevenly distributed and relational, structured as it is by sexuality, gender, class, caste and culture. Participants in this project commented that open dating, for example, is largely restricted to certain (but not all) heterosexual men and women; the same applies to negotiations of marriage. For others, particularly those experiencing same-sex desire or wishing to explore and experiment with sex before or outside heterosexual marriage, liberation tends to involve a more complex negotiation of religion. For such non-normative Muslims there are more constraints about what can be said, by who and to whom. Other norms and expectations are gendered, typically affecting women more than men. These include rules about premarital virginity (there is more tolerance of male promiscuity) and marrying young (women are typically expected to marry at a younger age than men). Other freedoms are class specific. Given the importance of higher education in postponing marriage and in finding one's own spouse, the freedoms to live as a single adult and then to choose one's own husband or wife (perhaps rejecting family proposals for transnational cousin marriage), are dependent on having the economic and cultural capital needed for admission to university. Put differently, since British higher education is largely the privilege of the middle classes, these freedoms are more readily available to better-off Muslims. In short, the sexual storying explored in this book tells a good news story, but one that needs to be qualified: kept in proportion, and painted in fine rather than broad brushstrokes.

To imagine a world

We want to end this book on a note of cautious optimism. Our research shows that even for young Muslims with the least freedom to assert themselves and make decisions, stories open doors. This is true not only for those who tell and write stories but also for those who hear and read, share and discuss them. Crucially, the stories we have discussed in this book are finding readers, just as the spoken words are finding listeners, and taking their places within wider exchanges. These audiences include young Muslims and others too: friends, parents, aunties, imams, neighbours, members of their communities and of the wider society. Throughout this book, we have paid great attention to those who tell stories, but their listeners and readers have always been with us too. We have developed a sense of stories in motion and in circulation, thus showing interest in the retelling as much as the telling. Whether because they did not wish to disclose personal histories or because they felt they were still waiting for their own stories to begin, many of the people we interviewed retold other peoples' stories. They spoke, as we have seen, of happy and unhappy marriages, of good and bad sex, of young people sent on correctional visits 'back home', of rumours and hearsay. In each case, they decant other people's stories into their own lives. Something similar applies to stories in print. Young Muslims, reading the stories we have explored in the course of this book, may recognize something of themselves and their own lives, and participate in something bigger than their own experiences and lives: a collective storying of sexual relationships.

The indirectness of storytelling – including possibilities of writing and speaking anonymously, of working with fiction and fantasy, of transposing one's desires and experiences onto characters – establishes possibilities and 'enables us to imagine a world' (Cheah 2016: 44). For those who are telling and sharing them, these spoken and written words and stories 'provide, if not answers, at least milestones and signposts' (Solnit 2017/2005: 15). Stories may not be the last word, but they allow for play on words in pleasurable and hopeful ways.

Conclusion

Table C.1 Interviews quoted in Conclusion

Name	Gender	Age	Relationship Status	Location
Ifrah	Female	21	Single	Yorkshire
Hiba	Female	27	Married	Glasgow
Hassan	Male	29	Single	Yorkshire
Tahir	Male	20	Single	Glasgow
Aqeelah	Female	29	Married	Glasgow

Table C.2 Workshop participants and convenors quoted in Conclusion

Name	Gender	Age	Workshop Series	Role in Workshop	Title
Noura	Female	28	5. Fiction, Glasgow 6. Blogging, Glasgow	Participant	'Untitled' 'Finding Your Power'
Yusuf	Male	22	7. Fiction, Rochdale	Participant	'What If?'
Mobeen	Male	26	7. Fiction, Rochdale	Participant	Untitled
Heena	Female	25	4. Playwriting, Glasgow	Participant	Untitled play
Haris	Male	25	7. Fiction, Rochdale	Participant	'"Qabool" – The Happily Never After'

GUIDE TO LITERARY SOURCES

Rehana Alam, The Tea Trolley: A Novel *(2017)*

Prior to the publication of her debut novel *The Tea Trolley*, Rehana Alam wrote two children's books in Urdu. Born and brought up in Pakistan, Alam pursued her higher studies in both her home nation and the United States, and has also lived in several other countries including Turkey, Nigeria, Italy, Kenya and Indonesia. She currently lives between Pakistan and the US. *The Tea Trolley* is related from the perspective of a first-person narrator protagonist who recalls her experiences of going through the 'meeting' procedures and rituals around arranged marriage. Often light-hearted in tone, the novel reveals the funny and absurd etiquette relating to matchmaking and, in Bildungsroman style, shows how the teenage protagonist matures as a result of her experiences.

Nadeem Aslam, Maps for Lost Lovers *(2004)*

Born in 1966 in Gujranwala, Pakistan, Nadeem Aslam moved to Huddersfield when he was fourteen. He left his undergraduate degree in biochemistry to devote himself to writing. Aslam's lyrical novel *Maps for Lost Lovers* is set in a fictitious British Pakistani town called Dasht-e-Tanhaii ('the Desert of Loneliness'), a poetic name bestowed on the locality in northern England by its homesick immigrant inhabitants. The narrative pivots on the 'honour' killing of the eponymous lovers, Jugnu and Chanda, excavating the intricate webs of religious orthodoxy, gender segregation and systemic racism in this impoverished part of the UK.

Fatima Bhutto, The Runaways *(2019)*

Fatima Bhutto hails from Pakistan's powerful yet tragic political dynasty. Her grandfather Zulfikar Ali Bhutto was Pakistan's prime minister who was usurped and then executed by President Muhammad Zia-ul-Haq in the late 1970s. Her leftist father Murtaza Bhutto was killed near the family home in 1996 when she was just fourteen. Blaming her uncle Asif Ali Zardari for the murder, Fatima Bhutto became estranged from his wife, her aunt Benazir, who was herself assassinated in 2007. In her 2010 memoir *Songs of Blood and Sword*, Bhutto recounts her father's murder during Benazir's premiership. A powerful and political writer, in her latest novel *The Runaways* Bhutto addresses social inequities, sexual relations and youths' vulnerability to radicalization in our divided contemporary age.

Roopa Farooki, Bitter Sweets *(2007) and* The Flying Man *(2012)*

Born in Lahore to a Pakistani father and Bangladeshi mother, Roopa Farooki grew up in London where her parents moved when she was a few months old. Farooki's debut novel *Bitter Sweets* was nominated for the Orange New Writers Award. A family saga, this novel primarily explores the concurrent presence of love and deceit and their associated complexities that mark generations of the same family. Her fourth novel, *The Flying Man*, follows the life of an unusually adventurous man – the titular protagonist – who refuses stability and certainty in life for the sake of his freedom to be anything and go anywhere he likes, even at the expense of love and familial bonds.

Mohsin Hamid, Exit West *(2017)*

Born in 1971 in Lahore, Pakistan, Mohsin Hamid spent a period in his childhood in the US where his father was pursuing his PhD. He later returned to America for his own studies at Princeton and Harvard Law. Hamid's critically acclaimed bestseller *The Reluctant Fundamentalist* was shortlisted for the Man Booker Prize and has been adapted into a film of the same name. *Exit West* is Hamid's fourth and latest novel – a finalist for the Man Booker Prize in 2017 – and scrutinizes the global refugee crisis. In it, he presents snapshots of the lives of anonymous people in different locations around the globe, including San Diego, Tijuana and Dubai. These snapshots are juxtaposed with the detailed narrative trajectory of the novel's only named characters, protagonists Nadia and Saeed, as they fall in love, begin to cohabit, flee the city of their birth and experience the migrant or refugee's precarious existence.

Shelina Zahra Janmohamed, Love in a Headscarf: Muslim Woman Seeks the One *(2009)*

A British Muslim of East African Asian heritage, Shelina Janmohamed was born and grew up in north London, graduating from New College, Oxford. She has been listed among the UK's 100 most influential Muslim women by *The Times* newspaper (UK). A writer and commentator on Muslim issues, especially the concerns of Muslim youths, Janmohamed writes regular columns for the *The Daily Telegraph*, *The Guardian* and the BBC. Published in 2009, her memoir recounts the author's search of love as a young British Muslim woman for whom faith is a central pillar in her life. The book has garnered positive critical appreciation because of its insight into British Muslim youth, and the work's wit and freshness stands in contrast to the popular perception of dour Muslims oppressed by their faith.

Amjeed Kabil, Straightening Ali *(2007)*

Amjeed Kabil's parents came to the UK from Pakistan in the 1950s. Kabil acknowledges that some of his personal experiences of life in a second-generation British Pakistani family make their way into his debut novel *Straightening Ali.* The text is about Ali, whose homosexuality is unacceptable to his orthodox family. He goes through a series of humiliations hurled at him by his family members, including his elder brother's violent homophobic assaults and his mother's emotional blackmail, which force him into marriage with a woman he barely knows. The novel was the first of its kind, and its discussion of queer identities in the British Muslim context was a significant literary landmark. However, Kabil's writing has rightly been criticized for its relative lack of complexity, stemming from the narrative's reliance on mostly stereotypical, flat characters.

Tabish Khair, Just Another Jihadi Jane *(2016)*

Born and raised in the small town of Gaya in Bihar, India, Tabish Khair is a noted literary critic, poet and novelist. He moved to Denmark to pursue his academic career and is currently an associate professor at Aarhus University. In his 2012 novel *How to Fight Islamist Terror from a Missionary Position*, Khair takes a comic and astute stance on Islamic extremism and popular portrayals of Muslims in the Western world from the perspective of a young man based in Denmark. *Just Another Jihadi Jane* again grapples with the issue of religious extremism but from a different perspective. This time the story is told through the focalization of a British Muslim teenage girl, who, with a teenage friend, leave their homes in West Yorkshire to marry ISIS jihadists. The much-lauded novel was nominated for the Kirkus Prize in the United States and the Tara Book of the Year Award in India.

Almas Khan, Poppadom Preach *(2011) and* Chapati and Chips *(1993)*

British Pakistani writer Almas Khan was born and raised in West Yorkshire. Her debut novel *Chapati and Chips* was published by the independent publisher Yorkshire Art Circus and gained popularity in her hometown of Bradford. Set in this multicultural city, the novella follows the life of the mixed-race British adolescent Stacey who tackles both her racist maternal grandfather's dictates and the conservative extended family on her late Pakistani father's side. Her second novel *Poppadom Preach* is also set in Bradford in the 1970s. The novel charts the coming of age of its teenage protagonist, Dilly, who is indomitable despite her experiences of 'casual racism', her dangerously ill-tempered father and verbal abuse from her mother.

Muhammad Khan, I Am Thunder *(2018)*

YA (Young Adult) author Muhammad Khan wears many hats: not only does he write but he has a background in engineering and teaches mathematics in a south London school. Khan says that he derives inspiration from his students, and this is particularly apparent in his young characters' confident, codeswitching use of Multicultural London English (MLE). His debut novel *I Am Thunder* centres on a teenage schoolgirl, Muzna. Torn between her own aspirations and her parents' different expectations, she gradually becomes radicalized by her attractive boyfriend who, it transpires, has been 'brainwashed' (2018: 264) by his jihadist brother. Khan's most recent book *Kick the Moon*, published in January 2019, presents a teenage boy as its protagonist, and deals with the issue of gang membership.

Hanif Kureishi, The Black Album *(1996/1995)*

Born in Kent to a white English mother and an Indian Muslim father (whose family migrated to Pakistan after partition in 1947), Hanif Kureishi was one of the first authors to write about Muslim and mixed-heritage characters in contemporary Britain. A novelist, filmmaker and playwright, Kureishi's *My Beautiful Laundrette* (1985) won Best Screenplay nominations from the Academy Awards and BAFTA. *The Black Album* is Kureishi's second novel. It is set in 1989, the year of the Rushdie affair and the rave music craze. Both of these phenomena are discussed at some length in this humorous novel of ideas, attuned as it is to popular culture. The novel also takes its title from pop artist Prince's album of the same name that came out the preceding year. The novel was adapted as a play and staged at the National Theatre and other playhouses in 2009 and again in 2019.

Ayisha Malik, Sofia Khan is Not Obliged *(2015) and* The Other Half of Happiness *(2017)*

British Muslim writer Ayisha Malik casts herself as a 'lifelong Londoner'. Marketed as the 'Muslim Bridget Jones', her debut novel *Sofia Khan is Not Obliged* shatters many stereotypes about today's young Muslims through its funny account of her caustic protagonist's dating experiences. Sofia decides to date as part of her personal quest to find a life partner and her professional commission to write a book about the Muslim dating scene. Her next novel *The Other Half of Happiness* is a sequel that follows Sophia Khan's post-wedding misunderstandings and subsequent divorce.

Maria Qamar, Trust No Aunty *(2017)*

An illustrator and writer, Maria Qamar describes the style of her work as 'American pop art mixed with Indian soap opera' (qtd in Khan 2016). Qamar was born in Pakistan and grew up in Canada, where her family moved when she was nine years old. In 2015, she started her Instagram account @Hatecopy that features comic illustrations of young women's experience of growing up in the South Asian diaspora. Later she adapted these illustrations into her book *Trust No Aunty*. The genre-defying book is a 'survival kit' containing strategies to manage the often conflicting demands of diasporic life and, of course, how to handle the ever-present inquisitive 'Aunties'.

Kamila Shamsie, Home Fire *(2017)*

Kamila Shamsie was born and raised in Karachi and later moved to the US where she pursued creative writing degrees at Hamilton and Amherst. Coming from an illustrious family of literary doyennes (her mother is the Pakistani literary critic Muneeza Shamsie, and her great-aunt was Attia Hosain), Shamsie too is a prolific and acclaimed author. Having been awarded the Women's Prize for Fiction, her recent novel *Home Fire* reworks the Sophoclean tragedy *Antigone*. Her British Muslim Antigone, Aneeka, dares to defy the state in order to bring back the body of her jihadist brother, who was killed in Istanbul as he tried to escape from the Islamic State. Among its many strengths, the novel imagines a British Muslim Home Secretary stripping a fellow British Muslim of citizenship, which is prescient given Sajid Javid's similar repudiation of Shamima Begum's rights eighteen months later.

REFERENCES

Abboud, S., L. S. Jemmott and M. S. Sommers (2015), '"We are Arabs": The Embodiment of Virginity through Arab and Arab American Women's Lived Experiences', *Sexuality and Culture*, 19(4): 715–36.
Abraham, I. (2009), '"Out to Get Us": Queer Muslims and the Clash of Sexual Civilisations in Australia', *Contemporary Islam*, 3(1): 79–97.
Abraham, M. (1999), 'Sexual Abuse in South Asian Immigrant Marriages', *Violence Against Women*, 5(6): 591–618.
Abu Dawud, S. (2009), 'Online Hadith Collection, Book 33, Prescribed Punishments, Hadith 4448'. Available online: http://www.hadithcollection.com/abudawud.html (accessed 10 September 2019).
Abu-Lughod, L. (2013), *Do Muslim Women Need Saving?*, Boston, MA: Harvard University Press.
Adams, T. E. (2016), *Narrating the Closet: An Autoethnography of Same-Sex Attraction*, Abingdon: Routledge.
Afshar, H., R. Aitken and M. Franks (2006), 'Islamophobia and Women of Pakistani Descent in Bradford: The Crisis of Ascribed and Adopted Identities', in H. Moghissi (ed.), *The Muslim Diaspora: Gender, Culture and Identity*, 167–85, Abingdon: Routledge.
Ahmad, F. (2001), 'Modern Traditions? British Muslim Women and Academic Achievement', *Gender and Education*, 13(2): 137–52.
Ahmad, F. (2012), 'Graduating Towards Marriage? Attitudes Towards Marriage and Relationships among University-Educated British Muslim Women', *Culture and Religion*, 13(2): 193–210.
Ahmed, R. (2015), *Writing British Muslims: Religion, Class and Multiculturalism*, Manchester: Manchester University Press.
Ahmed, S. (2010), *The Promise of Happiness*, Durham, NC: Duke University Press.
Ahmed, S. (2012), *Secrets of the Henna Girl*, London: Puffin.
Ahmed, S. (2013), 'Single Muslim women on dating: "I don't want to be a submissive wife"', *The Guardian*, 15 July. Available online: https://www.theguardian.com/lifeandstyle/2013/jul/15/single-muslim-women-dating (accessed 1 December 2019).
Ahmed, S. (2014), 'Wiggle Room', Feminist Killjoys Blog, 28 September. Available online: https://feministkilljoys.com/2014/09/28/wiggle-room/ (accessed 30 November 2019).
Alam, M. Y. and C. Husband (2006), *British-Pakistani Men from Bradford*, York: Joseph Rowntree Foundation.
Alam, R. (2017), *The Tea Trolley: A Novel*, Denver, CO: Outskirts.
Alexander, C. E. (2000), *The Asian Gang: Ethnicity, Identity, Masculinity*, Oxford: Berg.
Ali, A. (1987/1984), *Al-Qur'ān: A Contemporary Translation*, Delhi: Oxford University Press.
Ali, A. H. (2006), *The Caged Virgin: An Emancipation Proclamation for Women and Islam*, New York: Simon & Schuster.
Ali, N., R. Phillips, C. Chambers, K. Narkowicz, P. Hopkins and R. Pande (2019), 'Halal Dating: Changing Relationship Attitudes and Experiences among Young

British Muslims', *Sexualities*. Available online: https://tinyurl.com/szbt87h (accessed 28 December 2019).

Alibhai-Brown, Y. (2019), 'The Islam of my youth was open-minded, curious, and joyful. Where has it gone?', *I-News*, 26 February. Available online: https://inews.co.uk/opinion/shamima-begum-islam-iranian-revolution-98387 (accessed 28 December 2019).

Amer, A., C. Howarth and R. Sen (2015), 'Diasporic Virginities: Social Representations of Virginity and Identity Formation amongst British Arab Muslim Women', *Culture and Psychology*, 21(1): 3–19.

Amis, M. (2001), *The War against Cliché: Essays and Reviews 1971–2000*, New York: Vintage.

Anderson, L., ed., (2006), *Creative Writing: A Workbook with Readings*, Abingdon: Routledge and the Open University.

Aslam, N. (2004), *Maps for Lost Lovers*, London: Faber & Faber.

Atkinson, R. (1998), *The Life Story Interview*, London: SAGE.

Atwood, M. (2003), *Negotiating With the Dead*, London: Time Warner Books.

Bacchus, N. S. (2017), 'Shifting Sexual Boundaries: Ethnicity and Premarital Sex in the Lives of South Asian American Women', *Sexuality and Culture*, 21(3): 776–94.

Bakht, N. (2008), *Belonging and Banishment: Being Muslim in Canada*, Toronto: TSAR.

Balzani, M. (2006), 'Transnational Marriage among Ahmadi Muslims in the UK', *Global Networks*, 6(4): 345–55.

BBC (2003), 'Speed dating first – Muslim Style', *BBC News*, 19 August. Available online: http://news.bbc.co.uk/1/hi/wales/south_east/3164067.stm (accessed 17 January 2017).

BBC (2011), 'Jack Straw criticised for "easy meat" comments on abuse', *BBC News*, 8 January. Available online: http://www.bbc.co.uk/news/uk-12142177 (accessed 3 February 2017).

BBC (2019a), 'Shamima Begum: IS bride set to be granted legal aid'. *BBC News*, 15 April. Available at: https://www.bbc.co.uk/news/uk-47934721 (accessed 1 December 2019).

BBC (2019b), 'Brunei says it won't enforce death penalty for gay sex', *BBC News*, 6 May. Available online: https://www.bbc.co.uk/news/world-asia-48171165 (accessed 27 December 2019).

Berelowitz, S. (2012a), 'Too many children are victims of sexual abuse. It's our duty to protect them', *The Guardian*, 21 November. Available online: https://www.theguardian.com/commentisfree/2012/nov/21/children-sexual-abuse-duty-to-protect (accessed 10 September 2019).

Berelowitz, S., C. Firmin, G. Edwards and S. Gulyurtlu (2012b), '"I Thought I Was the Only One. The Only One in the World": The Office of the Children's Commissioner's Inquiry into Child Sexual Exploitation in Gangs and Groups'. Available online: https://static.lgfl.net/LgflNet/downloads/online-safety/LGfL-OS-Research-Archive-2012-Childrens-Commissioner-CSE.pdf (accessed 3 October 2020).

Bhopal, K. (2009), 'Identity, Empathy and "Otherness": Asian Women, Education and Dowries in the UK', *Race Ethnicity and Education*, 12(1): 27–39.

Bhutto, F. (2019a), *The Runaways*, London: Viking.

Bhutto, F. (2019b), *New Kings of the World: Dispatches from Bollywood, Dizi, and K-Pop*, New York: Columbia Reports.

Bochner, A. P., C. Ellis and L. M. Tillmann-Healy (1997), 'Relationships as Stories', in S. Duck (ed.), *Handbook of Personal Relationships: Theory, Research and Interventions*, 307–24, Oxford: Wiley.

Bolognani, M. (2014), 'Visits to the Country of Origin: How Second-Generation British Pakistanis Shape Transnational Identity and Maintain Power Asymmetries', *Global Networks*, 14(1): 103–20.

Boswell, J. (1980), *Christianity, Social Tolerance and Homosexuality*, Chicago, IL: University of Chicago Press.

Britton, J. (2018), 'Challenging the Racialization of Child Sexual Exploitation: Muslim Men, Racism and Belonging in Rotherham', *Ethnic and Racial Studies*, 42(5): 1–19.

Buitelaar, M. W. (2002), 'Negotiating the Rules of Chaste Behaviour: Re-Interpretations of the Symbolic Complex of Virginity by Young Women of Moroccan Descent in the Netherlands', *Ethnic and Racial Studies*, 25(3): 462–89.

Bullock, K. (2010), *Rethinking Muslim Women and the Veil*, Richmond: International Institute of Islamic Thought (IIIT).

Burns, T. R. (2015), 'Two Conceptions of Human Agency', in P. Sztompka (ed.), *Agency and Structure: Reorienting Social Theory*, 197–250, New York: Routledge.

Cable, A. and K. Connolly (2006), 'A forced marriage? I'd rather kill myself', *Daily Mail*, 9 June. Available online: http://www.dailymail.co.uk/femail/article-389831/A-forced-marriage-Id-kill-myself.html (accessed 1 December 2019).

Calhoun, C. (2005), 'Foreword', in T. Modood (ed.), *Multicultural Politics: Racism, Ethnicity and Muslims in Britain*, ix–xii, Edinburgh: Edinburgh University Press.

Cameron, E. (2012), 'New Geographies of Story and Storytelling', *Progress in Human Geography*, 36(5): 573–92.

Carbajal, A. F. (2019), *Queer Muslim Diasporas in Contemporary Literature and Film*, Manchester: Manchester University Press.

Casey, L. (2016), *The Casey Review: a review into opportunity and integration*. Available online: https://www.gov.uk/government/publications/the-casey-review-a-review-into-opportunity-and-integration (accessed 13 September 2019).

Chambers, C. (2013), 'Countering the "Oppressed, Kidnapped Genre" of Muslim Life Writing: Yasmin Hai's *The Making of Mr Hai's Daughter* and Shelina Zahra Janmohamed's *Love in a Headscarf*, *Life Writing*, 10(1): 77–96.

Chambers, C. (2019), *Making Sense of Contemporary British Muslim Novels*, London: Palgrave Macmillan.

Chambers, C. and M. White (2019), 'Essay: Christchurch and Other Stories', *Dawn*, 31 March. Available online: https://www.dawn.com/news/1472932 (accessed 10 September 2019).

Chambers, C., N. Ali and R. Phillips (2020), *A Match Made in Heaven*, London: HopeRoad.

Chambers, C., R. Phillips, N. Ali, P. Hopkins and R. Pande (2018), '"Sexual Misery" or "Happy Muslims"? Contemporary Depictions of Muslim Sexuality', *Ethnicities*, 19(1): 66–94.

Change Institute (2009), *Pakistani Muslim Community in England: Report Commissioned by DCLG (Department for Communities and Local Government, Home Office)*, London: Office of Public Sector Information.

Charsley, K. (2005a), 'Unhappy Husbands: Masculinity and Migration in Transnational Pakistani Marriages', *Journal of the Royal Anthropological Institute*, 11(1): 85–105.

Charsley, K. (2005b), 'Vulnerable Brides and Transnational Ghar Damads: Gender, Risk and "Adjustment" among Pakistani Marriage Migrants to Britain', *Indian Journal of Gender Studies*, 12(2–3): 381–406.

Charsley, K. and M. Bolognani (2017), 'Being a Freshie Is (Not) Cool: Stigma, Capital and Disgust in British Pakistani Stereotypes of New Subcontinental Migrants', *Ethnic and Racial Studies*, 40(1): 43–62.

Charsley, K. and A. Liversage (2015), 'Silenced Husbands: Muslim Marriage Migration and Masculinity', *Men and Masculinities*, 18(4): 489–508.
Charsley, K. and A. Shaw (2006), 'South Asian Transnational Marriages in Comparative Perspective', *Global Networks*, 6(4): 131–45.
Cheah, P. (2016), *What Is a World? On Postcolonial Literature as World Literature*, Durham, NC: Duke University Press.
Cockbain, E. (2013), 'Grooming and the "Asian Sex Gang Predator": The Construction of a Racial Crime Threat', *Race and Class*, 54(4): 22–32.
Cvetkovich, A. (2012), *Depression: A Public Feeling*, Durham, NC: Duke University Press.
Dale, A. and S. Ahmed (2008), *Migration, Marriage and Employment amongst Indian, Pakistani and Bangladeshi Residents in the UK*, Manchester: University of Manchester, CCSR Working Paper, 2: 1–10.
Daneshpour, M. and E. Fathi (2016), 'Muslim Marriages in the Western World', *Journal of Muslim Mental Health*, 10(1): 51–64.
Daoud, K. (2016), 'The sexual misery of the Arab world', *The New York Times*, 12 February. Available online: http://www.nytimes.com/2016/02/14/opinion/sunday/the-sexual-misery-of-the-arab-world.html?_r=0 (accessed 17 January 2017).
Dearden, L. (2017), 'One of first Muslim same-sex marriages takes place in UK', *The Independent*, 11 July. Available online: https://www.independent.co.uk/news/uk/home-news/muslim-same-sex-marriage-uk-first-walsall-west-midlands-islam-homosexual-jahed-choudhury-sean-rogan-a7835036.html (accessed 13 September 2019).
Desai, J. and R. Dudrah (2008), 'The Essential Bollywood', in J. Desai and R. Dudrah (eds), *The Bollywood Reader*, 1–17, Maidenhead: Open University Press.
Dialmy, A. (2010), 'Sexuality and Islam', *The European Journal of Contraception and Reproductive Health Care*, 15(3): 160–8.
Duffy, J. (2014), 'The changing face of Muslim matchmaking', *The Herald*, 30 November. Available online: http://www.heraldscotland.com/news/13191876.The_changing_face_of_Muslim_match_making/ (accessed 17 January 2017).
Dwyer, C. (2000), 'Negotiating Diasporic Identities: Young British South Asian Muslim Women', *Women's Studies International Forum*, 23(4): 475–86.
Eaton, C. L. G. (2008), *The Book of Hadith: Sayings of the Prophet Muhammad from the Mishkat Al Masabih*, Bristol: Book Foundation.
El Feki, S. (2013), *Sex and the Citadel: Intimate Life in a Changing Arab World*, New York: Pantheon.
Eşsizoğlu, A., A. Yasan, E. A. Yildirim, F. Gurgen and M. Ozkan (2011), 'Double Standard for Traditional Value of Virginity and Premarital Sexuality in Turkey: A University Students Case', *Women and Health*, 51(2): 136–50.
Evans, M. (2013), 'The Meaning of Agency', in S. Madhok, A. Phillips, K. Wilson and C. Hemmings (eds), *Gender, Agency, and Coercion*, 47–63, London: Palgrave.
Farooki, R. (2007), *Bitter Sweets*, London: St. Martin's.
Farooki, R. (2012), *The Flying Man*, London: Hachette.
Federico, A. (2016), *Engagements with Close Reading*, Abingdon: Routledge.
Fekete, Liz (2006) 'Enlightened Fundamentalism? Immigration, Feminism and the Right'. *Race and Class*, 48(2): 1–22.
Franceschelli, M. and M. O'Brien (2015), '"Being Modern and Modest": South Asian Young British Muslims Negotiating Multiple Influences on their Identity', *Ethnicities*, 15(5): 696–714.
Fraser, M. M. (2012), 'Once upon a Problem', *Sociological Review*, 60(1): 84–107.
Garland-Thomson, R. (2009), *Staring: How We Look*, New York: Oxford University Press.

Gleeson, K. (2004) 'From Centenary to the Olympics: Gang Rape in Sydney', *Current Issues in Criminal Justice*, 16(2): 183–201.
Gopinath, G. (2000), 'Queering Bollywood: Alternative Sexualities in Popular Indian Cinema', *Journal of Homosexuality*, 39(3–4): 283–97.
Gubrium, J. F. and J. A. Holstein (2008), *Analyzing Narrative Reality*, London: SAGE.
Habib, S., ed. (2009), *Islam and Homosexuality*, Santa Barbara, CA: ABC-CLIO.
Hall, S. (1990), 'Cultural Identity and Diaspora', in J. Rutherford (ed.), *Identity: Community, Culture, Difference*, 222–37, London: Lawrence and Wishart.
Hamid, M. (2017), *Exit West*, London: Hamish Hamilton.
Hamid, T. (2017), 'Islamic Tinder', in Mahfouz, S. (ed.), *The Things I Would Tell You*, 81–4, London: Saqi.
Harding, E. (2019), 'Primary school AXES anti-homophobia lessons after protests from Muslim parents who withdrew 600 children from lessons', *Mail Online*, 5 March. Available online: https://www.dailymail.co.uk/news/article-6771317/Primary-school-AXES-anti-homophobia-lessons-protests-Muslim-parents.html (accessed 10 September 2019).
Harper, G. (2019), *The Desire to Write: The Five Keys to Creative Writing*, London: Red Globe.
Harvey, M. R., E. G. Mishler, K. Koenen and P. Harney (2000), 'In the Aftermath of Sexual Abuse: Making and Remaking Meaning in Narratives of Trauma and Recovery', *Narrative Inquiry*, 10(2): 291–311.
Hasan, A. G. (2002), 'Halal, Haram, and Sex in the City: A Young Muslim Lawyer on the American Dating Scene', in M. Wolfe (ed.), *Taking Back Islam: American Muslims Reclaim Their Faith*, 117–26, Emmaus, PA: Rodale.
Hélie, A. and H. Hoodfar (2012), *Sexuality in Muslim Contexts: Restrictions and Resistance*, London: Zed.
Honesty Policy (2014), *Happy British Muslims*, YouTube. Available online: https://www.youtube.com/watch?v=gVDIXqILqSM (accessed 3 October 2020).
Hussain, S. (2020), *The Family Tree*, London: HQ.
Hussain, Z. (2006), *The Curry Mile*, Manchester: Suitcase.
Hussein, K. (forthcoming), *The Muslim Speaks*, London: Zed/Bloomsbury.
Ijaz, A. and T. Abbas (2010), 'The Impact of Inter-Generational Change on the Attitudes of Working-Class South Asian Muslim Parents on the Education of their Daughters', *Gender and Education*, 22(3): 313–26.
Islamophobia Definition (2019), 'Islamophobia | Islamophobia is rooted in racism and is a type of racism that targets expressions of Muslimness or perceived Muslimness'. Available online: https://islamophobia-definition.com (accessed 28 December 2019).
Jamal, A. (2001), 'The Story of Lot and the Qur'an's Perception of the Morality of Same-Sex Sexuality', *Journal of Homosexuality*, 41(1): 1–88.
Janmohamed, S. Z. (2009), *Love in a Headscarf: Muslim Woman Seeks the One*, London: Aurum.
Janmohamed, S. (2019), 'Long before Shamima Begum, Muslim women were targets', *The Guardian*, 1 March. Available online: www.theguardian.com/commentisfree/2019/mar/01/shamima-begum-muslim-women-targets (accessed 10 September 2019).
Jaspal, R. and M. Cinnirella (2010), 'Coping with Potentially Incompatible Identities: Accounts of Religious, Ethnic, and Sexual Identities from British Pakistani Men who Identify as Muslim and Gay', *British Journal of Social Psychology*, 49(4): 849–70.
Jay, A. (2014), *Independent Inquiry into Child Sexual Exploitation in Rotherham (1997–2013)*, Rotherham: Rotherham Council.

Kabbani, R. (1986), *Imperial Fictions: Europe's Myths of Orient*, London: Pandora.
Kabil, A. (2007), *Straightening Ali*, Herndon, VA: STARbooks.
Kabir, N. (2005), *Muslims in Australia: Immigration, Race Relations and Cultural History*, London: Kegan Paul.
Kandiyoti, D. (1988), 'Bargaining with Patriarchy', *Gender and Society*, 2(3): 274–90.
Karma Nirvana (2019), 'Supporting victims of honour-based abuse and forced marriage'. Available online: https://karmanirvana.org.uk/about/ (accessed 28 December 2019).
Kersting, K. (2003), 'What Exactly is Creativity?', *American Psychological Association*, 3410(40): 1–40.
Khair, T. (2017/2016), *Just Another Jihadi Jane*, Northampton, MA: Interlink.
Khan, A. (1993), *Chapati and Chips*, Castleford: Yorkshire Art Circus.
Khan, A. (2011), *Poppadom Preach*, London: Simon & Schuster.
Khan, H. H. (2012), 'Moral Panic: The Criminalization of Sexuality in Pakistan', in A. Hélie and H. Hoodfar (eds), *Sexuality in Muslim Contexts: Restrictions and Resistance*, 79–97, London: Zed.
Khan, M. (2019), *It's Not about the Burqa: Muslim Women on Faith, Feminism, Sexuality and Race*, London: Picador.
Khan, M. (2018), *I Am Thunder*, London: Macmillan.
Khan, N. (2016), 'Pakistani Hatecopy artist Maria Qamar shares advice and vision', *Brown Girl Magazine*, 6 January. Available at: https://www.browngirlmagazine.com/2016/01/pakistani-hatecopy-artist-maria-qamar-shares-advice-and-vision/(Accessed: 10 September 2019).
Kindon, S., R. Pain and M. Kesby, eds (2007), *Participatory Action Research Approaches and Methods: Connecting People, Participation and Place*, Abingdon: Routledge.
Krishnadas, J. (2006), 'The Sexual Subaltern in Conversations "Somewhere in Between": Law and the Old Politics of Colonialism', *Feminist Legal Studies*, 14(1): 53–77.
Kumar, S. (2013), 'Constructing the Nation's Enemy: Hindutva, Popular Culture and the Muslim "Other" in Bollywood Cinema', *Third World Quarterly*, 34(3): 458–69.
Kureishi, H. (1990), *The Buddha of Suburbia*, London: Faber & Faber.
Kureishi, H. (1996/1995), *The Black Album*, London: Faber & Faber.
Kureishi, H. (2011), *Collected Essays*, London: Faber & Faber.
Leavy, P. (2010), 'Poetic Bodies: Female Body Image, Sexual Identity and Arts-Based Research', *LEARNing Landscapes*, 4(1): 175–87.
Leavy, P. (2015), *Method Meets Art: Arts-Based Research Practice*, New York: Guildford.
Lewis, P. J. (2011), 'Storytelling as Research/Research as Storytelling', *Qualitative Inquiry*, 17(6): 505–10.
Lewis, P. (2007), *Young, British and Muslim*, London: Continuum.
Lewis, P. and S. Hamid (2018), *British Muslims: New Directions in Islamic Thought, Creativity and Activism*, Edinburgh: Edinburgh University Press.
Leyshon, C. (2016), 'Mohsin Hamid on the migrants in all of us', *The New Yorker*, 7 November. Available online: https://www.newyorker.com/books/page-turner/this-week-in-fiction-mohsin-hamid-2016-11-14 (accessed 10 September 2019).
Mahfouz, S. (2017), *The Things I Would Tell You: British Muslim Women Write*, London: Saqi.
Mahmood, S. (2001), 'Feminist Theory, Embodiment and the Docile Agent', *Cultural Anthropology*, 16 (2): 202–36.
Malik, A. (2016/2015), *Sofia Khan is Not Obliged*, London: Twenty7.
Malik, A. (2017), *The Other Half of Happiness*, London: Zaffre.
Maqsood, R. W. (1994), *Islam*, London: Hodder Headline.
Massad, J. (2007), *Desiring Arabs*, Chicago, IL: University of Chicago Press.

Massad, J. (2015), *Islam in Liberalism*, Chicago, IL: University of Chicago Press.
Mattu, A. and N. Maznavi (2012), *Love, InshAllah: The Secret Love Lives of American Muslim Women*, Berkeley, CA: Soft Skull.
Mattu, A. and N. Maznavi (2014), *Salaam, Love: American Muslim Men on Love, Sex, and Intimacy*, Boston, MA: Beacon.
McClintock, A. (1995), *Imperial Leather: Race, Gender and Sexuality in the Colonial Contest*, London: Routledge.
McNay, L. (2018), 'Agency', in L. Disch and M. Hawkesworth (eds), *The Oxford Handbook of Feminist Theory*, 39–60, New York: Oxford University Press.
Meghani, S. (2015), 'Queer South Asian Muslims: The Ethnic Closet and Its Secular Limits', in C. Chambers and C. Herbert (eds), *Imagining Muslims of South Asia and the Diaspora: Secularism, Religion, Representations*, 172–84, Abingdon: Routledge.
Mohammad, R. (2015), 'Transnational Shift: Marriage, Home, and Belonging for British-Pakistani Muslim Women', *Social and Cultural Geography*, 16(6): 593–614.
Mohdin, A. (2018), 'Sajid Javid lambasted for "Asian paedophiles" tweet', *The Guardian*, 20 October. Available online: https://www.theguardian.com/politics/2018/oct/20/sajid-javid-lambasted-for-asian-paedophiles-tweet-huddersfield (accessed 23 December 2019).
Mondal, A. A. (2008), *Young British Muslim Voices*, Oxford: Greenwood.
Morgan, E. (2000), 'Transgression in Glasgow: A Poet Coming to Terms', in R. Phillips, D. Watt and D. Shuttleton (eds), *De-centring Sexualities: Politics and Representations beyond the Metropolis*, 278–91, London: Routledge.
Morris, N. (2006), 'Hate crime inquiry into "anti-gay" Sacranie', *The Independent*, 12 January. Available online: https://www.independent.co.uk/news/uk/crime/hate-crime-inquiry-into-anti-gay-sacranie-6112027.html (accessed 3 October 2020).
Mort, G. (2013), 'Transcultural Writing and Research', in J. Kroll and G. Harper (eds), *Research Methods in Creative Writing*, 201–22, London: Palgrave Macmillan.
Muslim Council of Britain (2015), 'British Muslims in Numbers: A Demographic, Socio-economic and Health Profile of Muslims in Britain Drawing in the 2011 Census', London: Muslim Council of Britain.
Neale, D. (2006a), 'Writing What You Know', in L. Anderson (ed.), *Creative Writing: A Workbook with Readings*, 44–55, Abingdon: Routledge and the Open University.
Neale, D. (2006b), 'Writing What You Come to Know', in L. Anderson (ed.), *Creative Writing: A Workbook with Readings*, 56–69, Abingdon: Routledge and the Open University.
Newns, L. (2017), 'Renegotiating Romantic Genres: Textual Resistance and Muslim Chick Lit', *Journal of Commonwealth Literature*, 53(2): 284–300.
Norfolk, A. (2012), '"Media prejudice" claim as child sex report turns a blind eye to Asian gangs', *The Times*. Available online: https://www.thetimes.co.uk/article/media-prejudice-claim-as-child-sex-report-turns-a-blind-eye-to-asian-gangs-f6qk3tfdsf9 (accessed 24 December 2019).
Norfolk, A. (2016), 'Home Office "covered up racism of abuse judge', *The Times*, 21 November. Available online: https://www.thetimes.co.uk/edition/news/home-office-covered-up-racism-of-abuse-judge-cpct9clq3 (accessed 24 December 2019).
Office for National Statistics (ONS) (2015), *2011 Census analysis: Ethnicity and religion of the non-UK born population in England and Wales*. Available online: https://www.ons.gov.uk/peoplepopulationandcommunity/culturalidentity/ethnicity/articles/2011censusanalysisethnicityandreligionofthenonukbornpopulationinenglandandwales/2015-06-18 (accessed 1 December 2019).

Ouis, P. (2007), 'Muslim Marriage in Europe: Tradition and Modernity', *Global Dialogue*, 9(3–4): 108–17.
Owens, N. and N. Wilkinson (2013), 'Forced marriage: Ayesha was repeatedly beaten, raped and then twice almost murdered by her own family', *Mirror*, 10 November. Available online: https://www.mirror.co.uk/news/real-life-stories/forced-arranged-marriage-young-british-2715692 (accessed 1 December 2019).
Pande, R. (2014), 'Geographies of Marriage and Migration: Arranged Marriages and South Asians in Britain', *Geography Compass*, 8(2): 75–86.
Peach, C. (2006), 'Islam, Ethnicity and South Asian Religions in London 2001 Census', *Transactions*, 31(3): 353–70.
Phillips, D. (2007), 'Creating Home Spaces: Young British Muslim Women's Identity and Conceptualisations of Home', in P. Hopkins and R. Gale (eds), *Muslims in Britain: Race, Place and Identities*, 23–36, Edinburgh: Edinburgh University Press.
Phillips, L. G. and T. Bunda (2018), *Research through, with and as Storying*, Abingdon: Routledge.
Phillips, R. (2012), 'Interventions against Forced Marriage: Contesting Hegemonic Narratives and Minority Practices in Europe', *Gender, Place & Culture*, 19(1): 21–41.
Phillips, R. (2016), 'Islam in Sexuality', *Dialogues in Human Geography*, 6(2): 229–44.
Phillips, R. and H. Kara (2021), *Creative Writing for Social Research*, Bristol: Policy Press.
Phillips, R., C. Chambers, N. Ali, R. Pande and P. Hopkins (2020), 'Mobilizing Pakistani Heritage, approaching Marriage', *Ethnic and Racial Studies*, 43(16): 1–19.
Plummer, K. (1995), *Telling Sexual Stories: Power, Change and Social Worlds*, London: Routledge.
Poynting, S., G. Noble, P. Tabar and J. Collins (2004), *Bin Laden in the Suburbs: Criminalising the Arab Other*, Sydney: Sydney Institute of Criminology.
Puar, J. K. and A. Rai (2002), 'Monster, Terrorist, Fag: The War on Terrorism and the Production of Docile Patriots', *Social Text*, 20(3): 117–48.
Qamar, M. (2017), *Trust No Aunty*, New York: Touchstone.
Qureshi, I. (2018), *The Funeral Director*, London: Nick Hern.
Qureshi, K., K. Charsley and A. Shaw (2014), 'Marital Instability among British Pakistanis: Transnationality, Conjugalities and Islam', *Ethnic and Racial Studies*, 37(2): 261–79.
Ramadan, T. (2004), *Western Muslims and the Future of Islam*, Oxford: Oxford University Press.
Rich, A. (1980), 'Compulsory Heterosexuality and Lesbian Existence', *Signs*, 5(4): 631–60.
Richards, R. (2007), *Everyday Creativity and New Views of Human Nature*, Greenwich, CT: Ablex.
Rouhani, F. (2007), 'Religion, Identity and Activism: Transnational Queer Muslims', in K. Browne, J. Lim and G. Brown (eds), *Geographies of Sexualities: Theory, Practices and Politics*, 169–80, Farnham: Ashgate.
Runnymede Trust (1997), *Islamophobia: A Challenge for Us All*, London: Runnymede Trust.
Runnymede Trust (2016), *Islamophobia – 20 Years on, Still a Challenge for Us All*, London: Runnymede Trust. Available online: https://www.runnymedetrust.org/blog/islamophobia-20-years-on-still-a-challenge-for-us-all (accessed 30 November 2019).
Rushdie, S. (1998/1988), *The Satanic Verses*, London: Vintage.
Sahih Bukhari (2009), 'Online Hadith Collection, Volume 007, Book 062, Wedlock, Marriage (Nikah), Hadith Number 004'. Available online: http://www.hadithcollection.com/sahihbukhari (accessed 10 September 2019).

Sahih Muslim (2009), 'Online Hadith Collection, Book 008 Marriage, Hadith 3233'. Available online: http://www.hadithcollection.com/sahihmuslim.html (accessed 10 September 2019).
Samad, Y. and J. Eades (2002), *Community Perceptions of Forced Marriage: Foreign and Commonwealth Office Report*, London: Stationery Office.
Sandelowski, M. (1991), 'Telling Stories: Narrative Approaches in Qualitative Research', *Journal of Nursing Scholarship*, 23(3): 161–6.
Sanjakdar, F. (2011), *Living West, Facing East: The (De)construction of Muslim Youth Sexual Identities*, New York: Peter Lang.
Santesso, E. M. (2013), *Disorientation: Muslim Identity in Contemporary Anglophone Literature*, Basingstoke: Palgrave Macmillan.
Saqi (2019), 'Publisher's Blurb'. Available online: https://saqibooks.com/books/saqi/the-things-i-would-tell-you/ (accessed 28 December 2019).
Savage, T. M. (2004), 'Europe and Islam: Crescent Waxing, Cultures Clashing', *Washington Quarterly*, 27(3): 25–50.
Scott, J. C. (2008 [1985]), *Weapons of the Weak: Everyday Forms of Peasant Resistance*, New Haven, CT: Yale University Press.
Shah, S. (2017), *The Making of a Gay Muslim: Religion, Sexuality, and Identity in Malaysia and Britain*, London: Palgrave Macmillan.
Shamsie, K. (2017), *Home Fire*, London: Bloomsbury.
Shannahan, D. S. (2009), 'Sexual Ethics, Marriage and Sexual Autonomy: The Landscapes for Muslimat and Lesbian, Gay, Bisexual, and Transgendered Muslims', *Contemporary Islam*, 3(1): 59–78.
Shaw, A. (2000), *Kinship and Continuity: Pakistani Families in Britain*, Abingdon: Routledge.
Shaw, A. (2001), 'Kinship, Cultural Preference and Immigration: Consanguineous Marriage among British Pakistanis', *Journal of the Royal Anthropological Institute*, 7(2): 315–34.
Shaw, A. (2006), 'The Arranged Transnational Cousin Marriages of British Pakistanis: Critique, Dissent and Cultural Continuity', *Contemporary South Asia*, 15(2): 209–20.
Shryock, A. (2010), *Islamophobia/Islamophilia: Beyond the Politics of Enemy and Friend*, Bloomington: Indiana University Press.
Siraj, A. (2009), 'The Construction of the Homosexual "Other" by British Muslim Heterosexuals', *Contemporary Islam*, 3(1): 41–57.
Solnit, R. (2017/2005), *A Field Guide to Getting Lost*, Edinburgh: Canongate.
Tan, Y. (2019), 'Brunei implements stoning to death under anti-LGBT laws', *BBC News*, 3 April. Available online: https://www.bbc.co.uk/news/world-asia-47769964 (accessed 27 December 2019).
Taqî-ud-Din Al-Hilâlî, M. and M. M. Khân, eds (1985), *Interpretation of the Meanings of the Noble Qur'ān in the English Language*, Riyadh: Al-Haramain Islamic Foundation.
Tufail, W. (2015), 'Rotherham, Rochdale, and the Racialised Threat of the "Muslim Grooming Gang"', *International Journal for Crime, Justice and Democracy*, 4(3): 30–43.
Vickers, M. H. (2002), 'Researchers as Storytellers: Writing on the Edge – and without a Safety Net', *Qualitative Inquiry*, 8(5): 608–21.
Warner, M. (2012), *Stranger Magic: Charmed States and the Arabian Nights*, London: Vintage.
Werbner, P. (2007), 'Veiled Intervention in Pure Space: Honour Shame and Embodied Struggles among Muslims in Britain and France', *Theory, Culture and Society*, 24(2): 161–86.

Whitlock, G. (2007), *Soft Weapons: Autobiography in Transit*, Chicago, IL: University of Chicago Press.
Wood, P. (2018), 'Marriage and Social Boundaries among British Pakistanis', *Diaspora*, 20(1): 40–64.
Yip, A. K. T. (2004a), 'Embracing Allah and Sexuality? South Asian Non-heterosexual Muslims in Britain', in K. A. Jacobsen and P. P. Kumar (eds), *South Asians in the Diaspora: Histories and Religious Traditions,* 294–310, Leiden: Brill.
Yip, A. K. T. (2004b), 'Negotiating Space with Family and Kin in Identity Construction: The Narratives of Non-heterosexual Muslims', *Sociological Review*, 52(3): 336–50.
Yip, A. K. T. (2007), 'Sexual Orientation and Discrimination in Religious Communities', in M. V. L. Badgett and J. Frank (eds), *Sexual Orientation Discrimination: An International Perspective*, 209–44, Abingdon: Routledge.
Zaidi, M. (2020) *A Dutiful Boy: A Memoir of a Gay Muslim's Journey to Acceptance.* London: Penguin.
Zakiyyah, U. (2016), *Let's Talk about Sex and Muslim Love: Essays on Intimacy and Romantic Relationships in Islam*, College Park, MD: Al-Walaa.

INDEX

Note: Page locators in italics refer to figures.

Abraham, Ibrahim 88, 95, 135
abuse & violence 86, 87–9, 91, 96, 109, 120
   see also Islamophobia
affairs 11, 47, 131
affirming and validating experiences 9–10
Afshar, Haleh 133
ahadith 128, 135, 139, 140
   seee also hadith
Ahmed, Rehana 3
Ahmed, Sameera 93, 132, 133
Ahmed, Sara 97, 130
Alam, Rehana 34–5, 174, 179, *186*
Alexander, Claire 7, 86, 130
Al-Hilâlî, Muhammad Taqî-ud-Din 128
Alibhai-Brown, Yasmin 96
Amis, Martin 49
angraiz (English) 118
animation (*Halal Dating*) 13, 31–2, 62–5, *126*, 133–4
Antigone figures in literature 152–4
apps/online meetings 12, 42–3, 93
arranged marriages 33, 90, 115
   anxiety 151
   dreaming 161–2
   experiences 116
   versus love marriage 80
Aslam, Nadeem 11, 101, 110–12, *186*
autobiographies 10
   Love in a Headscarf (Shelina Janmohamed) 3–4, 7, 11, 20–5, 91
ayat 128

Barelwi traditions 129–30
becoming/dreaming 163–5
Begum, Shamima 90
Berelowitz, S. 88–9
Bhutto, Fatima 11, 49, 73, 76–8, 120, *186–7*
Bitter Sweets (Roopa Farooki) 115, 122–3, *187*

Black Album, The (Hanif Kureishi) 11, 144–6, *189*
blogs 10, 150–1
Bollywood 45, 47–50, 119–20, 161, 167–8
Bolognani, Marta 6–7, 96, 130
Buddha of Suburbia, The (Hanif Kureishi) 11

careers 87, 110, 132–3
Casey, Louise 8, 95
caste 108–9
casual sex/dating 62
Catholicism 6–7
cautionary tales 6–7, 121–2
Chapati and Chips (Almas Khan) 122, *188*
Charsley, Katharine 8, 96, 130, 133–4, 139
chastity, premarital 137–9
checklist of qualities to look for in relationships 168–9
chick flicks 76
chick lit 3–4, 7, 11, 20–5, 91
Child Sexual Abuse (CSA) 88–9
Child Sexual Exploitation (CSE) 88–9
Christchurch, New Zealand terrorist attacks 86
Christianity 4, 6–7, 46
Cinderella 48
cinema 45, 47–50, 119–20, 161, 167–8
clichés 47–50
closet 47
clothing 3–4, 7, 11, 20–5, 34, 68, 90–1, 151–4, 158–9
cohabitation 121–2
colonial discourse 85
coming of age stories 11
commitment 79
commodity racism 109
compulsory heterosexuality 130–4
confidence 25
consummation of marriage 105–6

conversations 1–2, 13–14, 133–4
courtship 32
   see also dating
creative workshops 12–13
creative writing 10–11, 53–6
creative writing journals 5
curiosity about sex 148
Curry Mile, The (Zahid Hussain) 11

Daily Mail 3, 90–1, 95
Dale, Angela 132, 133
Daoud, Kamel 89–90, 96
dating 46–7, 59–72
   disillusionment 82–3
   Halal Dating 13, 31–2, 62–5, *126*, 133–4
Deobandi traditions 129–30
desire 75–6, 149–50, 158–9
disillusionment 82–3
Disney 48, 161
divorce 82, 83, 121–2, 162
double standards 61–2, 106–7
dreaming 157–70

EastEnders (British soap opera) 49–50, 52–3
education 19–20, 132–3
empathy 79
erotica 120, 145
escapism 165–6
Exit West (Mohsin Hamid) 59, 69–71, *187*
expectations 24–5, 59–60, 106–7
   see also dreaming
experimenting sexually 132–3
extramarital affairs 11
   see also infidelity

faith 67–9, 83
family
   interference 80–1, 92–4
   meeting stages 31–4, 39–40
   premarital relationships 59–60
   secretive relationships 60–1, 62
   shame 47
   transnational relationships 8
   see also arranged relationships
fantasies 157–9
   see also erotica
Farooki, Roopa 115, 122–5, *187*

fatwa 144–5
fetishes 120
fiction 10, 11, 37–9, 117–20, 152–4
film 45, 47–50, 119–20, 161, 167–8
Finsbury Park Mosque 86
first loves 75–6
flirting 41–3
Flying Man, The (Roopa Farooki) 123–5, *187*
free-writing exercises 53–5, 73–4
friends and strangers 50–1
friendships/online meetings 42–3
fulfilment and happiness 46, 81–3, 96–8, 109
Funeral Director, The (Imam Qureshi) 45, 47–50

gameshows 13, 31–2, *32*, 62–5, *63*, *126*, 133–4
gay relationships *see* homosexuality
gendered pressures 110–12
Glasgow Women's Library 12
Goddard, Dame Lowell 88–9
Guardian, The 93, 97, *187*

hadith 128, 131, 135, 137
   see also ahadith
Halal Dating (animation) 13, 31–2, 62–5, *126*, 133–4
halal 47, 59–60, 63, 64
Hamid, Mohsin 59, 69–71, 93, *187*
Hamid, Triska 12
happily ever after clichés 47–50, 74, 82–3, 160–2
happiness 46, 81–3, 96–8, 109
Happy British Muslims (YouTube Video) 97–8
   see also Honesty Policy
haram 47, 59–60, 63, *64*
Hasin, Sarvat 117
   see also published stories
hatred
   homophobia 94–5
   Islamophobia 1–2, 85–7
   racism 86, 87–9, 109, 120
headscarves 3–4, 7, 11, 20–5, 90–1, 151–4
   see also hijab
Hélie, Anissa 9, 132
heteronormativity 11, 130–4

higher education 19–20
hijab 3–4, 7, 11, 20–5, 90–1, 151–4
    see also headscarves
Home Fire (Kamila Shamsie) 152–4, *190*
homonegativity 130–1, 134–7
homophobia 94–5
homosexuality
    cautionary tales 6
    clichés 49–50
    closeted 47
    dating 61–2
    gendered pressures 111–12
    homophobia 94–5
    honour/shame 101–3
    intolerance 94–5
    language/speech 46
    lesbian and gay rights 95
    literature 8
    meeting stages 31, 37–9
    published stories 11
    singlehood 17, 25–6
    speaking about 1
    televised depictions 49–50, 52–3
    temptation/marriage 131
Honesty Policy 97–8
    see also Happy British Muslims
honour 46–7, 91, 101–3, 104–6, 110, 137–9
Hoodfar, Homa 9, 132
human rights 95
Hussain, Sairish 55–6
Hussain, Zahid 11

I Am Thunder (Muhammad Khan) 101, 104–7, 110, *189*
idealization of love 47–50, 74, 82–3, 160–2
Independent Inquiry into Child Sexual Abuse 88–9
Independent Inquiry into Child Sexual Exploitation in Rotherham 88
infidelity 11, 47, 131
internet dating 42–3
interviews 13–14
intimacy 79
introductions *see* meeting stages
ISIS (Islamic State in Iraq and Syria) 22–3, 90
Islamic Tinder 12
Islamophilia 9, 98

Islamophobia 1–2, 85–7
    anti-Muslim hatred groups 86
    homophobic intolerance, stereotype of 94–5
    Islamophobia: A Challenge for Us All (Runnymede Trust) 86
    Islamophobia/Islamophilia 98
    joylessness, stereotype of 98
    Runnymede Trust 86, 90–1
    see also stereotypes
izzat (honour) 46–7, 91, 101–3, 104–6, 110, 137–9

Jamaat-e Islami movement 129–30
Jamal, Amreen 95, 134, 135–6
Janmohamed, Shelina 3–4, 7, 11, 20–5, 87, 91, 97, 119, 127, *187–8*
Javid, Sajid 89
Jay, Baroness Alexis 88
joylessness 96–8
Judaism 46
Just Another Jihadi Jane (Tabish Khair) 21, 22–4, 26–7, *188*

Kabil, Amjeed 11, 31, 37–9, *188*
Kandiyoti, Deniz 137–8
Khair, Tabish 21, 22–4, 26–7, *188*
Khan, Almas 122, 157, 165–6, *188–9*
Khan, Muhammad 8, 101, 104, 106–7, 110, *189*
Khân, Muhammad Muhsin 128
Koran *see* Qur'an
Kureishi, Hanif 11, 144–6, *189*

lesbian relationships *see* homosexuality
Let's Talk About Sex and Muslim Love: Essays on Intimacy and Romantic Relationships in Islam (Umm Zakiyyah) 9
Lewis, Philip 130
Living West, Facing East: The (De)construction of Muslim Youth Sexual Identities (Fida Sanjakdar) 9
loneliness 24–5, 47, 83
loss 81–3
love 73–84, 115
    conquers all adage 83
    down-to-earth romance 166–9
    happily ever after clichés 47–50, 74, 82–3, 160–2

marriage 80, 81–3, 122–3
    norms 128–9
    religious diversity 129–30
    social acceptance of love relationships 168
    unexplainability of love 75–6
Love in a Headscarf (Shelina Janmohamed) 3–4, 7, 11, 20–5, 91, *187–8*
Love, InshAllah: The Secret Love Lives of American Muslim Women (Ayesha Mattu and Nura Maznavi) 8
lust 149–50

Mahfouz, Sabrina 8, 92
Making of a Gay Muslim, The (Shanon Shah) 8, 95
Malik, Ayisha 59, *67–9*, 73, *81–3*, *119*, *127*, *189*
Maps for Lost Lovers (Nadeem Aslam) 11, 101, 110–12, *186*
marriage 1, 115–27
    arranged experiences 116
    caste 108–9
    conflict *126*
    dreaming 160–5
    everyday togetherness 125–6
    expectations 106–7
    fictional depictions 117–20
    flawed 123–5
    fragility 115, 122–3
    hadith 131
    higher education 19–20
    honour 105–6
    premarital chastity 137–9
    premarital relationships 18–19, 59–60, 68, 137–9
    religious diversity 129–30
    sex/love norms 128–9
    statistics 131–2
    talking about 133–4
    wedding night/anxiety 150–1
    see also premarital relationships
Match Made in Heaven, A (Claire Chambers et al., eds) 56, 117, 127, 164
matchmaking websites 12, 42–3, 93
Maznavi, Nura 8, 140
meeting stages 31–44
    Halal Dating (animation_ 13, 31–2, 62–5, *126*, 133–4

love 80–1
    tea trolley meetings 34–7, *39*, *56–7*, *63*, *64*, 107–8, 133
memoirs (such as *Love in a Headscarf*) 3–4, 7, 11, 20–5, 91
men
    gendered pressures 110–12
    oversexed, stereotype of 87–9
Mills and Boon 146–7
Mirpuri-heritage Muslims 132–3
misery/unhappiness 96–8
Mohammad, Robina 8, 130, 133–4
Mondal, Anshuman 7, 52, 130
Morgan, Edwin 14, 46, 58
mosques 3, 83, 86

newspapers 3, 89–92, 93, 95, 96, 97
It's Not About the Burqa: Muslim Women on Faith, Feminism, Sexuality, and Race (Mariam Khan, ed.) 8

One Thousand and One Nights, The 47
online relationship practices
    fetishes 120
    matchmaking websites 12, 42–3, 93
    meetings 12, 42–3, 93
    suitors 65–6
Orientalism, sexualized 85
Other Half of Happiness, The (Ayisha Malik) 73, 81–3, *189*
otherness 88

paedophilia 88–9
parents
    economic interest in children 132–3
    meeting stages 34–7
    meetings 39–40
    overbearing 92–4
    see also family; pressures
patriarchy 118, 127, 137–8
Phillips, Louise 10
Plummer, Ken 2–3, 10, 46, 49
Polari 46
Poppadom Preach (Almas Khan) 157, 165–6, *188–9*
predatory behaviour 87–9, 95
premarital relationships
    dating 59–60, 68
    singlehood 18–19

pressures 23–4, 101–13
  premarital chastity 137–9
prohibitions on dating 46–7
promiscuity 11, 20–1, 23, 47, 87, 131
published stories 11–12
  in Chambers et al. *A Match Made in Heaven*:
    'Boneland' (Shaista Sadick) 120, 127
    'Cat That Came in with the Dark, The' (Sarvat Hasin) 117
    'Heartbeat' (Ayisha Malik) 119, 127
    'Her Trials' (Mariam Naeem) 56
    'Love Letter' (Shelina Janmohamed) 119, 127
    'Marriage of Convenience' (Sabyn Javeri) 117–18
    'Moments in Time' (Sunah Ahmed) 164–5
    'Peter Pochmann Goes to Dinner' (Bina Shah) 118, 127
    'Rearranged' (Noren Haq) 65–7, 158–60
    'Simple Nature, A' (Inayah Jamil) 33, 56–7

Qamar, Maria 157, 166–9, *190*
queer 11, 88, 95, 135
Qur'an 81, 128, 135, 139
Qureshi, Imam 45, 47–50
Qureshi, Kaveri 8, 133–4

racial profiling 87–9
racism 86, 87–9, 109, 120
  see also Islamophobia
rape/sexual abuse 88–9, 91, 96
relationships and sex education (RSE) 95
renunciation of Islam 90–1
repression 97–8
researching stories 9–14
Rich, Adrienne 130–1
rishtas (relationships) 34–7, 39, 56–7, 63, *64*, 107–8, 133
romance 146–7, 166–9
  Love in a Headscarf (Shelina Janmohammed) 3–4, 7, 11, 20–5, 91
Rouhani, Farhang 94, 136
Runaways, The (Fatima Bhutto) 11, 73, 76–8, 120, *186–7*

Runnymede Trust 86
Rushdie, Salman 144–5

Sadick, Shaista 120, 127
  see also published stories
Santesso, Esra Mirze 165
Satanic Verses, The (Salman Rushdie) 144–5
secretive relationships 11, 47, 60–1, 62, 131
  see also premarital relationships
Secrets of the Henna Girl (Sufiya Ahmed) 11
self-harm 109
sex 143–55
  Home Fire (Kamila Shamsie) 152–4
  honour 104–6
  norms 128–9
  premarital chastity 137–9
  religious diversity 129–30
  speaking about 1–2
  thinking about 148
  see also premarital relationships
sexual abuse 88–9, 96
sexual assaults in Germany 96
sexual fantasies 157–9
sexual questioning 11
sexual stories 10
sexualised Orientalism 85
sexuality
  experimentation 132–3
  Home Fire (Kamila Shamsie) 152–4
  joylessness/repression, stereotype of 97–8
  as marker of difference 85
  premarital chastity 137–9
  see also homosexuality
Shah, Bina 118, 127
Shah, Shanon 8, 95
Shamsie, Kamila 152–4, *190*
sharam (shame) 47, 101–3
Shaw, Alison 8, 133–4
Shia Muslims 129–30
Shryock, Andrew 9, 86, 98
Siddique, John 4–5
singlehood 17–29, 93
  strategic singlehood 19–20
Siraj, Asifa 134, 135, 136
Sleeping Beauty 48
Snow White 48

soap operas 49–50, 52–3
Sofia Khan is Not Obliged (Ayisha Malik) 59, 67–9, *189*
stereotypes 1–2, 9, 47–50, 85–99
   counter-stereotypes 96–8
   overbearing parents 92–4
   oversexed men 87–9
   passive wives 89–92
Straightening Ali (Amjeed Kabil) 11, 31, 37–9, *188*
strangers, chatting with 50–1
Straw, Jack 87–8, 89
suitability of partner 108–9
Sunni Muslims 129–30, 131
support networks 79
   see also family
Sûrah 128

Tablighi Jamaat movement 129–30
Tatchell, Peter 95
Tea Trolley, The (Rehana Alam) 34–5, 174, 179, *186*
television programmes 49–50, 52–3
Tell MAMA 86
terrorism 86, 120
Things I Would Tell You, The (Sabrina Mahfouz, ed.) 8, 92
Tinder app 12
tolerance 79
transnational relationships 8, 115
   see also arranged marriages
Trust No Aunty (Maria Qamar) 157, 166–9, *190*

uncertainty, expressions of 51–3
unhappiness 96–8, 109
   see also happiness

unpublished stories
   'Cake and Eat It' (Meena) 163–4
   'A Day of Love' (Bilal) 4–5
   'Dreams' (Farid) 158
   'Entry, The' (Asmah) 37
   'How to Be a Man' blog post (Nazia) 150–1
   'Last Paragraph of a Romantic Novel, The' (Aleeha) 125–6
   'Life As We Know It' (Sofia) 107–8, 159
   'Qabool: The Happily Never After' (Haris) 93–4, 161
   'What If?' (Yusuf) 17

Vaz, Keith 89
veiling 3–4, 7, 11, 20–5, 90–1
violence 47, 86, 87–9, 91, 96, 109, 120
   see also Islamophobia
virginity 110–11, 137–9

Werbner, Pnina 7, 130
women
   chastity 137–9
   employment 87
   gendered pressures 110–12
   ideal beauty standards 109
   overbearing parents 92–3
   passive wives, stereotype of 89–92
   premarital relationships 59–60
   undersexed women, stereotype of 89–92
Women's Prize for Fiction 152

Yip, Andrew K. T. 7, 46, 94, 136
Young Adult (YA) fiction 11